ENGLISH POPULAR ART

ENGLISH POPULAR ART

Margaret Lambert & Enid Marx

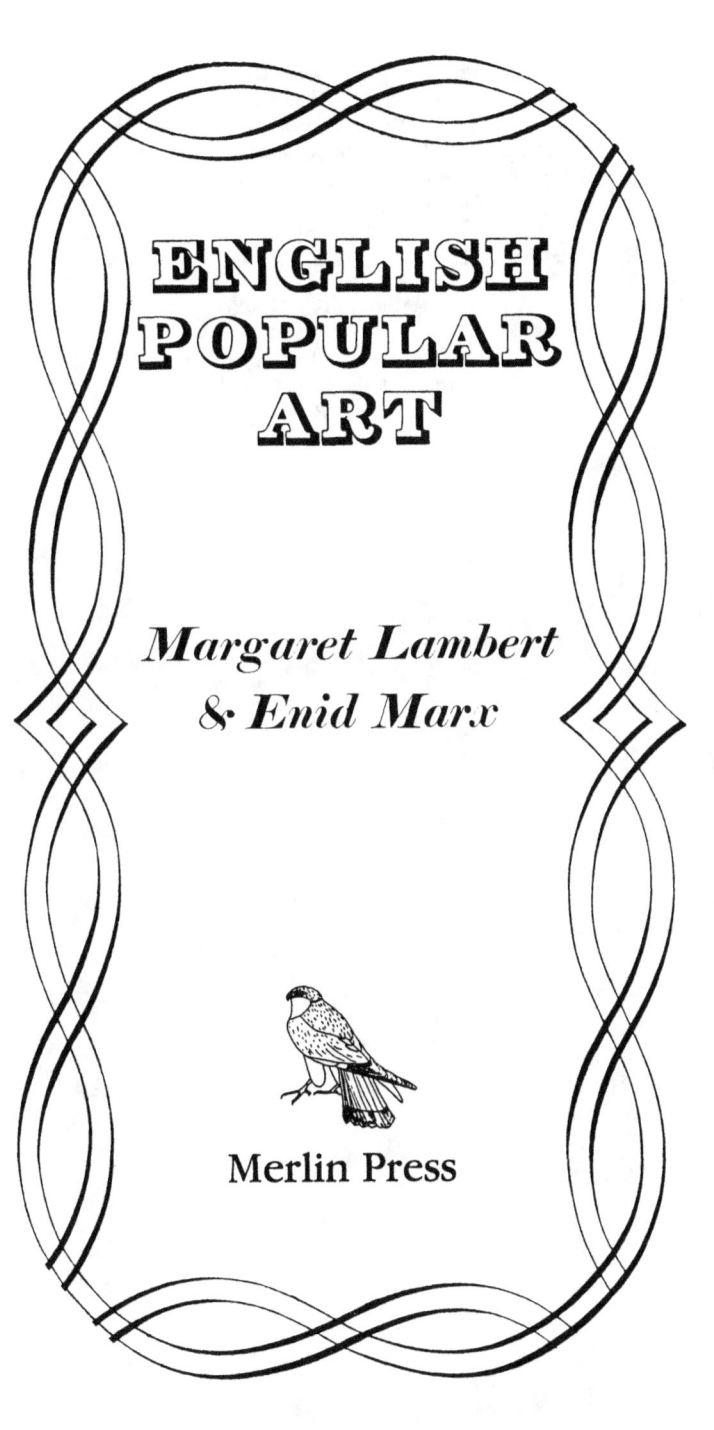

Merlin Press

This edition with additional illustrations
published in 1989 by
The Merlin Press Ltd.
10 Malden Road,
London NW5 3HR
Originally published in 1951
by B.T. Batsford Ltd
New Material © 1989 by Margaret Lambert and Enid Marx

ISBN: 0-85036-597-X

Printed in Great Britain by
Whitstable Litho Printers Ltd.,
Millstrood Road,
Whitstable, Kent

FOREWORD to new edition 1989

WE wish to acknowledge our great debt to the late Mrs Nicholl who gave us generously of her help from the time when we first began to write about the English tradition in the popular arts; she lent lavishly from her own collection but perhaps more importantly showed us the many books and articles she had assembled during a lifetime of study.

This volume is our third attempt to further public interest in the traditions of English popular art, and once again we have had help from many friends whom we would like to thank especially the photographers Brenda Herdman and Olive Smith, widow of Edwin Smith who took some of the photographs for our first book, Frank Atkinson, the founder of the Beamish Open Air Museum and now also of the Berwick Trust, Margaret Hall of the British Museum, Michael Taylor of Rare Books and Mrs Jean Mellanby, to name a few who share our interest in what is possibly a minor but nevertheless an important aspect of the British Heritage and Dr E.C.M. Brenning for invaluable help on the proofs.

Looking back to the period when our first book was written it comes as something of a surprise to realize how much social life, on which the traditions of popular art were based, has changed.

For instance, no longer does one often come across a village smithy, or a wheelwright, a saddle maker, a local printer, and now even less a local baker. Few village shops now set out their wares in fanciful displays, such as the ironmongers of old and a well remembered fishmonger who daily drew with coloured chalks on a blackboard advising 'Today's BEST Buy', while his fish were displayed on ice and embellished with sprigs of parsley and slices of lemon so enchantingly as to be fit to be painted by a Dutch master.

On the canals no longer can one see the barges with their gaily printed castles and roses, equipped with matching buckets and spades, or the giant tea pots at the barges' resting places. To see them now one has to visit the Waterways museum at Stoke Bruerne near Towcester.

The painted caravans of the gipsies have been displaced by the motor car, and the face of the fairground too has altered: instead of finely carved and brightly coloured steeds and fierce fantastic birds there are plastic aeroplanes for would-be future aeronauts to ride through space, for science fiction is the fairy tale of to-day.

A few village craftsmen, thankfully, remain; there are thatchers who decorate cottage roofs and dovecotes with straw birds, shepherds who carve their crooks and others who make decoy ducks.

Happily there is a growing interest in local history, and small museums are springing up, not only in country districts but also some in urban areas there local traditions are being honoured. Though, sadly, much is labelled as 'bygones', not a few of these local treasures are in fact minor works of art.

M.L. & E.M.
September 1988

ACKNOWLEDGMENT

THE authors would particularly like to thank the following, who have been most helpful in providing information on particular aspects of their subject: Mr. Thomas Balston (Staffordshire figures); Mr. Harry Batsford; Mr. Bembrose, Curator of Hanley Museum (pottery); the Director of the Western Region of the B.B.C.; Mr. W. A. Gay, of Exeter: Miss Innes Hart (tombstones); Mr. Robert Harcourt; Miss Hobbs; Lady MacGregor of MacGregor; Admiral and Mrs. Middleton; Mr. Gerald Morice; Miss Jocelyn Morris, Curator of Shire Hall, Warwick (wall-paintings); Mrs. Nicholl; Miss K. B. Outhwaite; M. A. Poignard, of Antwerp; Mr. George Speaight; Mr. Threadgill, Sexton of Abbotts Ann (Maidens' Garlands); Miss Upright, Curator of St. Nicholas Priory, Exeter; and Mr. Sidney Vaux, of Ilchester.

They are most grateful also to the curators and staff of museums which have helped them, in particular to the following: Mr. Maxwell, of the City Art Gallery, Bristol; Mr. Musgrove and his staff, at Brighton; Major Gay, of Exeter; Mr. Collar, and the present director of Saffron Walden Museum; Mr. Shortt, of Salisbury; and Mr. W. Seaby and the retiring director, Mr. St. George Gray, of Taunton.

For the use of photographs, etc., reproduced in the illustrations, they have to thank: Thomas Balston, for fig. 12; Beamish Museum, for fig. 83; Brighton Museum, the Willett Collection, for figs. 18, 30, 31, 33, 34 and 41; Bristol City Art Gallery, for figs. 28, 42 and 56; Castle Museum, Norwich, for fig. 1; Castle Museum, Nottingham, for Fig.40; Brian C. Clayton for Fig. 14; Georgian House, Bristol, for figs. 19 and 23; Miss Innes Hart, for figs. 4-6; Miss Brenda Herdman, for figs. 60-62, 66-69, 74, 77, 84, 86-7, 90-7, 104, 106-109; the Viscountess Lambert, for fig. 44; Luton Museum, for fig. 53; Maggie Milders for the use of toys etc.; Gerald Morice, for figs. 2 and 3; Reginald A. Muxlow, for fig. 119; Mrs Nicholl, for figs. 10, 13, 22 and 55; Royal Albert Memorial Museum, Exeter, for figs. 35-7; Saffron Walden Museum, for figs. 8, 15, 16, 20, 46 and 47; Salisbury Museum, for fig. 43; Edwin Smith, for figs. 59, 64, 71, 78, 98, 101, 105; Taunton Museum, for figs. 27 and 32; Mrs Vaux of Ilchester, for fig. 29; the Victoria and Albert Museum, for figs. 7, 21, 24, 54, 70, 73 and 89; Wiltshire Gazette, for fig. 57; The World of Interiors, for figs. 102-3.

PREFACE

The study of Popular Art in the various countries, especially in England, is still only in its infancy. We do not claim that this book, although four times as long as our first, written in 1945, is still anything more than a brief survey. It has many more illustrations and includes subjects not touched in our earlier book. Even so, it covers only a small section of a vast field. Lack of space and lack of time have forced us to be ruthlessly selective in our choice of examples and illustrations. It remains for some one else, possibly one of our American friends, to make a comprehensive study of English Popular Art.

We have kept the title "Popular Art" as the nearest English equivalent of the neat French term "imagerie populaire"; and have again used it to cover not only handicrafts but also machine production, such as printing, in the popular idiom. Our researches go to show how many popular motives have filtered down from more sophisticated levels, becoming transmuted in the process into something different with qualities of its own, and also how some exceptionally gifted craftsman may influence a whole region or even a generation. In a few cases we have been able to trace names, but the bulk of popular art will probably always remain anonymous.

It is to other countries, notably to the Scandinavians and Americans, that we must be grateful for taking the lead in the study of Popular Art, both by special museums, like the famous open-air ones at Copenhagen and Stockholm, and also by publications such as the great American Index of Design. From America too have come some of the best books on individual subjects, such as patchworks, figureheads, primitive paintings; often in these American subjects we can see traces of English origins.

It would be interesting, for comparative purposes, to see examples of the popular art of different countries side by side. Many things, like fairground art, painted boats and carts, shepherds' carvings, cakemoulds, would be found in common. So would certain types of decoration and often a delight in similar subjects, such as giants and monsters, which is shared by all simple people. What seems to be indigenous to each country is their sense of humour and their choice of colours. Typically English, for instance, are our potters' jokes: jugs and mugs with a toad inside or holes in the rims or handles, making it hard to drink without spilling or even drink at all.

The "innocent eye" is disappearing in England, not, we think, entirely due to mechanisation, but rather from changing social habits, bringing a certain lack of initiative and interest in things with a distinctive individual character. As the countryside becomes more urbanised and we buy more from chain stores, the country craftsmen are dying out and with them that individuality in design and decoration that gave life to the old popular art.

Preface

This is not a thing that can be artificially revived; to try to do so would be to get the antithesis of the genuine tradition. But by preserving examples from the past for study and enjoyment we may, through our designers of the future, possibly regain some of the old individual qualities and delight in simple forms.

Spring, 1951   M. L.
                                                                       E. M.

CONTENTS

Chapter One – CARVING   *page*

   Giants and Marionettes   1
   Ships' Figureheads   6
   Roundabout and Rocking Horses   8
   Shop and Inn Signs   11
   Tombstones   16
   Crooks and Sticks   19
   Presents and Love Tokens   20
   Sailors' and Apprentices' Work   22
   Gingerbread Stamps and Moulds   24
   Tunbridge Ware   25

Chapter Two – METAL

   Sign Brackets and Frames   27
   Weathercocks and Vanes   28
   Club Poleheads   30
   Horse Brasses and Harness Ornaments   31
   Pilgrim Badges   34
   Fakes and Forgeries   35
   Fire Insurance Signs   35
   Trade Tokens   37
   Firebacks and Hearth Implements   38
   Household Ornaments   40

Chapter Three – PAINTING

   Wall Paintings   44
   Wattle-and-Daub Parge Work   47
   Sign Painting and "Primitive" Painting   47
   Silhouettes and Cut Paper   50
   Parlour Pastimes   51
   Glass Paintings   52
   Fairground Painting   52

Chapter Four – TEXTILES

   Printing   56
   Coventry Ribbons   58
   Quilting and Patchwork   59
   Knitting   60
   Smocking   62
   Embroidered Pictures and Samplers   62
   Sailors' Embroideries   66

Contents

Chapter Five – POTTERY   *page*
    Slipwares   67
    English Delft   71
    Staffordshire Figures and Chimneypiece Ornaments   72
    Stoneware Bottles and Flasks   76
    Painting and Transfer Printing   78
    Giant Teapots   82

Chapter Six – GLASS AND MISCELLANEOUS
    Nailsea Special Pieces   83
    Spun and Twisted Glass   84
    Lustred Glass   85
    Love Tokens in Glass   86
    Engraved and Brilliant Glass   86
    Straw Marquetry   87
    Corn Dollies   88
    Easter Eggs   88
    Maidens' Garlands   89
    Toys   90
    Pipes and Smoking   91

Chapter Seven – PRINTING
    Ballads and Broadsides   93
    Chapbooks and Children's Books   98
    Bills, Trade Cards and Advertisements   101
    Pictures and Paper Games   106
    The Toy Theatre   108
    Tinsel Pictures   112
    Valentines and Christmas Cards   112

INDEX   117

CORRIGENDA

page	line	
4	verse 1.1	for "mightly" read "mighty"
8	14	for "positon" read "position"
22	12	for "Waldon" read "Walden"
23	4 up	for "patterns" read "pattens"
31	4 up	for "teacup" read "teacups"
48	1	for "Dab" read "Daub"
57	26	for "Charta" read "Carta"
60	4 up	for "knitting" read "singing"
63	2nd verse	
	1.3	for "ne'er" read "near"
66	2	for "others" read "other"
67	bottom	for "wares" read "ware"
68	8	for "percursors" read "precursors"
69	20	for "Donyatt" read "Donyat"
70	2nd verse	
	1.2	for "macking" read "making"
79	8 up	for "engavings" read "engravings"
84	12	for "flour" read "water"
88	17	for "Persophene" read "Persephone"
94	2 up	for "acuracy" read "accuracy"
95	1 up	for "Catnatch" read "Catnach"
106	30	for "Couché" read "Coucher"
106	31	for "Levée" read "Lever"

LIST OF PLATES

Between pages 40 and 41

1. Procession Dragon.
2,3. Marionettes.
4,5,6 Carved Tombstones.
7. Hand Brace in Carved Wood.
8. Carved Cherry Wood Walking Stick.
9. Sign Painting of Single-Stick Contest.
10. Cast-iron Door Stop.
11. Wall painting.
12. Silhouette portrait.
13. Water-colour Portrait.
14. Weather Vane.
15. Brass tobacco Stopper.
16. 19th Century False Antiquities.
17. Glass painting over print.
18. Staffordshire Earthenware Group.
19. A Darning Sampler of 1820.
20. A Sailor's Embroidered Picture in Wool.
21. Printed Cotton Square.
22. Countryman's Smock.
23. Stuart Embroidered Picture.
24. Coverlet, Applique Work.
25, 26. Coventry Ribbon Book Marks.
27. Earthenware *sgraffito* Dish.
28. English Bristol Delft Tile.
29. Staffordshire Earthenware Castles and Windmill.
30. Staffordshire Figure.
31. Staffordshire Earthenware Horse.
32. Earthenware Nun Pigeon Sauce Boat.
33, 34. Staffordshire Earthenware Figures.
35-37. North Devon Harvest Pottery.
38, 39. Hand Coloured Prints.
40. Nottingham Stoneware Bear Mug.
41. Sussex Pig.
42. Bristol Earthenware Barrel.

43. Farmer's Mug.

44. Election Mug.

45. Child's Decorated Writing Sheet.

46, 47. Plaited Straw Corn Dollies.

48, 49. Pull-up Valentine.

50. Welshwoman: Watercolour Painting.

51. "Pair of Gloves" Christmas Card.

52. Pictorial Alphabet.

53. Straw-work Group from Luton.

54. Toy Butcher's Shop.

55. Alphabet Counters.

56. Bristol Blown-glass Dog Jug.

57. Stone Carving of a Lamb.

Between pages 80 and 81

58. Wiltshire Woodcarving of a Bear.

59. Parge Figures.

60. Fish Formed From Bread or Dough.

61. Carved Figure of a Boer War Soldier.

62. Dutch Doll.

63. Captain Silver's Collection of Ship's Figureheads.

64. Stone Carved Head of a Grieving Figure.

65. Tombstone of a Craftsman.

66. Snuff Horn.

67. Toy Made From Horn.

68. Shepherd's Crook.

69. Eighteenth Century Rocking Horse.

70. Painted Dummy Board Pig.

71. Ancient Printing Press.

72. Cast Iron Dog Door Stop.

73. Friendly Society Emblems.

74. Fishmonger's Sign.

75. Shop Sign.

76. Farm Sign.

77. Cast Figure of a Poacher in Brass.

78. Easter Parade of Dray Horses.

79-82. Painted Panels.

83. Beamish Quilt with Applique Design.

84. Knitted Kettle Holder.

85. Early Rail Theme on Coventry Ribbon.

86. Sailor's Embroidery.

87. Bobbin Box and Bobbins.

88. Friendly Society Ribbon.

89. Printed Handkerchief.

90. Embroidery on a Baby's Garment.

91-92. Transfer Printed Children's Plates.

93. Staffordshire Figures.

94. Wally Dogs.

95. Stirrup Cup of a Janus Head.

96. Nelson's Funeral: A Glass Painting.

97. Pressed Glass Hands.

98. Spun Glass Ship.

99-100 Pressed Glass Containers.

101. Corn Dolly For Harvest Festival.

102. Shell Decor Summer Fireplace Cover.

103. Feather Work Border.

104. Hobby Horse.

105. Dog made from Cigarette Packets.

106. Horse and Cart.

107. Pebble Parge Decoration.

108. Ah Papa! Valentine.

109. Gin Advert of Cross Eyed Cat.

110. Chiaroscuro Collage.

111. Tobacco Label.

112. Silhouette of a Gentleman.

113. Bill Head for a General Election.

114. Figures From a Shadow-figure Show.

115. Stencil of a Head.

116. Cut Out Paper Scene.

117. Illustration of Grimaldi the Clown.

118. Carved Figure of Punch.

Chapter One

CARVING

Giants and Marionettes

Carving gives particularly good opportunities for the exercise of personal skill and taste, and, since wood and stone are comparatively durable, we can find examples of popular art surviving in these materials over a longer period than any other.

One way of expressing fantasy and humour is through disproportionate size; very big and very little things have a special appeal, so we find that giants and miniatures are favourite forms of popular art from earliest times. Our modern world has little place for giants, though in England they still survive in Christmas pantomime. But until at least the middle of the seventeenth century giants were a regular feature in civic processions here, particularly those held on Midsummer Day, the feast of St. John the Baptist. They were paraded round the town accompanied by the mayor and the town musicians, the "waits." Nor was this custom confined to England; these pageant giants appeared for civic festivals in a number of European countries, notably in Dutch, Belgian and northern French towns.[1] The duty of providing them usually devolved on one or other of the trade guilds, so that they were specially associated with the guilds.

To this day the traditional giants are regularly carried in procession in a number of Belgian towns, often accompanied by fantastic beasts, notably at Antwerp, Ath, Brussels, Dinant, Grammont, Hasselt, Malines, Namur, Nivelles, Ostend and Ypres (Mons has its dragon), and at Lille and Douai in northern France. The great seated Antwerp giant is so big that the fire brigade has to remove the overhead tram cables before he can be drawn round the town in his chariot. These pageant giants of Western Europe have a common ancestry in mediaeval legend and folklore; they represent saints, biblical personages like Samson or Goliath, or the popular heroes and villains of the romances.

Gog and Maygog, the Guildhall giants, beloved of many generations of London children, were originally pageant giants; they replaced an earlier pair of figures actually carried in the Lord Mayor's Show, and apparently used for other celebrations also, for we are told that at Queen Elizabeth's coronation procession the two London giants Gogmaygog and Corinaeus were stationed at Temple Bar. William Hone,[2] the early nineteenth

[1] Giant masks, carved in wood or made in *papier mâché*, are also used to celebrate carnivals in many places on the Continent, e.g. the Black Forest.

[2] See William Hone, *Ancient Mysteries Described*, London 1823. The *Gigantic History* is a chapbook and appeared in two miniature volumes, measuring 2¼ by 1¼ inches,

century pamphleteer and antiquarian, made a special study of these pageant giants, and quotes as the best authority on Gog and Maygog *The Gigantic History of the Two Famous Giants in Guildhall, London*, published in 1741. The *History* relates: "Before the present giants inhabited Guildhall, there were two giants made only of wickerwork and pasteboard, put together with great art and ingenuity: and those two terrible original giants had the honour yearly to grace my Lord Mayor's Show, being carried in great triumph at the time of the pageants; and when that eminent annual service was over, remounted their old stations in Guildhall—till by reason of their very great age, old Time, with the help of a number of city rats and

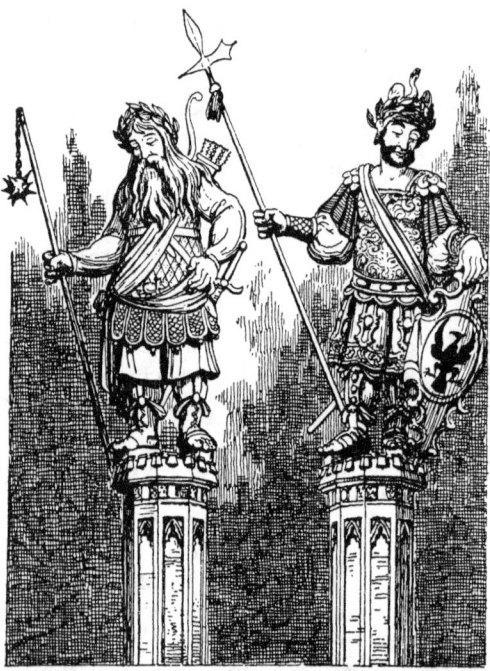

Gog and Maygog, the Guildhall Giants.
Drawn by George Cruikshank.

mice, had eaten up all their entrails. The dissolution of the two old, weak and feeble giants, gave birth to the two present substantial and majestic giants; who by order, and at the city charge, were formed and fashioned. Captain Richard Saunders, an eminent carver in King Street, Cheapside, was their father; who, after he had completely finished, clothed and armed these his two sons, they were immediately advanced to those lofty stations in Guildhall, which they have peacably enjoyed ever since the year 1708." There they remained until the night of Sunday, December 29th, 1940, when the Guildhall was gutted in the big fire raid on the City. Let us hope they may soon be replaced.

The accounts of cities like Chester and Coventry, both once famous for their civic pageantry, often show entries relating to the upkeep of their giants: Coventry seems to have had two and Chester four. From time to time the giants would be dropped from the processions, on grounds of

bound with green and gold embossed Dutch paper. It was printed for Thomas Boreman, bookseller, near the Giants in Guildhall, and at the Boot and Crown on Ludgate Hill, and was no doubt intended for sale to visitors, especially children.

economy or even morality, but they soon came back again. The Chester giants made one such brief exit in 1599, when the mayor altered many ancient customs, "as the shooting of the sheriff's breakfast, the going of the Giants at Midsommer," supplying instead a man in complete armour. The Chester giants were back again in 1601, but Hone suggests that their temporary replacement may perhaps explain the men in armour who, until recent times, always appeared in the Lord Mayor's Show. Nowadays even these substitutes for Gog and Maygog, if such they were, have been dropped. During the Commonwealth all British giants seem to have stopped going, only to reappear in fresh splendour at the Restoration.

To-day the last survivor of the once numerous band of perambulating giants in England is the Salisbury giant (*V*) who still goes in processions from time to time. The reason so many others have been lost seems to be that, in order to be transportable in spite of their size by a man walking inside them, they were necessarily made of very light materials. Though the heads might be carved in wood, as those of the old Antwerp giants are, the bodies were usually constructed of a light framework of wicker or wooden hoops, covered with cloth and reinforced with buckram. A writer in 1589, George Puttenham, in *The Art of English Poesie,* refers to "these midsommer pageants in London, where to make the people wonder are set forth great and uglie Gyants marching as if they were alive and armed at all points, but within they are stuffed full of browne paper and tow, which the shrewd boys underpeering, do guilefully discouer and turn to a great derision"; whilst the Chester city accounts contain an ominous item of 1s. 4d. for arsenic to put in the paste to save the giants from being eaten by rats. Once they ceased to be in regular use, and were no longer kept in repair, the giants easily fell to pieces.

The Salisbury giant's head (*V*), which is carved in wood (apparently walnut), has had to be repeatedly shaved to keep down the worm, so that now only a thin mask remains of the original carving, though a mid nineteenth century drawing shows him with a large expanse of bald pate. His lips have been restored at some more recent date, possibly owing to the practice at one stage of his career of putting a large wooden pipe in his mouth. Patched and restored as it is, the face with its bold, flat planes remains a superbly dramatic piece of carving. So far as is known, it is contemporary with the giant's first recorded public appearance, in 1496, for the visit of Henry VII to Clarendon. When the guild ceremonies with which he was originally associated were dropped, the giant still continued to appear for special festivities, changing his clothes and even the colour of his complexion with the centuries. For the celebration of peace after the American War of Independence in 1784 "the Giant was entirely new dressed, his coat alone taking 34 yards of cloth." Dressing the giant was evidently an important business, and we are told that for his more recent parades his admirers would present various pieces of costume. Contemporary illustrations show that even the rather incongruous nineteenth century clothes, a chintz robe with ruffed sleeves, huge cocked hat, pink face with white whiskers, and large pipe did not disguise the essential nobility of the original carving. The giant has now been dressed much more in keeping with his first appearance; his face is black (as it presumably began) and is surrounded with a mediaeval headdress of scarlet felt, emphasising its dramatic qualities.

Items of the giant's traditional equipment include a large wooden dagger carved with a lion's head hilt (probably eighteenth century workmanship) which he wears in his belt, a huge two-handed wooden sword and a mace which are carried beside him. The giant's swordbearer is no doubt a survival of the "Whifflers" of the old pageants, whose duties were to clear a way through the crowd with their wooden swords. They are mentioned in *Henry V*:

> . . . like a mightly Whiffler 'fore the King
> Seems to prepare the way.

The mace, which is lozenge-shaped and heavily studded with nails, is set on a long pole; it may perhaps originally have been a lantern or cresset light when the processions took place in the evening. Sword and mace are borne by two esquires in traditional costume; in front go the giant's "merrie men," morris dancers in braided suits sewn with bells, and round the procession frisks Hob Nob, the dragon, clearing a way. Hob Nob, the giant's traditional companion, is shaped like a large hobby-horse in folk dances; he has a long, narrow wooden head, with leather ears, and movable jaws, set with large nails. So far as is known, his head was carved at about the same time as the giant's. Besides the usual hobby-horse skirt, his performer wears a stout leather cap set with a plume of feathers, and a thick net veil, possibly to protect him against being pelted by the crowd, for Hob Nob used to be allowed considerable licence in his pranks, and is described as running at the spectators, snapping his jaws and ripping their clothes with his teeth, even driving some of them into the "channels" or canals which then flowed down the main streets of the city, to the vast delight of the rest.

Whereas Gog and Maygog represent characters associated with the legendary foundation of London as New Troy by Brutus, great grandson of Aeneas, who landed at Totnes in Devon and overcame a race of bad giants, the Salisbury giant represents one of the few saintly giants in history, St. Christopher, whose story is told in the *Golden Legend*, translated and published by Caxton in 1483. St. Christopher was a much-loved saint; he was a luck-bringer, and representations of him were frequent in the middle ages. A painting of him is in the chapel of St. John the Baptist of St. Thomas's Church in Salisbury. The Salisbury giant was originally owned by the Merchant Tailors' Guild, whose patron saint is St. John the Baptist, so that they invariably took a leading part in the civic midsummer processions, which fall on the eve of his day; they may perhaps have selected St. Christopher as the giant for their shows because of the picture in the chapel of their patron saint. The traditional giant of Hasselt in Belgium, the

"Langeman" or "long man," a huge seated figure in armour, also represents "Dom Christophe," but neither he nor the Salisbury giant has preserved any of the traditional symbols of St. Christopher.

Hob Nob, the dragon of Salisbury (*IV*), may once have formed part of the paraphernalia of the St. George's Guild, but has been associated with the giant for several centuries. He is evidently related to the large family of hobby-horses which play so prominent a part in folk dances, and also perhaps to the Hoddening Horse, with snapping jaws, which appears in the folk traditions of Cheshire and Kent. Fairy horses also play their part in mediaeval legends—for instance, Bayard, who would carry the four sons of Aymon on his back and who sometimes appears with the giants in Belgian processions.

The dragon of Norwich (1), "Old Snap," who regularly appeared in the corporation processions till the Municipal Corporations Act in 1835, is still preserved in the Castle Museum there. The earliest recorded appearance of the Norwich dragon is in 1451; he too had his Whifflers, in distinctive costume, and his allotted place in the civic processions, which at Norwich were particularly splendid. His body is constructed of painted canvas over wickerwork, with horsehair mane; and his jaws, which snap, are edged with horseshoe-shaped pieces of iron. In appearance he is a winged, scaly dragon, with a scarlet mane running down his back, and the inside of his jaws scarlet too, the whole making a very striking effect. There have been a number of lesser dragons at various times in Norwich, all in the same tradition, but as far as is known only two of these have been preserved; there is a smaller one in the Castle Museum and one in private possession. Though prohibited from civic processions, Old Snap has been brought out from time to time in aid of charity, collecting money with his jaws; models of him are still used in this way, so that he is still very much a feature of Norwich, as he has been for so many centuries.

Besides figures, the Guilds carried huge emblems of their crafts in their shows. Two examples of gigantic wooden axes, carried by the Shipwrights, may be seen in the Blaise Castle Folk Museum at Bristol. One of them, which is seven feet high, has Noah's Ark carved in low relief and gaily painted on the blade (*IV*). The carving is a very skilful piece of work, both in craftsmanship and design, carefully finished down to the smallest detail, obviously a labour of love by some ship's carver of the past.

The old legends, in which the giants play their part, are still performed in puppet and marionette shows, often with beautifully carved figures, in a number of Continental towns; Lille has a particularly fine set. Such shows once existed here also. Mr. George Speaight, the authority on the Juvenile Drama, has made a special study of English glove puppets and marionettes; he has managed to trace performances of these old folk-dramas, some religious such as the "Creation of the World," some secular like the chapbook romances, from Elizabethan times to the end of the eighteenth century. Even to-day we still find some of the old characters surviving in the traditional Mumming Plays. Giant Despair and the other personages in *Pilgrim's*

Progress must have appealed all the more vividly to Bunyan's contemporaries, who could see their secular prototypes appearing regularly in pageants and puppet shows.

By the 1850's the English marionettes had changed their repertoire from folkplays to the melodramas of the contemporary stage, though from time to time we still come across a piece of traditional folk humour, like "The Village Lawyer or Baa," the text of which has recently been published in *Puppet Plays and Pamphlets*; a village yokel tried for sheep-stealing outwits both the judge and his own lawyer by simply saying "Baa!" Mr. Punch himself, for all his remote Italian ancestry, has now become another such piece of folk wit, though an essentially urban one. It seems probable that he originally came to us as a marionette, but nowadays he invariably appears as a glove puppet, and is practically the sole survivor of a once proud tradition. For in their nineteenth century heyday so popular were our English marionettes, at fairgrounds and the like, both at home and abroad, that we hear of five wagons being needed to transport the equipment of one company, and even of foreign companies taking English names to acquire prestige. From the fairground the marionettes invaded the music-hall, and the older generation amongst us, though we may not have seen whole plays, can recall "trick" performances, such as the "Dissecting Skeleton," where each bone changed into a different character, or the Grand Turk in his voluminous skirts transformed into his many wives and their offspring.

A number of nineteenth century English marionettes and glove puppets survive in private collections, whilst a few are still treasured possessions of old showmen and appear from time to time. They deserve to be much more widely known. They are often admirable examples of design, moving most beautifully, whilst the carved heads are extremely dramatic and often witty characterisations of the more or less stock personages (**2, 3**).

Ships' Figureheads

Carving on ships, and especially the figureheads, is one of the most characteristic expressions of popular art in a seafaring nation like the English; it survived as long as ships were made of wood, right down to the end of the nineteenth century. Decoration of ships by painting and carving dates from earliest times; the Viking ships had carved prows, and it has been suggested that the figurehead may be derived from the conception of giving a ship eyes to find her way, as eyes are sometimes painted on Mediterranean fishing-boats. Howsoever this may be, there seems to be no doubt that, besides its purely ornamental value, the carving, and particularly the figurehead, had a special significance for the crew as personifying the ship. In *A Smile of Fortune* Joseph Conrad describes the indignation of a sea-captain at the suggestion that he should replace his own figurehead, which had been lost, by a casual one lying in a shipbuilder's yard. There was a long struggle in the Navy between the Admiralty, who wished to economise, and the sailors, who were determined to preserve their traditional "carved works."

The development of naval ships' decoration is described in Mr. L. G. Carr Loughton's *Old Ships' Figureheads and Sterns*, together with many amusing details of the feud between the Admiralty and the sailors. The form of the decoration is naturally much influenced by the design of the ships themselves. The figurehead as we know it made its appearance in Tudor times, when a combination of the sailing-boat and the oared galley led to the development of a beakhead, thereby providing a place where the figurehead could be set conspicuously. In its heyday the carving ran right round the ship, to end in a special blaze of magnificence at the stern. Styles varied with the changes in comtemporary taste in architecture and the fine arts. From the time of Elizabeth to the mid-eighteenth century, the royal lion formed the figurehead of all ships of the Royal Navy, except for first raters,

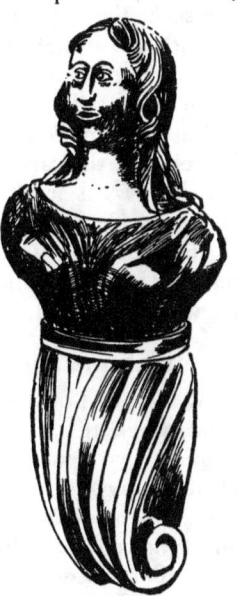

who had tremendously elaborate carved and gilded groups, often equestrian with supporting figures. In the full tide of baroque exuberance such groups, with the correspondingly rich ornamentation of the stern, were apt to lose their effect through overweight of detail, which could not be seen from a distance. The Admiralty drive for economy thus had aesthetically beneficient effects in compelling a certain degree of sobriety. By the end of the eighteenth century single figures were coming into fashion, the old gilding in the Navy was giving place to painting in vivid colours, the subjects even becoming more naturalistic and bearing a closer connection to the ship's name.

Few of the figureheads still to be seen to-day date from earlier than 1815; collections of naval ones have been preserved in the dockyards of Chatham and Portsmouth, the Royal Maritime Museum at Greenwich and elsewhere. In country churchyards near the coast, as at Bude and Morwenstow, figureheads of lost ships were sometimes set up as a memorial to the crew; sometimes they have been adapted to inn signs; whilst the large number in the Scilly Isles are a grim reminder of

Miniature Ships' Figurehead, height 8 inches, made as a sample

the dangers to navigation on this part of the coast. Whilst the Admiralty still strove to keep figureheads on the smaller vessels down to portrait busts or half or three-quarter figures, or even to billet-heads and scrolls, the merchantman was restricted only by the taste and generosity of her owners. Most first-class merchantmen seem to have carried full-length figures. As the century advanced, the figurehead grew in size, till by the 1850's three-quarter-lengths as much as fifteen feet high occur on naval vessels. Curiously enough, except in size figurehead designs appear to make no concession to the increasing vogue for opulent and elaborate decoration in Victorian times; if anything they tend to become more severe.

The trend towards naturalistic representation set the ships' carvers some pretty problems in interpretation when ships were given mythological or allegoric names, problems which are tackled with much verve and ingenuity (*III*). Portraits of royal personages and popular heroes often give good results; the fifteen-foot-high "Royal Albert" figurehead, complete with side-whiskers, shows the Prince Consort looking, for all his immense size, very like the little Staffordshire figure portraits of him. The vogue for portrait figureheads when merchantman were named after their owners sometimes gave a certain incongruity; the "James Baines" was carved buttoned up in a frock coat; the "Samuel Plimsoll" wore a top hat. Uniforms, with their bright colours, are more suitable. So, too, are the turbanned oriental figures which reflect British interests in the Far East; one such, the "Bencoolen," is set up in Bude churchyard.

With the arrival of the clipper, the positon of the figurehead inclined more to the horizontal; this new position, combined with the elegant lines of these fast sailing-ships, again influenced design. Since vessels of all sorts and sizes, from the largest warship to the humblest paddle-steamer, carried figureheads, the carvers were afforded plenty of scope for the exercise of individual skill and taste. Miniature figureheads a few inches high, and perhaps made as samples or souvenirs, can sometimes be found.

The figurehead went out, not with the advent of steam, but when iron replaced wood for shipbuilding; at the beginning of the twentieth century a few still survived.

Roundabout and Rocking Horses

At least one of the old ships' carvers, and probably others, turned his hand, when the ships' carving began to decline, to a form that became increasingly popular during the later years of the nineteenth century, the carved merry-go-round or carousel horses. These fairground ride decorations are one of the last and more flamboyant manifestations of popular art, all the more remarkable because they arose out of the industrial revolution. They afford evidence that mechanisation is not incompatible with popular art, and that the reasons for its present decline must be sought elsewhere.

Until some seventy or eighty years ago the only form of merry-go-round consisted of wooden horses on a revolving platform turned by hand. The advent of the steam engine revolutionised all this by making possible the huge roundabouts we know to-day, with horses that not only revolve but also go up and down. A country blacksmith and wheelwright, Frederick Savage from King's Lynn in Norfolk—where his statue stands to-day— seems to deserve most of the credit for the evolution of the steam-driven roundabouts, as a sideline to his work on agricultural machinery. The construction of the roundabout needs to be both light and strong; light so that it can be easily taken to pieces and packed in a small place for transport; strong so that it will stand up to the exuberance of a holiday-making public. A steam engine in the middle drives a revolving centre, from which project steel shafts, like the spokes of a huge wheel; platform and horses are hung from the shaft, whilst cranks give the horses their up-and-down motion.

But if the mechanical principle of the roundabout derives from agricultural machinery, the gorgeous decoration comes straight from the old fairground and circus tradition of magnificent display; the spirit of the "Greatest Show on Earth" ramps over everything. Because the roundabouts were developed in the heyday of the Victorian era, the prevailing style is that extraordinary hotchpotch of decoration, with motives culled from every possible time and place, which reached its zenith in the Great Exhibition of 1851. Glitter and brilliance are the keynotes, just as in the

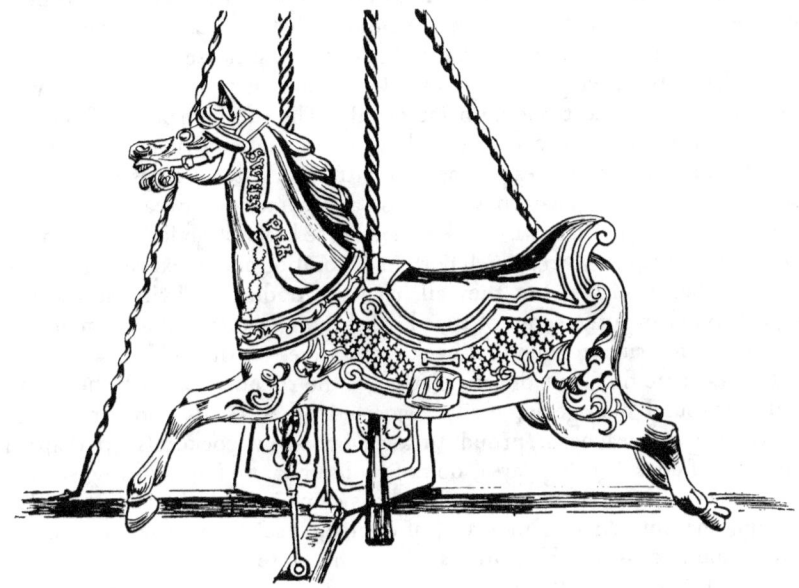

Merry-go-round or Carousel Horse

Victorian public-house or theatre. Every possible space is lavishly ornamented. The revolving centre, encased in carved and painted panels, is crowned, like the capital of a column, with elaborately carved and painted scroll work; from the lower edge depend scolloped or lozenge droppers, each carved and painted and often inset with a bit of cut "brilliant" mirror glass, to flash and sparkle as they swing. The paintings on the panels will, perhaps, depict the highspot of some tremendous adventure, a tiger hunt or the like, with a drama and gusto which suggest that they are directly descended from the old Raree- or Peep-shows of the fairground. Or in more idyllic mood, they may represent a romantic landscape, of moonlit rocks and waterfalls, perhaps, in the same vein as the castles painted on barges or the toy theatre scenes; in this they reflect the vogue for the picturesque in art at the turn of the eighteenth century. The owner's name supplies a further chance for decoration. It appears, painted in elaborately twirled and shaded lettering, on the curved or "rounding" boards which form the rim of the great wheel of shafts from which the platform is suspended. The many joins which must necessarily occur in the structure, so that it can be easily taken to pieces, are hidden by elaborately carved crestings.

Such is the magnificent *décor* which sets off the horses. These are hung four or five abreast from shiny, twisted brass rods, or, more recently, chromium plate. Their bodies are carved in wood, but the projecting ears are usually made of cast iron, and serve as grips for the riders. The eyeballs are usually made of glass and sparkle as they move. The horses are painted all over in shiny, highly varnished paint, with the details picked out in vividly contrasting colours. As a rule the outermost horse is also patterned with elaborate carving, though the decoration may grow progressively less and the innermost one be painted only. The carving spreads from the saddle and trappings all over the body of the horse, so that he may appear wreathed in acanthus leaves perhaps, or patterned with scollops and scrolls, or rose, thistle and shamrock designs, and sometimes wearing portrait medallions or grotesque masks, like huge horse brasses, on flanks and chest. Individual horses vary very much both in decoration and in expression, some fierce, others amiable, but they all have the traditional flying stance designed to enhance the sense of speed. Each horse has its name, sometimes inscribed on a ribbon round its neck, sometimes on the saddle.

Horses came first, but the association of the roundabout with the circus and fairground menagerie, easily suggested other beasts and birds. The birds, elegant peacocks, proud turkeys or perky cockerels (perhaps a memory of cock-fighting days), do not fly but adopt a fine strutting stance, sometimes with very fierce feet. Ostriches came in with the rise of ostrich farming in South Africa; they are, of course, specially associated with the fairground because of the feathers which the costermonger's donah wears in her hat. There are also fabulous creatures; scaly dragons, natural enough in a land where the patron saint is St. George, or sometimes grotesque hybrids with the tail of one added to the head of another.

We find the same basic fairground art all over Western Europe and in the United States, though with individual variations according to the different countries. It is essentially baroque in its exuberance and emphasis on movement, though it has its roots at least as far back as the Middle Ages.

Until about the 1920's, this fairground idiom could comfortably assimilate new ideas and motives, just as did the music-hall. The fairground artist took the Boer War in his stride, and the wide-brimmed hat of some contemporary military hero can appear on a portrait medallion alongside motives, such as a classical mask or helmeted Britannia, derived from perhaps as far back as the eighteenth century. But the super-cinema, with its stereotyped mass-production standards, has introduced a bogus modernism which is gradually destroying the old individual fantasy in both fairground and music-hall *décor*. The advance of mechanisation has brought about a curious change in taste. The roundabout remains a machine, as it always was, but the new spirit, instead of disguising its mechanical properties in fantastic fairytale trappings, emphasises them with austerely streamlined motor-cars and aeroplanes, all identical, in place of the old romantically individual horses and other beasts. The war has accelerated this disappearance of the old forms, and they are now mostly confined to roundabouts for small children, though here and there a thoroughly old-fashioned big roundabout survives.

Unlike the roundabout horses, the carved wooden rocking-horses (*II*) always seem to have retained a considerable degree of naturalism, and to have relied for extra decoration on their trappings and saddle. They too are often beautifully carved, and it is no small tribute to their workmanship that so many have survived. The earlier ones have wooden rockers like rocking chairs, which contribute greatly to their decorative appearance. The modern form swing from iron rods, but otherwise have kept a great deal of the old tradition.

Shop and Inn Signs

What the figurehead was to the ship, the sign was to the shop or inn. But whereas most inns have retained their signs in some form or other, shop signs have practically all disappeared now that everyone can read, city streets are numbered and distinctive emblems are no longer needed to guide the public. Signboards, with a picture painted on them, we discuss under painting and their decorative brackets under metalwork. But there is a large group of effigy signs, carved in the round, which have all the qualities of the figurehead and were probably often made by the same people. The effigy sign has the advantage over the signboard that it can be striking without taking up so much room, a point that appealed to the civic authorities, who were constantly trying to limit the size and projection of signboards to keep the narrow streets from being completely darkened, while naturally each shopkeeper wanted to make his sign bigger and project it further out than his neighbour's. After the great fire of London in 1666, many of the houses that were rebuilt had carved stone signs, painted or gilt, and let into the front of the house below the first-floor windows, in preference to the old swinging signboards. When Larwood and Hotton published their *History of Signboards*[1] (still the best book on the subject) some two hundred years later, many of these signs were still there, but have since disappeared, though the carved panel of the "Swan with Two Necks" in Cheapside survived until quite recently.

A fine example of the old carved stone signs, from the "Bull and Mouth,"

1 "Larwood" was the pen name of a Dutch artist and antiquarian, which accounts for the many references to Netherlands signs; his biography was given in *Notes and Queries* for 1920. He illustrated his *History*, which first appeared in 1866, with wood engravings of signs taken from old prints, broadsides. trade cards and tokens and the like, thus conveying little idea of what the actual signs looked like. A modern revised edition has been announced.

originally "Boulogne (Harbour) Mouth," a famous old coaching inn in St. Martin's le Grand, was transferred when the inn was pulled down to the façade of the Queen's Hotel, and is now preserved in the Guildhall Museum. It shows a disdainful bull standing over a broad-grinning face. But the typical nineteenth century attitude to the old shop and inn signs, apart from the small circle of antiquarians, seems to have been that they were ridiculous rubbish, unworthy of the age of universal knowledge, as we can see from passing references in Dickens. In *Dombey and Son* he mentions a carved wooden midshipman, which "thrust itself out above the pavement, right leg foremost," above Sol Gill's shop, and "bore at its right eye the most offensively disproportionate piece of machinery," as being one of many such "little timber midshipmen in obsolete naval uniform, eternally employed outside the shopdoors of nautical instrument makers, in taking observations of the hackney coaches." As for inn signs, and Dickens was a great lover of inns, the sign of the "Great White Horse" at Ipswich, where Mr. Pickwick spent an adventurous night, is guyed as "the stone statue of some rampacious animal, with flying mane and tail, distinctly resembling an insane carthorse, which is elevated above the principal door". Fortunately this spirited piece of popular art still survives. But it is small wonder that, in such an atmosphere of moral disapproval, most of the shop effigy signs should have been allowed to fall to pieces.

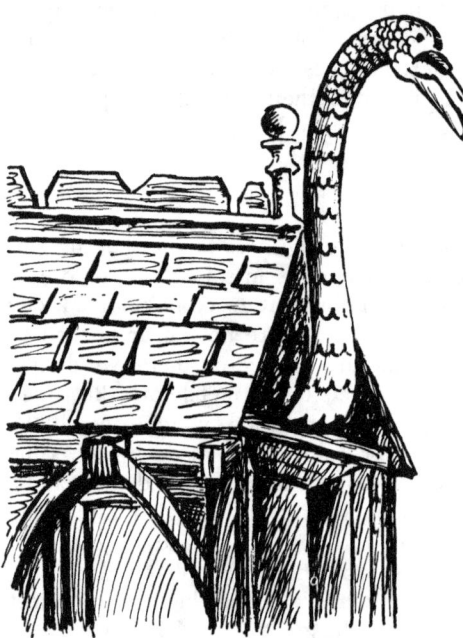

Figurehead serving as Inn Sign : "The Swan" between Ashford and Folkestone

Shop signs were intended to serve two purposes: to show the type of business, like the barber's striped pole, the glove-maker's golden hand or the shoemaker's golden foot, and to give the location, so that the shop could be picked out in a particular street, as for instance "at the Sun and Bible in Giltspur Street" or "at the Looking Glass on London Bridge," both early eighteenth century publishers' addresses. The location sign did not necessarily embody the trade emblem, and the amalgamation of businesses and the like often gave an even odder combination of objects than on the more familiar inn signs, as may be seen from Sir Ambrose

Heal's fascinating survey, *The Signboards of Old London Shops*, the only one on this particular subject, though inn signs have been much written about. Location signs have virtually disappeared from our shops, but effigies of trade emblems may sometimes still be seen, especially in country towns. A list of the emblems used by the various trades is given in Sir Ambrose Heal's book. Many of them, like the golden canister of the tea merchants, are immediately recognisable, though the association of tea merchants with a grasshopper, linen-drapers with a blackamoor's head or unicorn, or printers with an anchor seems remote to modern eyes, but to our ancestors they were probably as familiar as the three golden balls are to us.

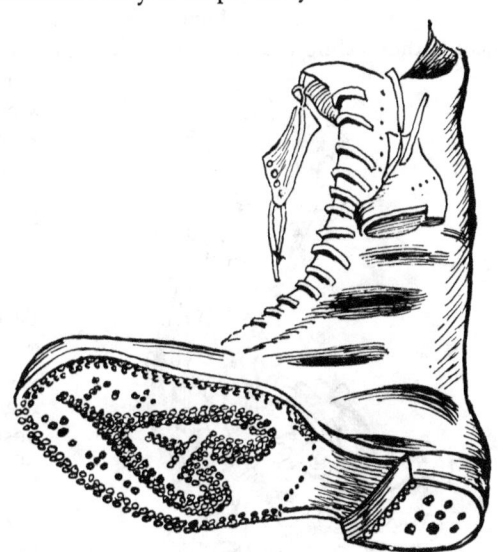

The red or gold hat in front of the hatters, the red plaster jars above the oil-and-colour merchant, the kettle or padlock over the iron-mongers, the gilt umbrella in front of the umbrella makers are still to be seen, and sometimes emblems such as the large gold key in front of the locksmiths or the golden trout of the fishing-tackle shop may be admirable examples of local carving. The best of these carved effigy signs that remain are usually the Highlanders of the tobacconist, meant to advertise Scotch snuff. They generally date from the eighteenth century,

Bootmaker's Sign in leather studded with brass nails

when Scotch snuff was much esteemed, and are (or at least originally were) gaily painted. They vary in size; some may be only two or three feet high, others five feet or more; often they wear a snuff horn in their belt and have one hand raised in an elegant eighteenth century gesture of snuff-taking. A bootmaker's sign, now preserved in the Horniman Museum, is a three-foot-high leather boot; the sole, the part most visible from below, is studded with shiny brass nails arranged in patterns and including the firm's initials. The practice of making patterns with brass nails on the soles of boots displayed in the bootmaker's window has only recently died out.

Two carved and painted wooden figures representing "Justice" and "Wisdom" taken from the old Town House (or Council Chamber) at Salisbury, which was burnt in 1782, are now in the Salisbury Museum; they are in the same simple idiom as the snuff Highlander, and provide admirable examples of popular carving of the eighteenth century. They too are, in a sense, emblem effigies, and give us some idea of what the more elegant eighteenth century carved shop sign looked like; actually Justice with her scales was one of the trade emblems of the scale-makers.

Of the carved inn signs that survive to us, few date from earlier than the seventeenth century, though the stone angel's-head bracket above the doorway of the "Angel and Royal" at Grantham is much older. These carved effigies are usually placed over the portico; but sometimes, like the magnificent "White Hart" at Salisbury, an eighteenth century carving, on the gable of the roof. The advantage of this position is that the sign can be seen from a much greater distance. Londoners will remember as a familiar landmark against the skyline the great stone lion (also eighteenth-century work and

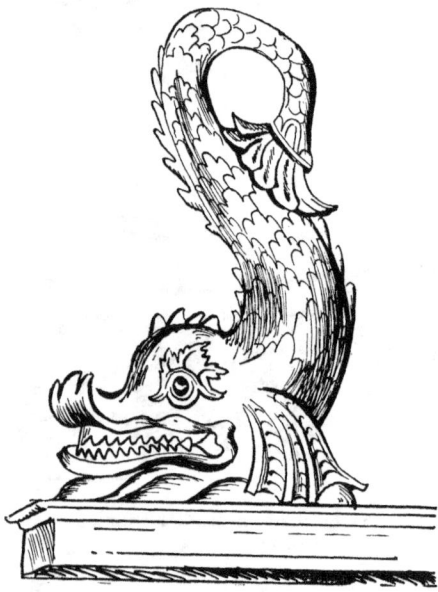

Carved Inn Sign: "The Dolphin" at Langport

made of artificial stone) which stood on the roof of the "Red Lion Brewery" on the south bank of the Thames; it survived all the bombing unscathed only to succumb to the post-war zeal of the Festival of Britain planners. The "Red Lion" at Barnet is precariously perched on the end of a wrought-iron bracket, projecting over the road, but this is an unusual position, though carved bunches of grapes, sugar loaves and similar symbols are sometimes hung from brackets, above or below a painted signboard. Where the inn has no portico, as many of the older ones have not, a carved sign may be set on a bracket over the doorway, like the dolphin at Langport

in Somerset, which is gaily painted and looks like the work of a ships' carver. Real figureheads make very attractive inn signs, like the Swan to be seen on the Ashford-Folkestone road (p. 12). We know from old illustrations that beam, or "gallows," signs stretching right across the road were once very popular, and would be elaborately decorated with carvings. Attractive examples survive at "The Fox and Hounds," Barley, Hertfordshire, and "The Four Swans," Waltham Cross.

These carved effigy signs do not show as great a range of subjects as the painted boards; the Royal Arms, so beautifully carved in relief, is frequent, so too are lions, horses, deer and bears in various attitudes. "The Bear" at Devizes carries a large bunch of grapes in his mouth; the same device appears on the owner's trade card when the inn was built in the eighteenth

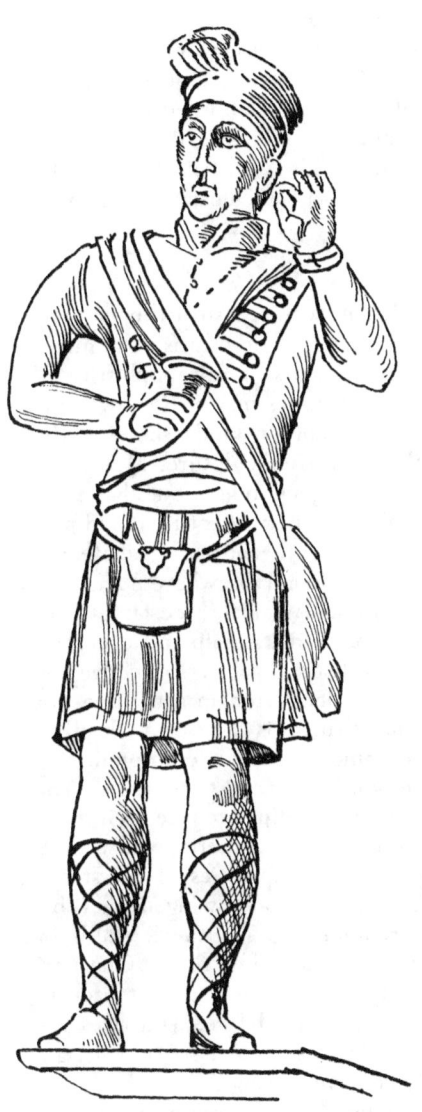

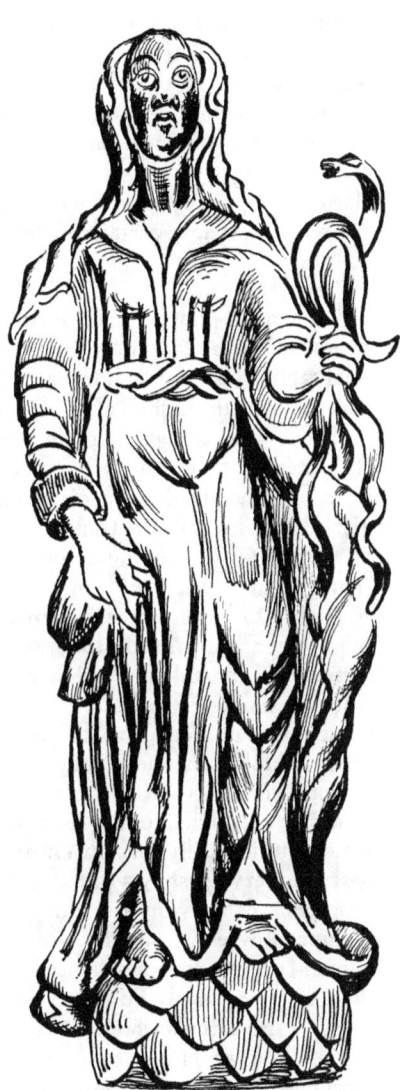

Eighteenth century Tobacconist's Sign
from Silver Street, Salisbury

Carved-wood Figure of "Wisdom" from
the old Town House, Salisbury

century, so presumably sign and house are contemporary. The "Dun Cow" at Shrewsbury fills the whole roof of the portico and sits looking placidly down on the public below. The style of carving ranges from simple to very elaborate, but it is rare to find a weak piece of work, and the majority show great character. Many of them are obviously local work, though towards the end of the eighteenth century and in the first quarter of the nineteenth, a sort of mass production of signs was established in London, in Harp Alley, off Shoe Lane, and the commoner emblems, like bunches of grapes or sugar loaves, were supplied to the whole country. But even the Harp Alley productions, such as the "Sugar Loaf" at Dunstable, are hand-carved and retain a certain quality.

Tombstones

A form of popular art carving which has received surprisingly little attention can be found on tombstones in country churchyards. The memorial tablets inside the churches are usually the work of more sophisticated craftsmen in the fashionable idiom, and tombstones may also show these qualities. But alongside them there exists another kind, showing the characteristics we usually associate with "primitive" sculpture. Miss Innes Hart, who has made a special study of this subject, points out that a remarkably homogeneous tradition exists in East Sussex, West Kent and part of Surrey (4, 6), amongst seventeenth, eighteenth and early nineteenth century tombstones, with forms of design not found elsewhere.[1] She suggests that for such an achievement in a particular area three factors are required: a good local stone, a tradition of craftsmanship and a certain number of individual craftsmen with an artist's capacity for conveying emotion in their work. The names of these local stonemasons have not come down to us and we can only surmise that, as is the case with other forms of folk art, there must have been among them a few dominating personalities who set their stamp on the work of several generations. The local stone, which does not lend itself to slabs, has helped to give their work a monolithic quality which enhances the emotional content, whilst at its best the carving shows great sensitiveness to the qualities of the stone. The symbols vary in the different districts; in some winged cherubs, trumpets, wreaths and rays of glory predominate; in others, skulls or human faces, sometimes incised only, sometimes in low relief. One persistent and curiously impressive type has the top of the stone cut back to form a semi-circular hood over an incised or carved face. The faces are stylised and simplified to a minimum of lines, so much so that in late examples they may have become merely concentric rings.

The skulls too vary very much in treatment; some are mere scratchings, others deeply carved, especially the eyeholes, giving full play to the effects of shadow. This austere and abstract idiom, concentrating as it does on conveying the essence of the symbols used, is curiously modern in feeling

[1] Miss Innes Hart has illustrated some of these strange carvings in the *Architectural Review* for November, 1939.

and probably makes a much more moving appeal to us than it will have done to previous generations accustomed to a more naturalistic interpretation. Used as we now are to abstract art, we can recapture something of the emotion, sometimes the dignity of peace and resignation, sometimes strange and rather sinister feelings, elsewhere jubilation in the hope of the

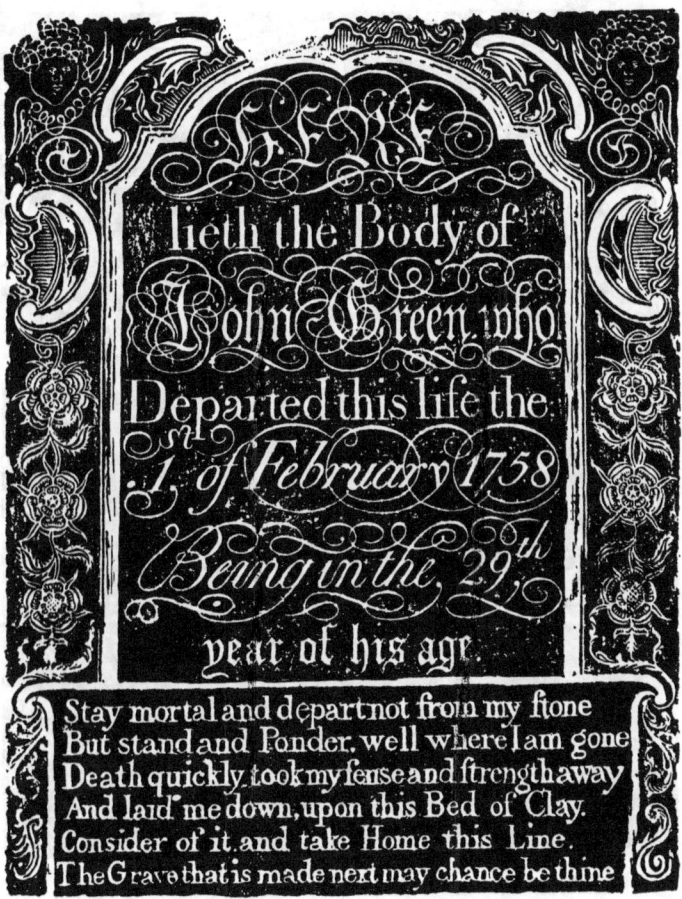

Slate Headstone from Farndon, Nottinghamshire, by
F. Lamb of Bottesford, 1758

Resurrection, which death brought to the very simple people for whom these stones were made.

Both this region and other districts also use less abstract interpretations. We sometimes find little scenes, perhaps of the Resurrection, or groups with angels and cherubs, and here it is interesting to see how the baroque motives of the late sixteenth and early seventeenth centuries are translated into the much simpler terms of popular imagery. Trade emblems may be used: the glover's gloves or the tailor's shears. Near the sea ships are sometimes found, especially in Norfolk; at Sheringham, near Cromer, there is a low-relief carving of an overturned boat, cut with an exquisite economy of line and making a poignantly dramatic statement. A feature of many, even of the simplest stones, is the lettering, often beautifully proportioned and

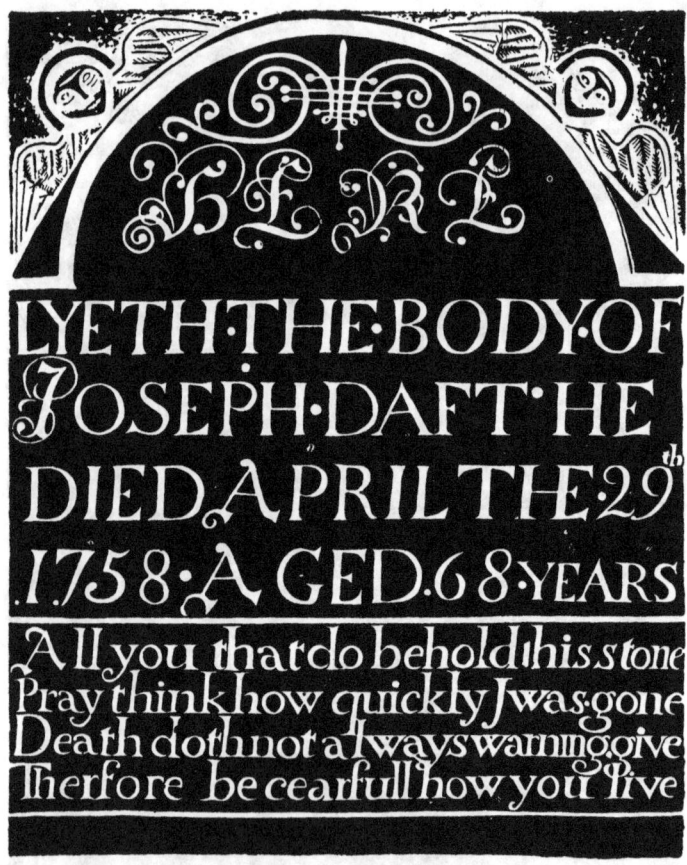

Slate Headstone from Whatton in Nottinghamshire, 1758

cut with great skill, giving a quiet dignity to simple and sometimes very naïve inscriptions. This superb lettering is a constant reminder of the long tradition of good writing in a great mercantile country like ours.

The tradition of good lettering is specially conspicuous on slate headstones, not only because slate is hard enough to take sharply defined incised or low-relief carving, but also because it resists the weather so that stones over two hundred years old may retain all their original precision. Remarkable in these slate slabs is the way in which their carvers try to get variety of texture in what is primarily a smooth, flat surface by carving the tops in low relief or raising some of the lettering whilst incising other parts. We come across slate headstones from time to time in most parts of the country; particularly fine ones occur in Leicestershire and Nottinghamshire, with a well-marked local tradition. From about the 1730's and 40's many Nottinghamshire ones are signed by their makers. Mr. M. W. Barley, in the *Transactions of the Thoroton Society* for 1948, has traced and analysed the work of a number of these named craftsmen and has worked out the evolution of local styles through the century. His record provides a fascinating miniature history of one branch of popular art. He shows the dominance of a few outstanding craftsmen, the influence of allied crafts like penmanship and engraving, the gradual filtering through of decorative idioms fashionable in the more sophisticated world but translated and simplified, and finally the all-too-familiar deadening impact of "elegant taste" on the sturdy vitality of village craftsmen, represented by the advent of foreign marbles in the nineteenth century.

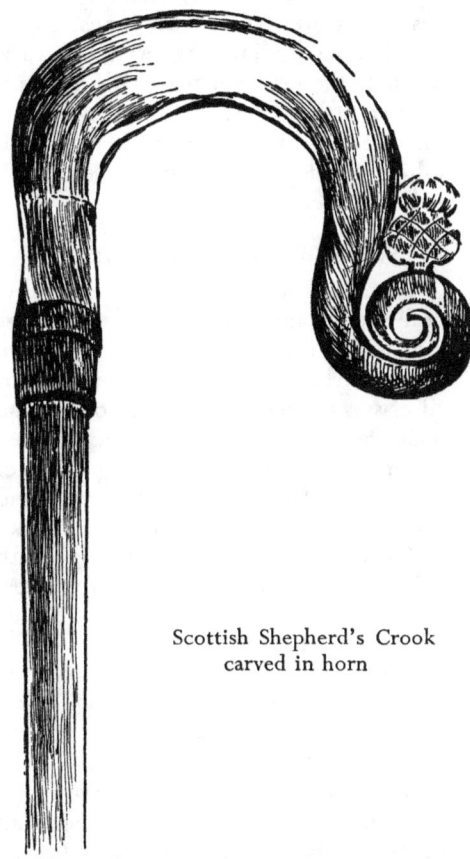

Scottish Shepherd's Crook
carved in horn

Crooks and Sticks

So far we have been considering the larger forms of carving. But small and intricate things too make a special appeal to the imagination. It is here, using the simplest materials and tools, that the amateur virtuoso comes into his own. Life in the country or at sea once gave the long intervals of leisure which are needed for the exercise of this special skill, and with the increasing tempo of modern life it is slowly dying out. All simple societies seem to have an urge to decorate even the humblest tools and utensils, for the sheer pleasure of doing it. Shepherds carve their crooks; Michael Drayton noticed that the Elizabethan shepherd took pride in "his sheep hook, once of price, that hath been carved with many a strange device." The carvings of the nomadic Wallachian shepherds, absent from their homes for months at a time, have produced some of the most interesting folk art in Roumania; and we can find examples from many other peasant countries. In the Scottish Highlands shepherds still carve crooks from a sheep's horn, making the curve three fingers broad for the width of a sheep's neck. The transparent colour of the horn and the simple decoration combine to produce the most subtle effects. Carving walking-sticks was also once a traditional shepherd's craft, though of course not confined to them only (8). Great care was needed to select a stick grown to the right shape for the design, with a natural curve perhaps or right-angled piece of root, and a good stick might need watching and coaxing for several years as it grew. Odd formations, like an ivy root twisting up the stem, could be incorporated as part of the carving. In the more elaborate forms not only the head but the whole stem of the stick is carved with patterns or even little scenes. The wooden handles of tools were sometimes beautifully carved by their owners, especially those used for carpentry and cabinet-making (7). Whip handles in wood or bone also lend themselves to carved decoration.

Presents and Love Tokens

The desire to give presents, especially love tokens, has created a great deal of popular art, particularly in carving, which the lover could do himself, using local, easily procurable materials and an ordinary pocket knife. When staybusks, those rather formidable articles of dress, were worn by all classes of the community, country lads often carved them in wood or bone for their sweethearts. The wooden ones mostly taper towards the lower end, and are either triangular in cross-section with a ridge running down the middle, or flat on the inside and slightly rounded on the outside. They are chip carved, with a date, linked initials, hearts and other love emblems, flowers and geometrical patterns, sometimes picked out in colour, or even made with a little recess to take a portrait protected by a piece of glass. The bone ones are usually slightly curved and tapered, rounded a little on the outside (a sheep's thigh bone was very suitable and easy to come by). They are ornamented with "scrimshaw" work, scratched decoration filled with red or black colour, and have the same devices as the wood ones. A sailing ship on a bone staybusk suggests a sailor's love token. Sailors were specially apt at this work and would sometimes use narwhale horn for scrimshaw. Normally staybusks were worn inside the corsage, but tradition has it that the country girl who was lucky enough to be given a handsomely decorated set would wear them outside to show them off properly.

A form of present which kept its vogue long after the staybusk had gone out of fashion was the knitting-stick, designed to be worn in the belt and take the ball of wool. These sticks were usually made of wood, all in one piece, the lower part slightly curved to fit the hip, a hook in the middle to go on the belt and a square head for the wool. The head and the front of the stick were elaborately carved, with the same sort of geometrical and floral patterns as the staybusks, though the hearts and other love symbols do not seem to be so frequent, which suggests that they may have been given to relatives also. Pinpoppets (*VIII*) and knitting-needle cases were also carved as love tokens; a very ingenious sailor-made pincushion has been carved out of the two halves of a coconut, decorated with fish; it has padding for the pins between. Coconuts could be put to all sorts of uses; one in the Taunton Museum has been made into a powderflask, carved in the likeness of some strange beast, perhaps an armadillo, and fitted with a silver nozzle.

A very simple form of love token was an apple corer or cheese taster, made of a piece of bone a few inches long, the knuckle serving as the handle, the stem decorated with hearts and linked initials in scrimshaw, filled in red, or even a bone shoe-horn, suitably inscribed. Many of these little carvings are extremely decorative and ingeniously take advantage of the natural forms of the materials. Milkmaids might be given a little tip of horn to keep fat in for smoothing rough hands on frosty mornings; indeed, these little carved love tokens show immense variety.

A *tour de force* in love tokens was to carve a spoon and fork linked together out of a single piece of wood or bone. They might be hinged (like a modern pair of salad servers) or, an even greater feat, attached by a chain with every link moving freely. Spoons are traditional courtship presents, as witness the word "spooning." This tradition seems to have been carried furthest in Wales;

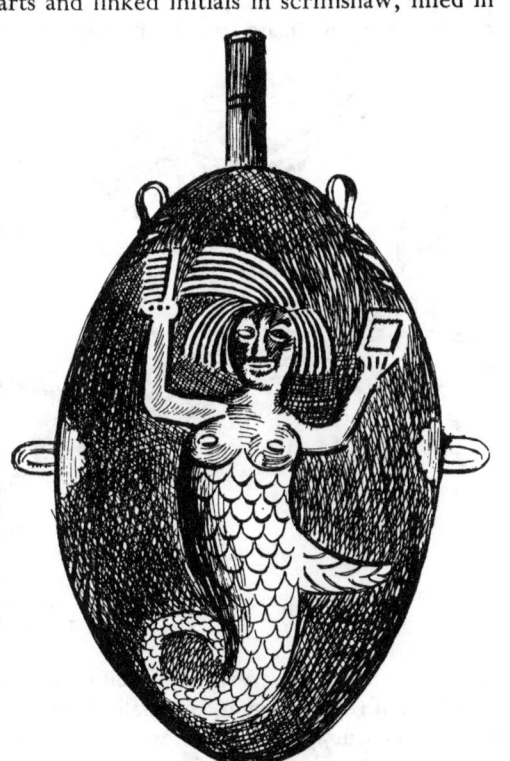

Flask carved from a Coconut, with silver nozzle.   Probably sailor's work

the Welsh love spoons are, in some of their more elaborate forms, only meant for ornament, and would be hung by the fireplace; they may have two or three bowls and handles, joined together like Siamese twins, with carved and pierced decoration; some have a knife and fork as well as the spoons. No doubt more practically minded suitors carved spoons and even forks that could be used. Some of these domestic utensils are beautifully made. Beech and sycamore were good woods for this form of work.

Of course not all these little amateur carvings were love tokens; it is hardly possible to imagine the many examples we find of carved pipe stoppers or even whip handles being given in this way. Quite a number may well have been done semi-commercially, for sale. Prisoners would often do such work; when the Vicar of Wakefield tried to reform his fellow prisoners, he started them on carving little objects as a means of earning money. The French prisoners of war, of whom there were large numbers here during the Napoleonic campaigns, were particularly skilful with wood and bone, and no doubt their work also influenced the English. There are, too, many things which seem to have been made purely for the pleasure of exercising skill, like a cherry stone beautifully carved and with an ivory stopper, made to hold nine dozen minute silver teaspoons, which

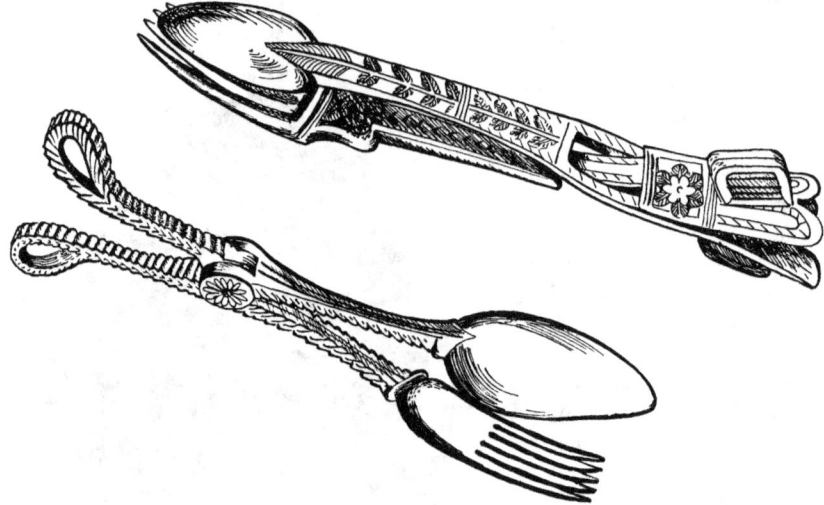

Hinged Spoons and Forks carved in one piece: the top pair in bone,
the lower in wood

is now in the Saffron Waldon Museum. This district had a particularly fine tradition of rustic carving, especially by shepherds, which survived into the present century; sometimes when objects have been presented to the museum, even the name of the craftsman has come down to us. Two remarkable examples of carving by shepherds are chain knitting-sticks, cut in holly, with every link separate; one has a single strand of chain, the other four.

Sailors' and Apprentices' Work

Specially associated with sailors are the carved and jointed models of ships fitted into bottles of all shapes and sizes. They were made in many different countries, and sometimes have a lighthouse and waves as well, though this kind is more common abroad. Ships are the most usual of the models fitted into bottles; an early railway engine is an unusual variation, and we sometimes find abstract devices of wood and coloured thread, stars, crosses and wheels, or wind bells hung on a wooden frame, which ring through the glass with a very clear tone. An extraordinarily ingenious model, made in Sweden, has two little dolls, each sitting weaving at a handloom, set one above the other in a large square-shaped bottle. Several examples of these weaving ladies in a bottle exist. A form of wood carving in birch very prevalent in Sweden is to cut very thin slices of wood and

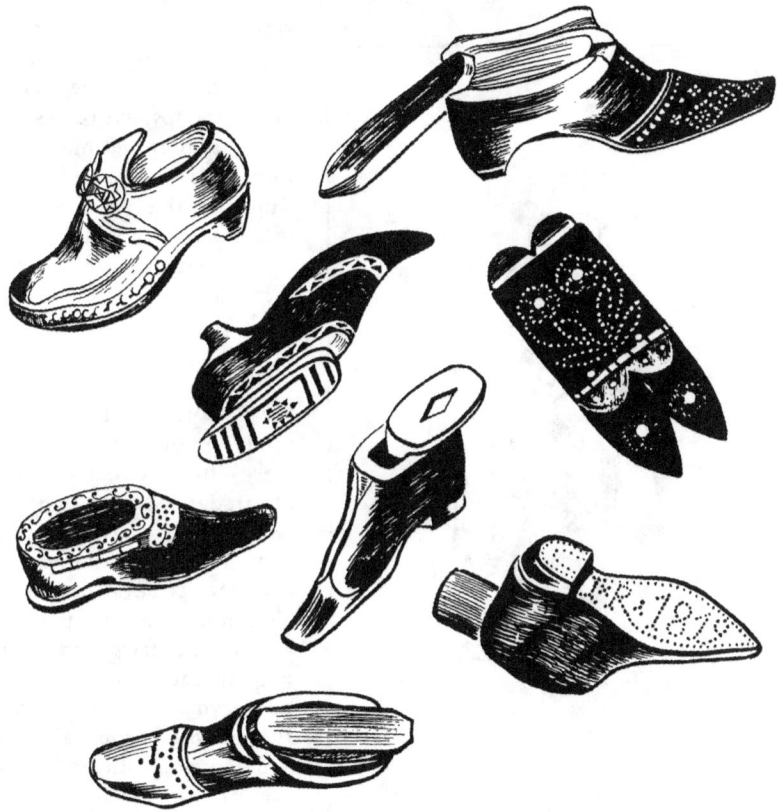

Shoe Snuff-boxes carved and studded

either spread them out, to form the wing and tail of a bird perhaps, or let them curl over to give a feathery effect. Curiously enough, this simple technique does not seem to have been much used in England, though the Salisbury Museum has some flowers made in this way by a shepherd.

In the days when the heels of shoes were hand cut out of wood, besides patterns and clogs, every shoemaker's apprentice could carve. To them we owe most of the little carved shoe snuff-boxes which came into vogue about 1800. We can trace half a century of fashions in shoes in these miniatures. Many of them have the soles decorated with tiny brass studs, as the

full-size sample shoes shown in the shoemaker's window once were. Some
of them are carved in horn or even ivory, others are beaten out of pewter.
The apprentices are also responsible for many of the miniature pieces of
furniture, at most some eighteen inches high, chairs, chests of drawers,
writing-desks and the like, which were made as trade samples or for practice.

Gingerbread Stamps and Moulds

Woodcarving was also used for making moulds and stamps for a great
variety of purposes—printing, pottery, even for stamping cakes and butter. The
butter stamps, with cows and roses, still sometimes used to-day, are humble descendants of the great age of monumental cookery, the towers, knights and dragons that the Elizabethan pastrycook delighted in, or the lighter and more Italianate confectionery ornament of the Restoration. The moulds used in the great houses were often extremely complicated pieces of carving on boxwood or pear, reflecting contemporary fashions in architecture and dress. Transmuted into the popular art of the fairground gilt gingerbread, household bun or dairymaid's butter stamp, the designs become simpler and less sophisticated. The stamps are usually cut in beech or, more often, sycamore, which has the great advantage for all culinary utensils that the more it is scrubbed the whiter it gets.

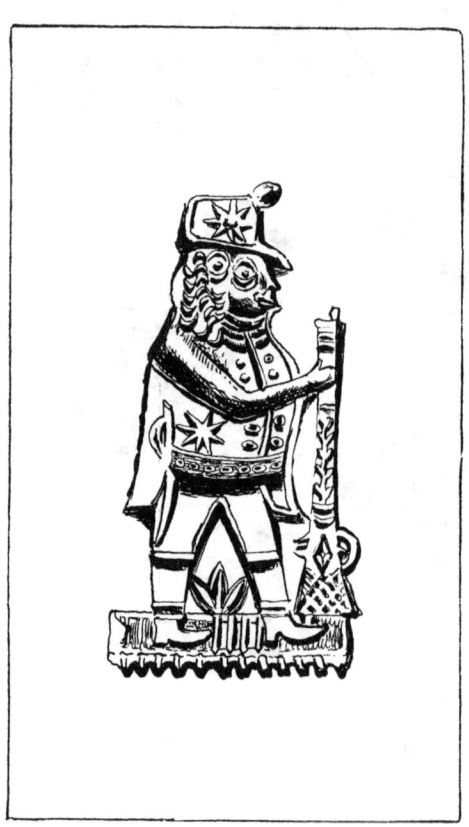

Gingerbread Biscuit Stamps from
Horsham in Sussex

Gingerbread rollers or platters, "cards" as they were sometimes called,
made by local craftsmen, were on sale at country fairs and markets, as
butter stamps still are, though nowadays they are apt to be machine made
with stereotyped designs. For everyday use they were carved with flowers,
fruit or birds, sometimes the letters of the alphabet—a pleasant way of
learning. A set of these stamps, used for making biscuits at Horsham

in Sussex is now in the Brighton Museum. The stamped gingerbread sold at fairs was decorated with thin gold leaf, which easily peeled off, hence the expression "the gilt has come off the gingerbread."

Special feasts had their appropriate symbols; the Easter lamb (which appears on the Pax cakes distributed at Hentland on Palm Sunday), for instance, or hearts for a betrothal. The famous "Biddenden Maids," the twin sisters Eliza and Mary Chulkhurst, have their names and portrait stamped on the "cakes" distributed as part of the Biddenden Dole on Easter Monday. This is one of the oldest surviving charitable distributions, though there seems to be some doubt whether the cake stamp was originally intended to represent the foundresses, or whether the local tradition that they were twins, joined together at the hips and shoulders, has arisen from the stamp.

Tunbridge Ware

The market for cheap mementoes or souvenirs to be sold to travellers, which must date from at least as early as the great mediaeval pilgrimages, has produced a great variety of little wood and bone objects, far too numerous for us even to attempt to list them. They retained their popular art qualities well on into the nineteenth century, when the increasing vogue for cheap mass-production imitation of more expensive articles brought about a complete collapse of the traditional standards. We

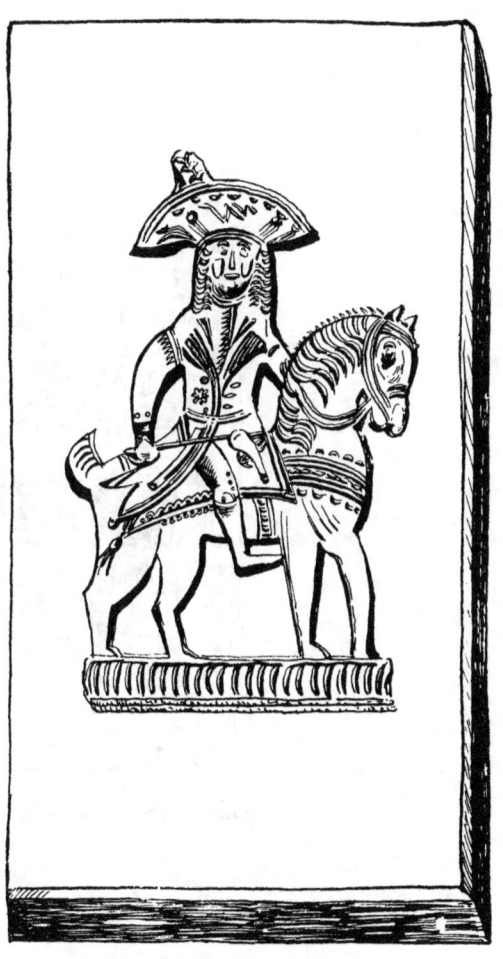

Gingerbread Biscuit Stamps from Horsham in Sussex

may single out, as examples of semi-manufactured articles, the little pressed horn objects, pinpoppets and the like, once sold in the streets of London, at the Thames Tunnel and elsewhere. Also the so-called "Tunbridge ware," a simple technique of veneering, made by glueing differently coloured strips of wood together and slicing them across horizontally. This technique, which was practised at Tunbridge Wells from at least the seventeenth century, involved the use of many different kinds of wood for colour effects—holly naturally white could be stained grey with Tunbridge Wells water. At its simplest it produced chequerboard patterns, at its most elaborate, floral and other picture patterns, which could be repeated by slices from the same block and gave very decorative effects.

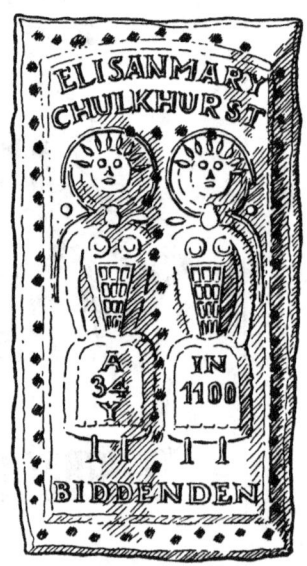

Stamp of the "Biddenden Maids"

Chapter Two

METAL

Sign Brackets and Frames

The blacksmith was, and indeed still is, an essential person in each rural community, possessing a skill and knowledge that range far beyond the mere shoeing of horses. He is the local engineer, making and repairing tools and machinery; indeed, to the ingenuity of country smiths we owe much of our modern agricultural machinery, and, as a by-product, that typical manifestation of popular art, the roundabout. Until recent years the smith was also the horse doctor, possessing a store of homely veterinary knowledge. Like all countrymen, the smith has his busy seasons, and during the slacker winter period often turns his hand to ornamental work.

One great opportunity for using ornamental wrought iron was provided by the many brackets and frames used for supporting lamps and signs. In large towns such as London, the ornamental iron work for lampholders, railings, gates and the like was normally the work of specialised craftsmen, using designs by an architect or taken from the pattern books published by famous smiths. But in country districts this fashionable idiom, so far as it existed at all, would be modified by the local smith to suit his own skill and taste. Street lighting was rare in the country, so it is to the wrought-iron brackets and frames for supporting signs, especially inn signs, that we must look to find the best examples in this form of popular art. Signs can be suspended on brackets projecting from the wall, the most usual position, which may well derive from the pole with a bush or hoop on it which was the earliest form of inn sign. Or they may be set up in an iron frame on a high wooden post, or even slung from an arch across the road in the now rare "gallows" form.

Our English wrought-iron sign supports are much simpler in design than the elaborate forms found on the Continent, in southern Germany, Switzerland and the Low Countries, for instance. But at their best they have plenty of vitality. Sometimes they repeat in metal the device painted on the board, as in the famous "Three Swans" bracket at Market Harborough which dates from about 1700, or the outline of a fox bracket from Huntingdon and now in the Victoria and Albert Museum. Sometimes the whole sign may be in wrought iron; smiths might make such signs for their own display, with devices such as three horseshoes or even the tools of their trade. More often, however, the brackets are made of abstract scroll work, though sometimes including a realistic bunch of grapes. Some are very big, as is for instance the elaborately scrolled and stayed triangular bracket of "The Ship Inn"

27

at Mere in Somerset which completely dwarfs the signboard; it is a late eighteenth century example and reflects the then fashionable decorative idiom. The West Country is particularly rich in examples of elaborate brackets. More effective perhaps are the earlier, smaller and simpler square types of bracket, though an exceedingly graceful arching one, mounted on a post, is outside "The Angel" at Aylesbury. Signboards mounted on posts were sometimes given hoods of decorative ironwork, like "The Bear" at Woodstock, but more often the board was framed in scrollwork of various shapes. Indeed, it is surprising to notice how much variety can be put into the simple purpose of hanging up a board. Much of this iron-bracket work dates from the eighteenth century, but as the old patterns were repeated, it is often difficult to date precisely.

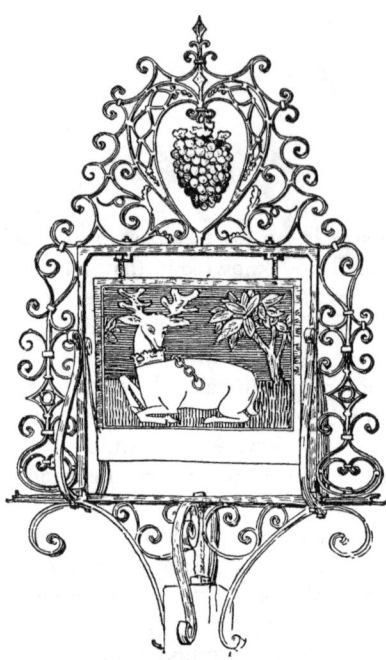

Sign of the "White Hart" of Bletchingly

Weathercocks and Vanes

Another form of sign in metal is the weathercock or weather-vane (**14**). Weathercocks are characteristically English, and were in use before the Norman Conquest; the Bayeux tapestry shows the weathercock on the newly built Westminster Abbey. The weather-vane, properly so-called, though "cock" and "vane" now seem to be interchangeable terms, derives from the common mediaeval practice of using pennants or "vanes"; it often has an armorial or other device pierced in it and, like flags, seems to have been originally intended only for display; pointers to show the direction of the wind are a later addition, and the letters marking the cardinal points of the compass, later still. In the days of sailing ships wind and weather were important topics in a country as much concerned with foreign trade as ours, as the wealth and variety of weather-vanes on the City of London churches bear witness. These elaborate works (for instance the

Blacksmith's Weather-vane made by John Hill Spreyton, Devon

famous dragon of Bow) were usually of copper gilt and made to the plans of
architects such as Wren or Inigo Jones. In the country districts, and on
humbler buildings, local talent had more scope; we often find the weathercocks on village churches in the more popular art idiom, and evidently the
work of some local craftsman. Cocks are, indeed, by far the most frequent
form; they seem to have had special religious associations (perhaps recalling
St. Peter), though we find them on secular buildings also. They range from
very primitive work, flat thick sheets of metal cut out in silhouette, with
pierced eye-holes, to birds with hollow bodies shaped in the round, the
wings, comb and wattles cut out of sheets and fitted on separately, as is the
tail, set at an angle to catch the wind. A fine sweeping tail is indeed the most

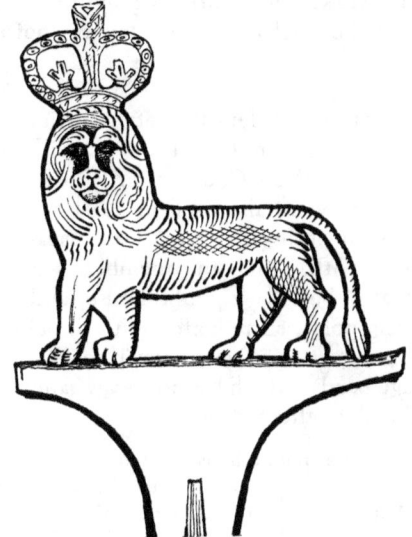

Village Club Polehead from Somerset

prominent feature of a good weathercock. On Axminster Church in Devon
it has become so tremendous as to make the cock look more like a peacock.

Other birds, such as swans and doves, have been used, but they are rare.
Fish are a particularly good shape to catch the wind, and might have been
expected to be specially popular in fishing towns, but we seldom find them.
The gilded fish over St. Andrew's Church at Charmouth in Dorset has its
body made of wood, with fins, teeth and tail of metal. Maidstone in Kent
has a fine dolphin. Ships too, a form of vane common in the Low Countries
and Baltic seaports, are surprisingly scarce here; most of those we see are
modern. Best known of the older ones, perhaps, are the detailed model of
Sir Cloudesley Shovel's frigate "The Rodney," on Rochester Town Hall,
which was specially commissioned as a memorial by the Town Council
(who found it very expensive), and another, rather simpler, of an early
eighteenth century man-o'-war, presented to Portsmouth by Prince

George of Denmark in 1710. But neither of these can really be classed as popular art.

The influence of heraldry has produced various heraldic beasts; but the famous golden grasshopper seems to be the only insect thus elevated, in this country at least. Then there are sporting subjects, especially on stables, such as horses, hounds, foxes or stags. Vanes have also been made in the form of trade signs, and are often pleasant examples of the work of local smiths. Norfolk is particularly rich in distinctive weather-vanes, many of them apparently local work.[1] Ingenious smiths might make their own weather-vane signs; a particularly good example used to surmount the smithy in the remote Dartmoor village of Spreyton: a sheet-metal outline of the blacksmith at work, with a little windmill to catch the wind, and make the hammer hit the anvil with a loud tapping noise.

Club Poleheads

Another form of sign or emblem in metal, particularly associated with rural life, is the polehead used in the ritual of the village clubs and friendly societies, especially in the West Country, in Wiltshire, Dorset, Somerset and Devon, though they were also used in other parts. These mutual aid societies held an annual outing or Great Day, usually at Whitsun or on Oak Apple Day, May 29th, when the members forgathered at the club headquarters, normally the village public house, and then walked in procession, carrying long poles, surmounted with the club's device. William Barnes, the Dorset poet, gives a lively description of the Club Walk (complete with the village band), which has nowadays fallen into disuse with the disappearance of the clubs themselves.

> Var up at public house by ten
> O'clock the pliace wer vull o' men,
> A-dress'd to goo to Church, an' dine,
> An' wa'ke about the pliace in line.
>
> Zoo off tha started, two an' two,
> Wi' painted poles, an' knots o' blue;
> An' girt silk flags . . .
> The fifes did squeak, the drum did rumble,
> An' girt biazzoons did grunt an' grumble,
> An' vo'ke that vollied in a crowd
> Kick'd up the doust in sich a cloud!
>
> An' then at church ther wer sich lots
> O' hats a-hung up wi' ther knots,
> An' poles a-stood so thick as iver
> Ya zeed bull rushes by a river . . .
> An' a'ter church tha went to dine
> 'ithin the girt long room behine
> The public house . . .

---

[1] In *The Weathervanes of Norfolk and Norwich* Mr. C. J. W. Messent has collected over a hundred examples, both old and new.

An' a'ter that tha went al out
In rank agien, an' wa'k'd about,
An' g'ied zome parish vo'ke a cal,
An' then went down to Narley Hal,
An' had zome beer an' danc'd between
The elem trees upon the green.[1]

At each place of call the procession was offered refreshments, so that by the end of the day the proceedings became very lively.

The poles carried in these processions were some six feet long and were often decorated with ribbons. The poleheads that have survived to us are most commonly of brass (below) (often made at Bristol), though there are also examples in strips of iron (evidently the work of a local smith) or even carved in wood. A pewter polehead has been found in York. The Nailsea Glassmakers Guild had their poleheads of blown glass, but these seem to be unique. Club stewards carried specially large and elaborate poleheads.

Most villages, however small, had their club; as each club had its distinctive emblem, often embodying the arms of the public-house where were its headquarters and where its regalia was stowed when out of use, the poleheads show a great variety of designs, some surprisingly elaborate. The favourite basic shape seems to have been the spear, decorated with floreated or curved edges and often pierced as well. Some heads are flat, others cast in the round, with a great variety of knobs, spherical, ovoid or elongated. Less frequent than the spear are the heads which show the actual device, either in outline or in the round: the royal lion, king's head, crown, fleur-de-lys, horse, horseshoe, anchor, dove, acorn and oakleaves, hand pierced with heart, star, sun and crescent moon; and so on. Sometimes the device might be engraved on the basic spearhead, as for instance a sailing-ship, or raised in relief. In some of the more complicated forms the initials of the club are included, sometimes with a date as well, presumably that of the club's foundation. The earliest of these dated poleheads belong to the mid-eighteenth century; indeed, many of the designs show an eighteenth-century elegance of curves and scrolls.

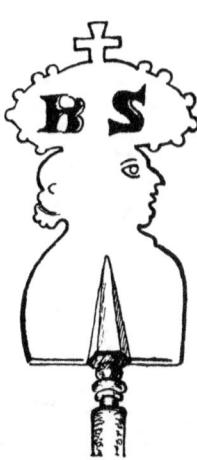

Village Club
Polehead

The clubs were primarily a masculine affair, though equipment seems also to have been provided for the ladies from time to time, in the form of specially inscribed teacup.

Horse Brasses and Harness Ornaments

Poleheads are no longer used, but horsebrasses still persist in their traditional forms. They are worn only by heavy draught horses, and may

[1] William Barnes, "Whitsuntide an' Club Wa'ken," in *Poems of Rural Life in the Dorset Dialect*, 1844.

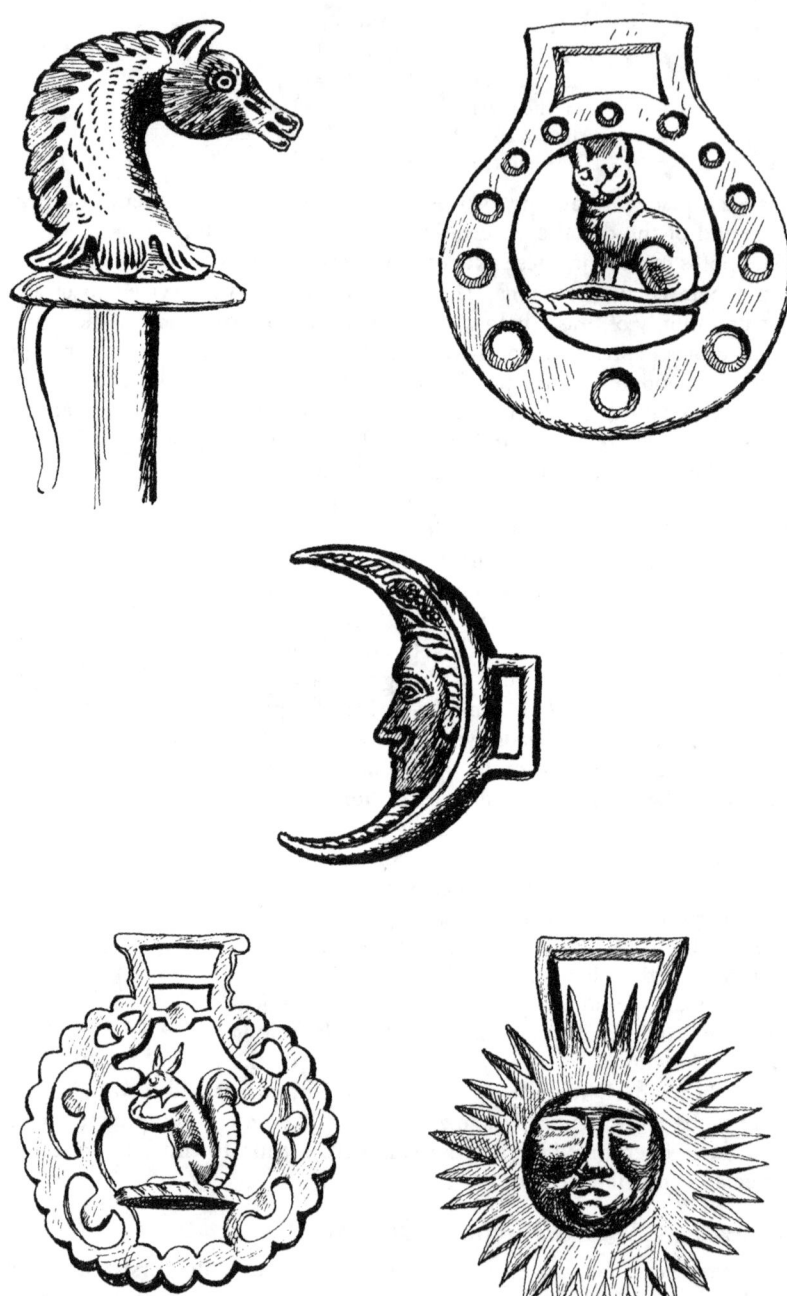

Horse Brasses and Harness Ornaments

still be seen all over the country, though in view of the shortage of labour and the time involved in polishing the brasses, horses nowadays generally only wear their full complement for special occasions, such as the horse show. A properly dressed horse wears a specially large brass, or even two, as a face piece on his forehead, hung from a strap buckled into his bridle. A set of smaller brasses on a wide leather strap is hung from his collar, and a whole row of them run down his martingale. He wears more brasses hung on short straps over his withers and on his backband. Set on his head is an upright three-tiered plume of coloured horsehair in a brass holder, with sometimes little bells attached, which fixes into his bridle. Or, in place of the plume, he may have, fixed to a short upright stand, a brass ring with a a swinging brass disc inside, which flashes in the sun as he walks; or perhaps a head ornament of little bells. His harness is lavishly decorated with brass studs, bosses, plates and buckles. For a show he also wears coloured ribbons and rosettes, with coloured worsted threads plaited into his mane.

All this finery still appears on occasion, though the sets of latten bells once carried by the teams of horses drawing the great farm waggons seem to have fallen completely into disuse. The bells were hung horizontally on a rod, set under a leather hood with a coloured fringe of thread. From the ends of the rod two long prongs ran down to fit into the collar. Each horse had his own set of bells, in fours or threes, tuned to a chord, and ideally each set rang a different chord. The bells served a certain useful purpose in giving warning of the approach of a large waggon in the narrow, twisting country roads where passing was difficult, though the creaking of the great wheels was probably enough in itself. The brasses are purely decorative, though the persistence of certain shapes, notably crescents, suggests that they originally served as amulets also.[1]

The brasses, as distinct from the harness, were often the property of the carter, and would be handed down in the family. The old ones were cast in solid metal, and are thus much heavier and more durable than the modern stamped brasses, which are thin and tend to lose in execution. Of the traditional shapes, the crescent is the most common, sometimes cast in relief, with a triangular cross-section, sometimes pierced in a circular or heart-shaped disc. Crescents are much used in combination with other symbols, sometimes surrounding a sun with rays, or, in a very effective and ancient form, three crescents may be joined back to back. There are many ways of representing the sun, sometimes pierced, sometimes as a whorl. Sun, moon, stars, hearts, interlacing circles and triangles, diamonds, crosses, fleur-de-lys, and other symbols with a certain esoteric significance attached to them, are freely combined with purely abstract decoration, scrolls, scollops, twists, axe- and wedge-shaped perforations, which may perhaps be modifications of earlier forms which once had a special meaning. But all this has long since been forgotten. The majority of the brass discs themselves are circular, though some have a heart-shaped or scolloped

[1] The origins and significance of horse brasses are traced in detail in an article in *The Reliquary and Illustrated Archaeologist*, vol. xii, 1906, by Miss Lina Eckstein.

form reminiscent of keyhole scutcheons. Some round discs have raised rings and twists or central bosses, and others again are quite plain.

The large class of pictorial subjects have a more obvious origin. There are many floral motives: a Tudor rose, or rose, thistle and shamrock, or acorn and oak leaves, are some of the most familiar. Another group has animal designs, sometimes the head only, as a lion or horse; sometimes the whole body, often in a recognisably heraldic stance; we find lions, horses, stags, swans, eagles and many more; oddly enough, sheep seem to be rare. A number have devices of the various trades: plough and harrow, wheat-sheaf, churn, barrel, anchor; there is even a railway engine. Others have portraits, perhaps a carter and horse, or heads of various celebrities, ranging from Queen Victoria to Lord Beaconsfield, Mr. Gladstone and Mr. Joseph Chamberlain, though these later heads lack the character and good workmanship of the earlier ones. In all, there are probably some thousands of different designs, for none of the many collectors claim to have a complete record.[1]

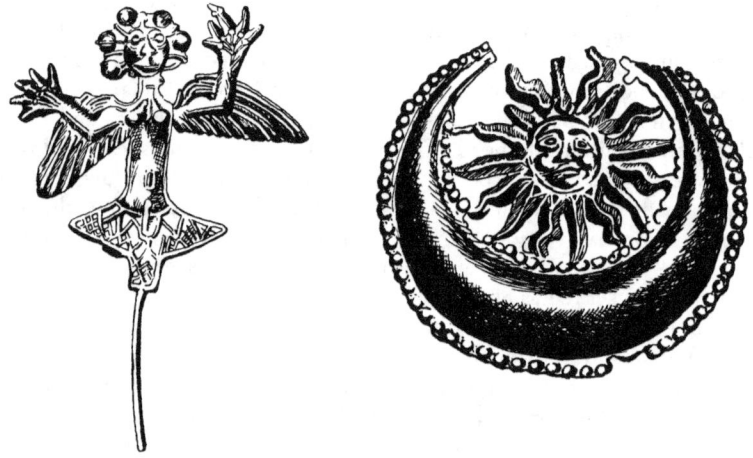

Mediaeval Pilgrim's Badges: St. Michael Archangel and St. John the Baptist

The polished brass devices decorating the front of steam rollers are possibly inspired by the horse brasses and harness plates. They are an attractive feature and we must hope that they will not be allowed to disappear.

Pilgrim Badges

It is interesting to compare the devices on horsebrasses with those of the mediaeval pilgrim's badges, in lead or pewter, some even in brass, of which quite a number survive. Each place of pilgrimage sold these emblems, sometimes of a particular saint or shrine, sometimes with more

[1] Mr. H. S. Richards, author of *All about Horse Brasses,* is publishing a series of illustrations of famous collections. His first volume contains over fourteen hundred different designs.

abstract symbolic motives, whilst other badges were secular and worn on liveries. We find, for instance, the same crescent moon surrounding a sun that is so frequent in the horsebrasses, and which also appears on the poleheads. The scollop shell was a very common motive, as were plumes, and there are many little figures of birds and beasts. Some of these badges show a very spirited sense of design.[1] It seems quite possible that some of the horsebrass patterns may have been derived from them, as also from the elaborate mediaeval horsetrappings.

Fakes and Forgeries

Interest in the many mediaeval relics, especially coins and medals, excavated during the late eighteenth and the nineteenth centuries, especially in London when new docks and embankments were built, led to an odd form of popular art—lead forgeries of such finds, made by workmen employed on building sites (**16**). These workmen were normally illiterate and jumbled together a number of quasi-mediaeval motives to suit their own fancies. Two workmen, known as Billy and Charlie, living in Rosemary Lane, Tower Hill, produced a very large number of these fakes during the 1850's, and for a time managed to impose even on the experts. Over eight hundred examples of their work were mentioned when their activities were exposed at a meeting of the British Archaeological Association in 1858, and they were by no means the only producers. Many of these fakes are flat and lifeless, but quite a few have their own vitality and fantasy. So much so, indeed, that they have been collected, which in turn gave rising to a faking of fakes,

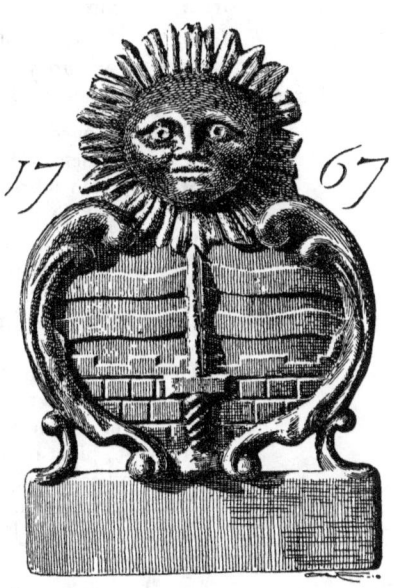

Fire Plate

though it would appear that too much expertise loses the old uninhibited, spontaneous qualities; for an illiterate workman capable of embarking on such fakes without directly copying the originals, who is compelled to call on his own imaginative conceptions and may well have a certain primitive vision.

Fire Insurance Signs

A device in metal more particularly associated with town life, is the firemark or firesign, which we find all over the country. These wall tablets

1 The London Museum's *Mediaeval Catalogue* illustrates a number of them.

were originally made of lead and served to identify property insured with a particular company and therefore entitled to protection from the company's privately maintained fire brigade, when this form of fire insurance was introduced shortly after the Great Fire of London. If the brigade, in those early days, turned out only to find that the burning property was not marked with their company's emblem, they were entitled to go home again. The mark thus served as a guide to the firemen. The old lead marks often still have the policy number pierced underneath the design and sometimes a fresh number has been stamped over the old one when the policy was renewed. When, towards the end of the eighteenth century, these restrictive practices were dropped and the companies' brigades might attend any fire, the companies dropped the lead fire mark and began issuing "fire plates," also to be affixed to the walls, but serving only as advertisement. These plates were usually made in copper or tinplate, whilst the firemen also wore their companies' badges in metal on their shoulders. Extinguishing an important fire must have been a picturesque if not very effective performance, as we may see from the description of the great Drury Lane Theatre conflagration of 1809 given in *Rejected Addresses*:

> The summoned firemen woke at call
> And hied them to their stations all;
> Starting from short and broken snooze
> Each sought his ponderous hobnailed shoes;
> But first his worsted hozen plied,
> Plush breeches next in crimson dyed
> His nether bulk embraced;
> The jacket then, of red or blue,
> Whose massive shoulders gave to view
> The badge of each respective crew
> In tin or copper traced.
> The engines thundered through the street,
> Firehook, pipe, bucket, all complete;
> And torches glared, and clattering feet
> Along the pavement paced.
> The "Hand-in-Hand" the race began,
> Then came the "Phoenix" and the "Sun,"
> Th' "Exchange" where old insurers run,
> The "Eagle" where the new . . .

Both marks and plates were gaily painted in colour, with gilt and scarlet predominating. The designs not only varied with each company, but the same company might issue variants at different times. Indeed the many patterns afford an interesting sidelight on the history of insurance. Sometimes the design shows some object connected with fire, like the "Phoenix" rising from flames, or the "Birmingham," showing a fireman and fire engine. Sometimes an emblem connected with the name of the company is introduced, like "Atlas" carrying the world, or "The Sun" with rays, or "The Hand-in-Hand" with two clasped hands. Others, especially where the company was named after some particular place, are heraldic, like "The

Kent," which has a white horse, or "London Assurance" with the arms of
the City. Others again, and some of the most attractive, are more or less
vaguely symbolic, like "The British" with a lion, or "The West of England"
with Alfred the Great.

Many of the old marks and plates show a high standard of execution,
with bold, broad treatment, though as the nineteenth century progressed,
they tend, like so much else, to become more stereotyped. In their heyday
they were very plentiful and must have formed an attractive decoration in
the city streets, placed as they usually were, between the windows of the
first floor. Nervous householders would insure with several companies
and display all their plates, as *The New Tory Guide* published in 1819 reports:

> For not e'en the Regent himself has endured
> Though I've seen him with badges and orders all shine
> Till he looked like a house that was over insured . . .

Curiously enough, though they must have been such a familiar feature, we
do not often see fireplates on walls in contemporary prints or engravings,
which suggests that they were little regarded.

Trade Tokens

Another interesting form of device in metal, reflecting the contemporary life and times of the seventeenth and eighteenth centuries, is the trade
token which John Evelyn, the diarist, prophesied might "in after times
come to exercise and busie the learned critic what they should signify."
Tokens were issued in great abundance by traders and businesses of all
kinds, to supply the lack of small change, which the State did not provide
for; they were exchangeable at their place of issue. They were stamped
with a great variety of designs, and besides serving the needs of customers,
were also useful as advertisements for particular wares. By no means all of
them, however, bore trade emblems or devices directly related to the
businesses issuing them; indeed, they provide a wonderfully varied pictorial record of popular interests and tastes. Sometimes they commemorate
places, by showing some historic building or local worthy: Coventry
tokens often have Lady Godiva and Dunmow tokens the famous flitch. Or
they may depict some local activity. A Lowestoft token shows a fishing
smack on one side and seabathing on the other, whilst a Rochdale one has
a weaver at work and, on the reverse, the golden fleece. Contemporary
celebrities were also portrayed: the admirals Howe and Jarvis; or religious
leaders, like Wesley and Whitfield; or politicians like Fox and Pitt, these
two sometimes appearing together on the same token, with a sarcastic
inscription like "Odd Fellows." There are tokens with stage celebrities
like Garrick or literary figures like Dr. Samuel Johnson, issued during their
lifetime, and of course, Shakespeare is not lacking

Surprisingly enough, a large number of political events are chronicled
on tokens, such items of domestic interest as the rise and fall of the price
of bread between 1795–6, represented by a pair of scales weighing a loaf

with the inscription "God deliver us" on the side with high prices and, more cheerfully, "God be praised" on the obverse, where the price has fallen. The horror aroused by the excesses of the French Revolution is reflected in many late eighteenth century tokens which depict the contrast between "French Slavery" and "English Liberty," with appropriate figures in the manner of the broadsides. Tom Paine's *Rights of Man* is satirised on a large number of tokens with the punning inscription "End of Pain" surrounding a figure hanging from a gibbet. The Anti-Slavery campaign is also illustrated, and so too is popular indignation at the neglect of disabled seamen when the wars were over. Here indeed is the same wide gamut of popular emotions and excitements that we find recorded in the street literature and Staffordshire figures.

Trade tokens vary very much both in design and execution, but many of them reach a surprisingly high standard considering what a transitory purpose they served. We do not know who was responsible for their design, but may perhaps assume, from general similarities of treatment and subject, that the artists of broadsides and the like also turned their hand to this work.

Firebacks and Hearth Implements

The domestic hearth needs metal implements and fittings, and here local ironwork has a special place. The earliest form of indoor fireplace is the down hearth, where the fire is made on a slightly raised slab of stone or iron. These down hearths were at first set in the centre of the hall, but a better place was back against the wall, so that the smoke could be carried away by a flue, running up the wall or through it. These wall hearths are still in use in cottages and farmhouses all over the country. But burning a fire against the wall will in time damage the fabric. Hence arose the use of "firebacks," thick iron plates to set up behind the fire and give protection. In England from about the fifteenth century onwards such firebacks were made of cast iron, by the simplest expedient of pressing a thick board into sand, and then ladling the molten metal into this cavity, so that in cooling it would take the shape of the sand mould.

We find these simply made firebacks in great profusion all over the country. But as Sussex was the great iron-working centre until coal replaced wood for smelting, it is from Sussex that the most interesting come. For the next step was to decorate these flat plates in some way. The first very primitive method was to press small objects into the face of the sand mould, to leave a raised pattern on the face of the plate: very simple little objects, like a twist of rope or even the palm of a hand or perhaps a small armorial device. These little imprints were arranged rather haphazardly at first, without much sense of spatial relationships. The next stage was to carve a wooden pattern as a stamp, large enough to fill the whole space. From now on we get coherent design and the beginning of those relief-decorated cast-iron firebacks which are so typical a Sussex product. Not only firebacks but grave-slabs too were made in this way, often with very fine lettering; oddly enough, grave-slabs were sometimes used as firebacks, presumably by unlettered cottagers who were not troubled by the inappropriateness of the inscription.

Beginning about the sixteenth century, these patterned firebacks were made in great numbers and variety until, in Georgian times, the introduction of dog grates and hob grates created a demand for a different type of iron work. The shapes and patterns vary with changing taste and fashion, and as Sussex is a coastal area foreign influences are strong. A very large

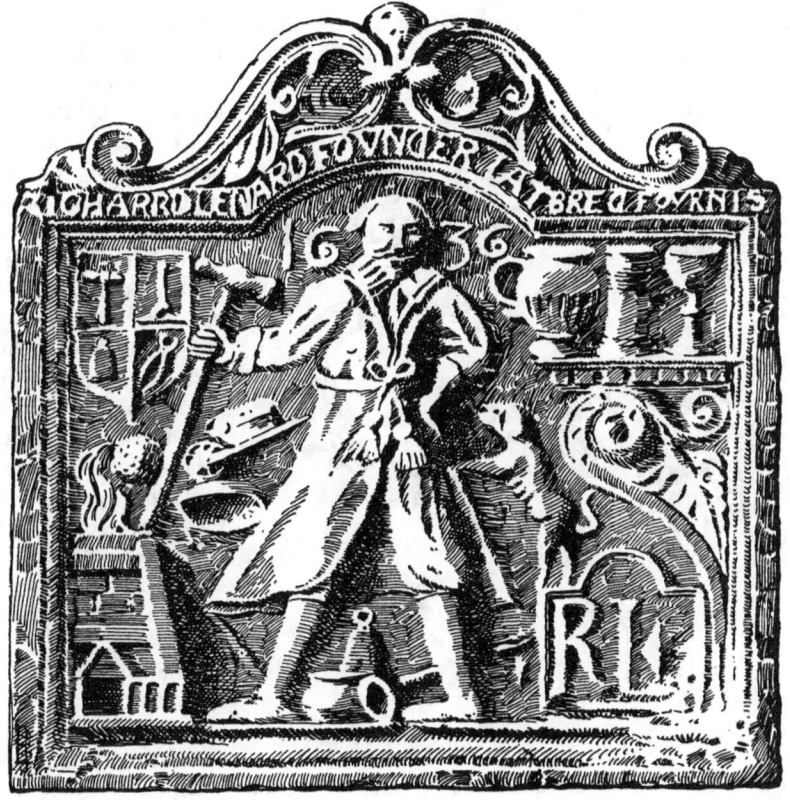

Sussex Fireback in cast iron

class, including some of the earliest, have armorial motives, which are specially well suited to cast iron. Less frequent are pictorial subjects, sometimes of local interest, but these are often particularly interesting as design: an outstanding one shows the ironmaster "Richard Lenard at Bred (Brede) Fournis" surrounded with the implements of his trade and accompanied by his dog (above), with the date 1636; another commemorates a pair of Sussex martyrs. Influence from Germany and the Low Countries shows itself in a number of biblical scenes, with crowded figures in contemporary dress; some may have been cast from imported carved stamps;

we even find inscriptions in German. Dutch fashions towards the end of the seventeenth century produced a more elegant form of design with subjects taken from mythology, as well as a thinner and lighter plate; these too seem at times to have been cast from imported stamps. Many of them are very decorative.

As characteristic of the open hearth as the firebacks are the andirons or firedogs, which were indeed even more essential as they served to raise up the logs and give a draught. They were at first made of wrought iron, and then, as the technique of casting was developed, were also cast; they too are a typical Sussex product. In Sussex cast iron andirons the basic

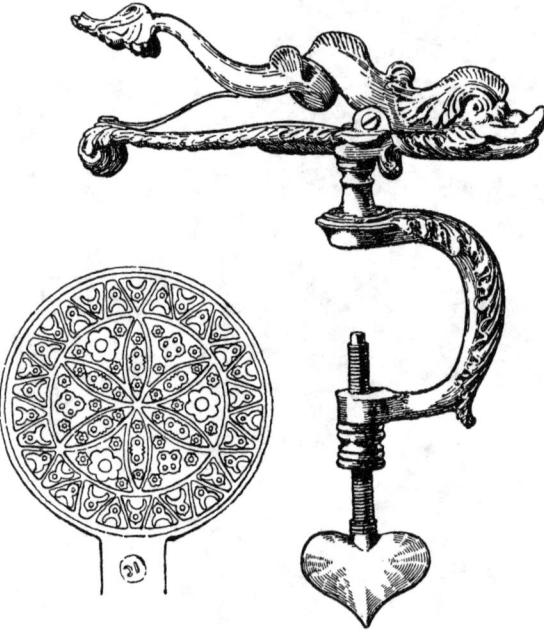

structure never seems to have been altered; there is always a rectangular upright post, with moulded cap and base, standing on two curved legs and supporting a horizontal bar with another leg at the back. The details vary very much: some forms are short and massive, others long and elegant, and we can trace the influence of changing fashions, from Gothic to Renaissance, in the moulding.

The many other items that went to furnish a well-equipped open hearth and chimney corner, fire irons and tobacco tongs, ratchets, chimney corner and wafering-irons, spits and cooking utensils, too numerous and varied to attempt to list here, were normally all of local manufacture, and often show not only ingenuity but a very considerable decorative sense, even in the most homely objects.[1] So strong indeed is this innate feeling for decoration that no amount of "fitness for purpose" can stifle it.

Wafering Iron   Embroidery Table Vice

Household Ornaments

Door furniture provides yet another example of this decorative sense. Locks, hinges and latches are essentially practical, yet their position makes

[1] Miss Gertrude Jekyll in *Old English Household Life* has illustrated many fine examples of such things.

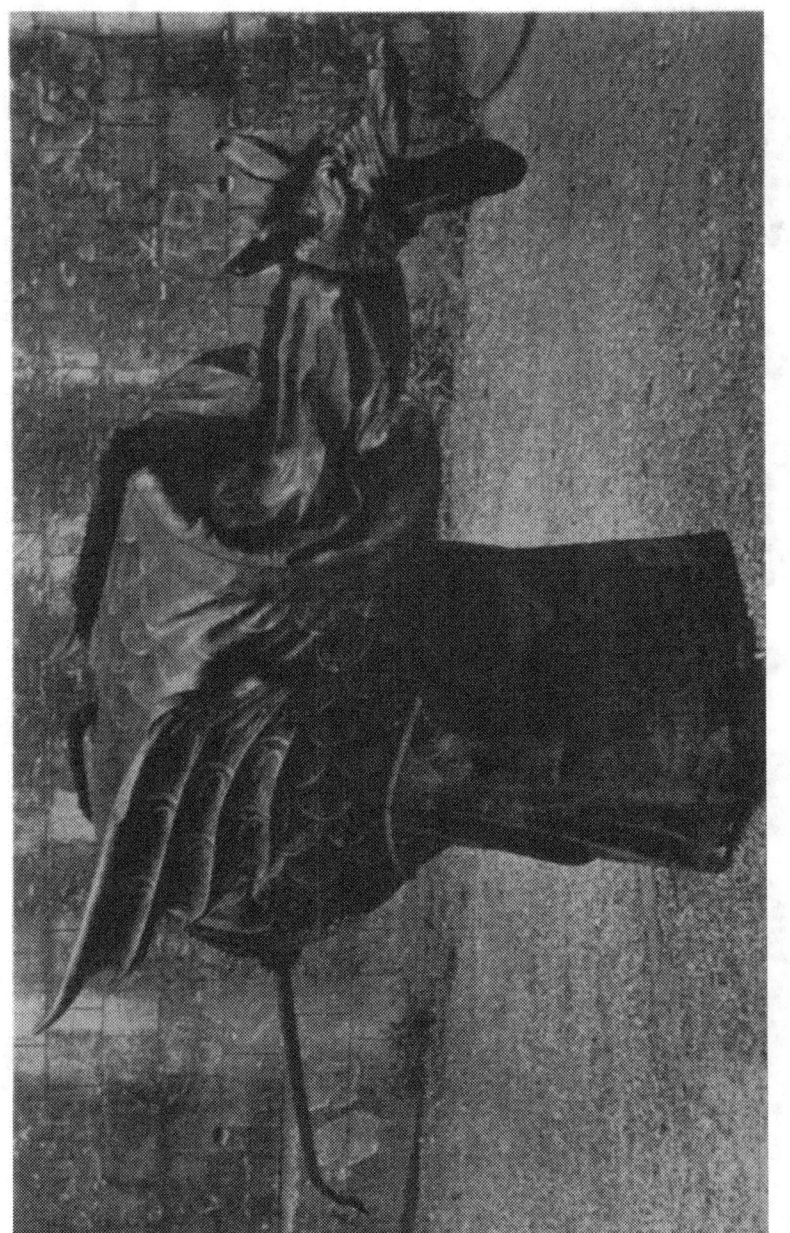

1   Procession Dragon: "Old Snap" of Norwich
      Painted canvas over wickerwork frame

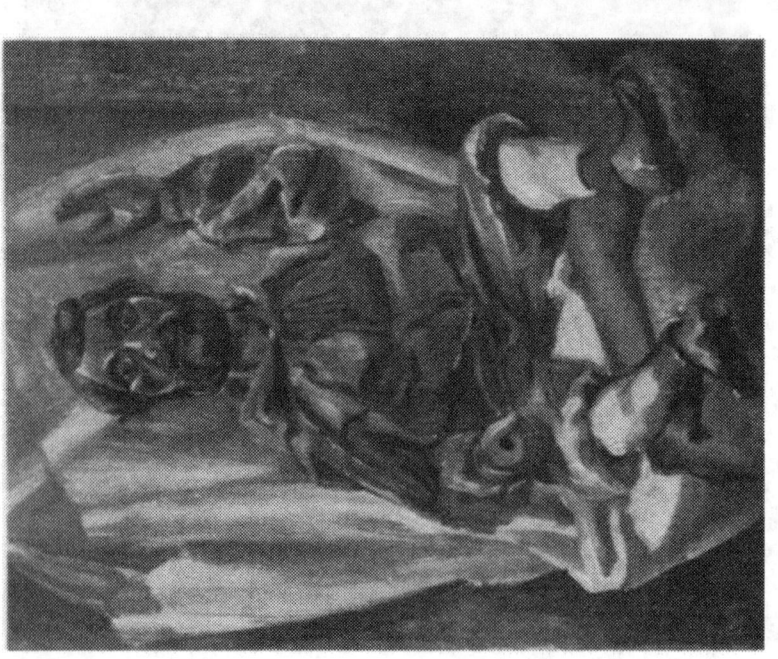

From paintings by Enid Marx

2, 3   Carved wood Marionettes (mid-nineteenth century)

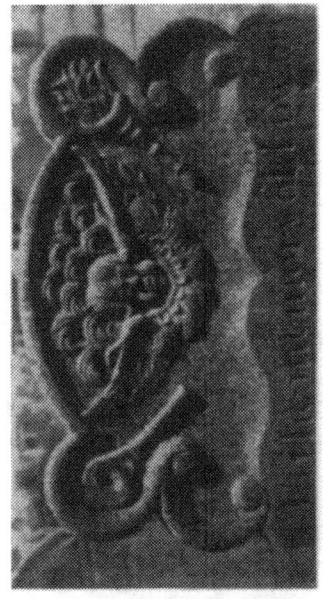

5 Sheringham, Norfolk (1790)

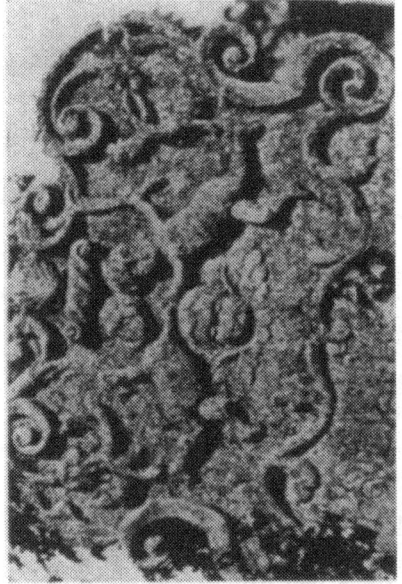

6 Darenth, Kent (late eighteenth century)

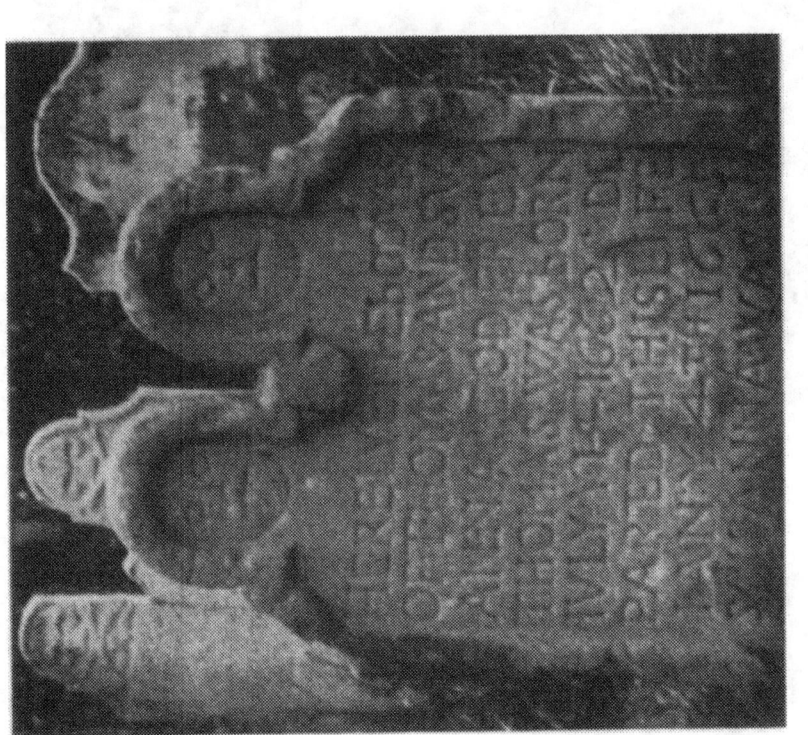

4 Faversham, Kent (1665)

CARVED TOMBSTONES

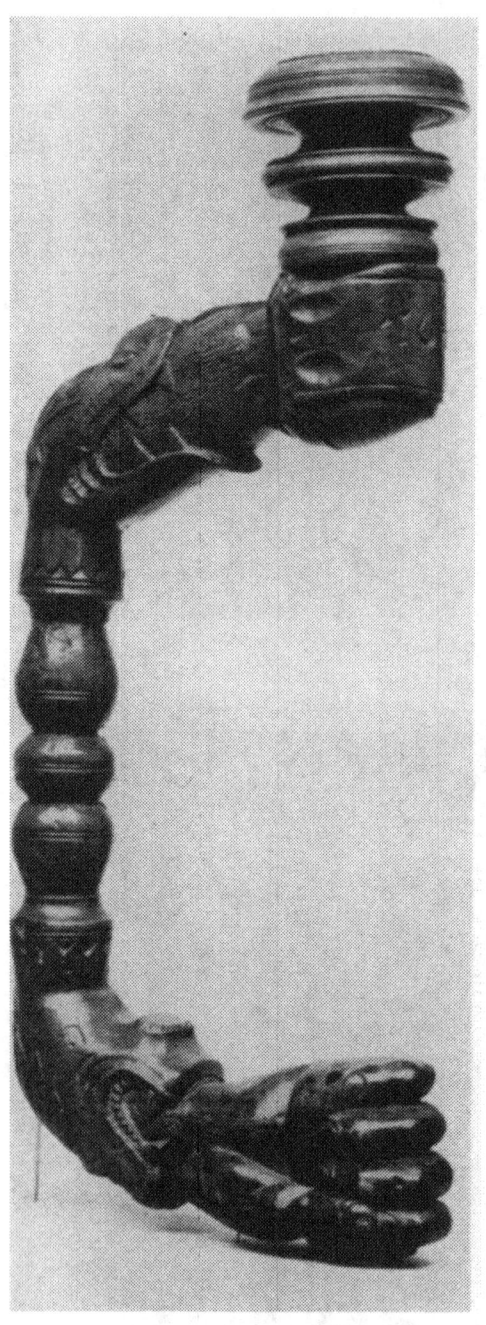

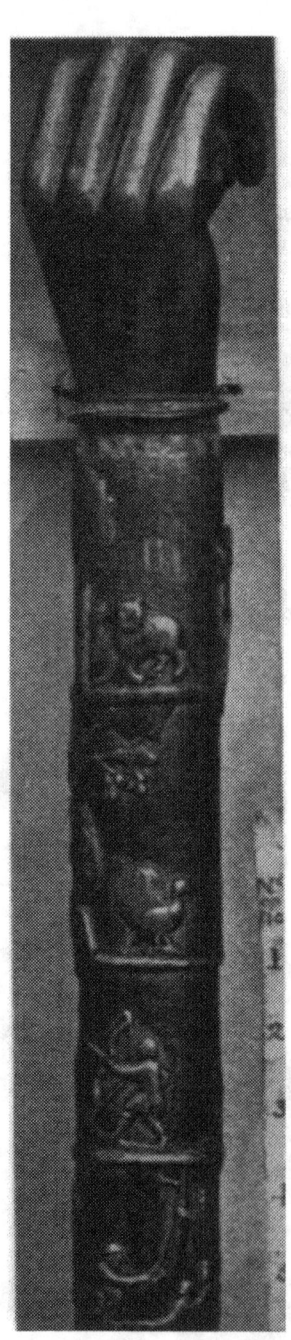

7 Hand Brace in carved
wood (1642)

8 Carved cherry wood
Walking Stick, showing
Old Testament scenes

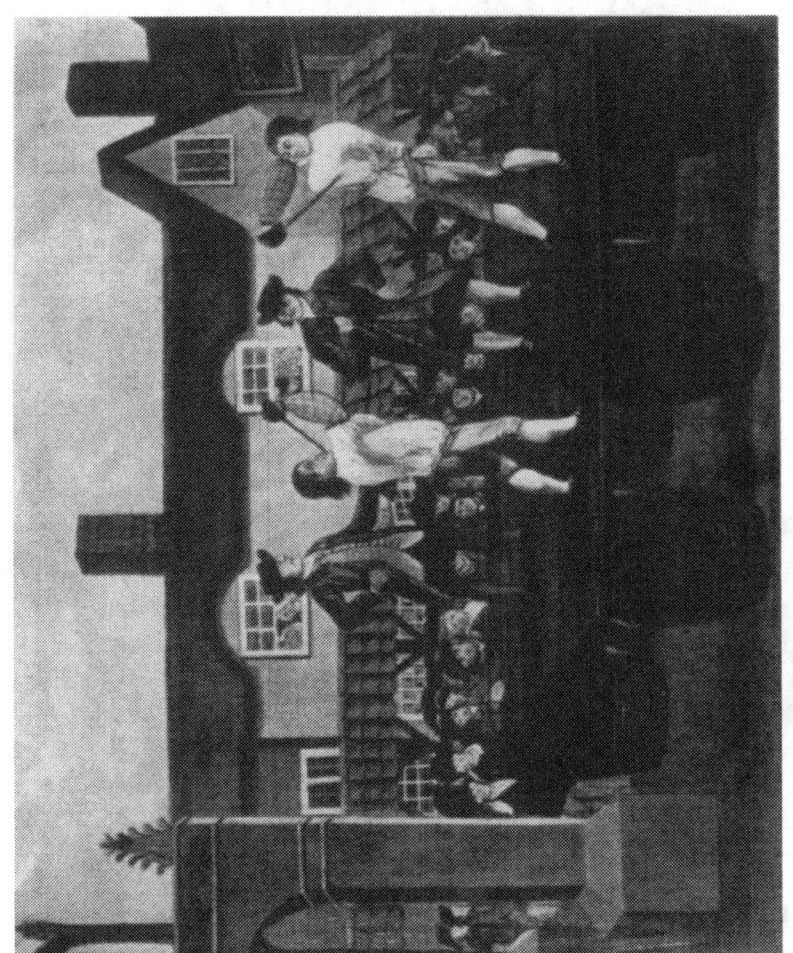

9   Sign-painter's Painting of a Single-stick Contest at Shepton Mallet

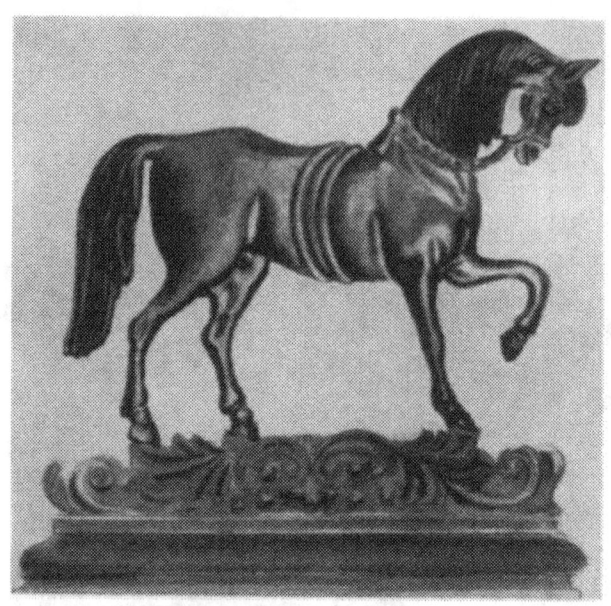

10   Cast-iron Door Stop (nineteenth century)

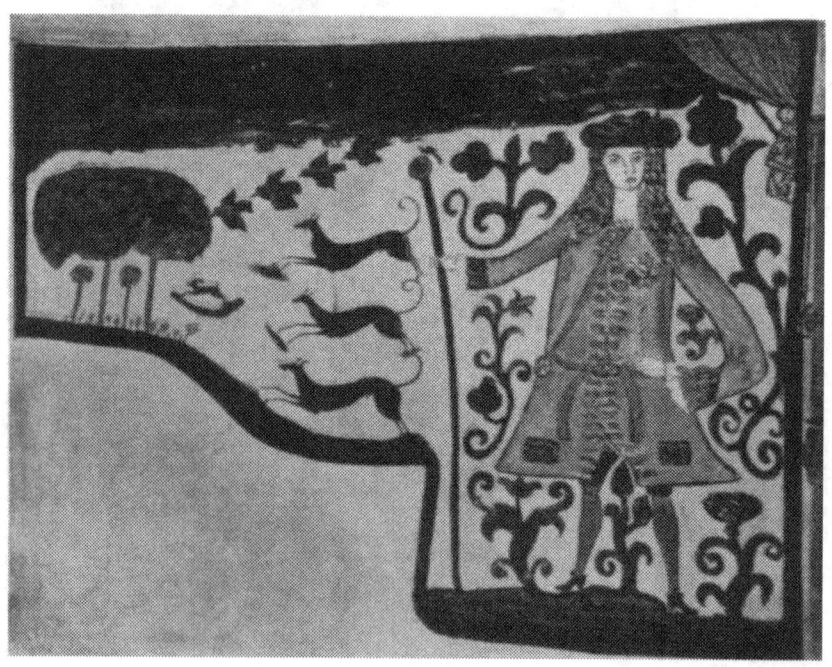

11   Eighteenth-century Wall Painting in the George Inn, Chesham, Buckinghamshire

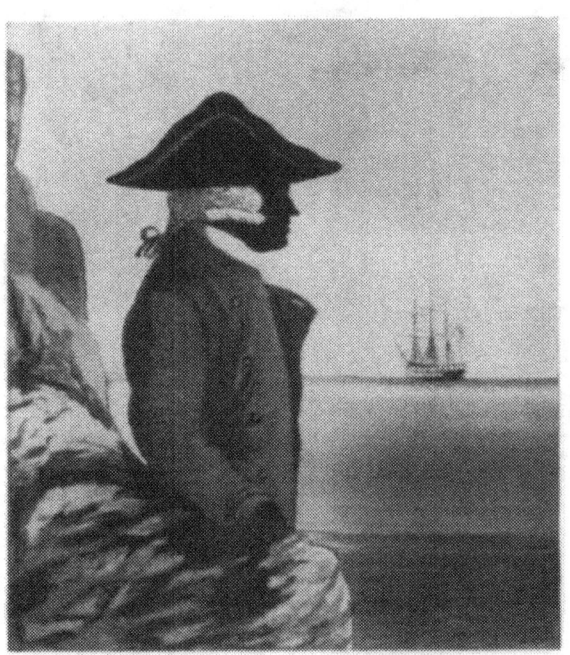

12 Silhouette Portrait, possibly of Admiral Rodney, in water-colour (eighteenth century). Size: 8½ by 7 inches

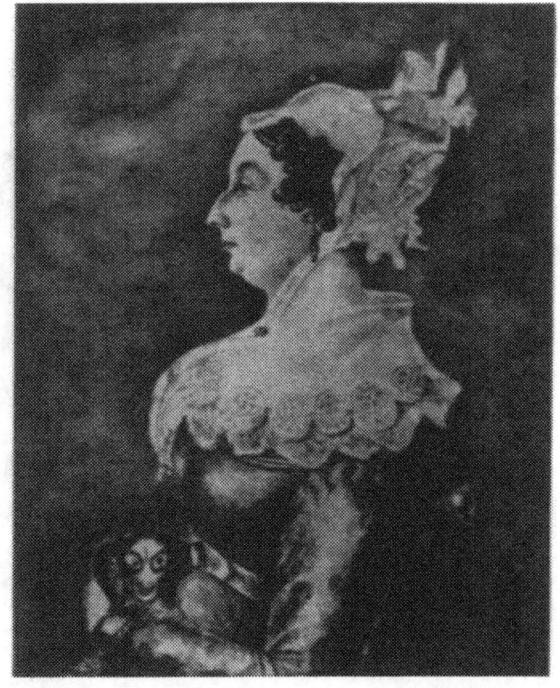

13 Water-colour Portrait of a member of the Drake family (mid-nineteenth century). Size: 6 by 5 inches. Inscribed: " *A. A. White, pinxit* "

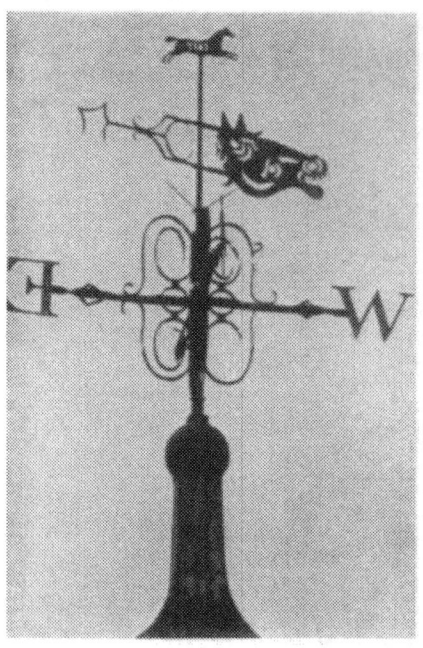

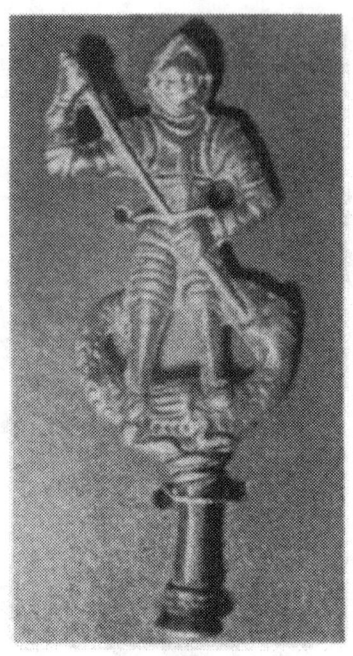

14 Weather Vane from Minster in Sheppey
(1817)

15 Brass Tobacco Stopper
(*c.* 4 inches high)

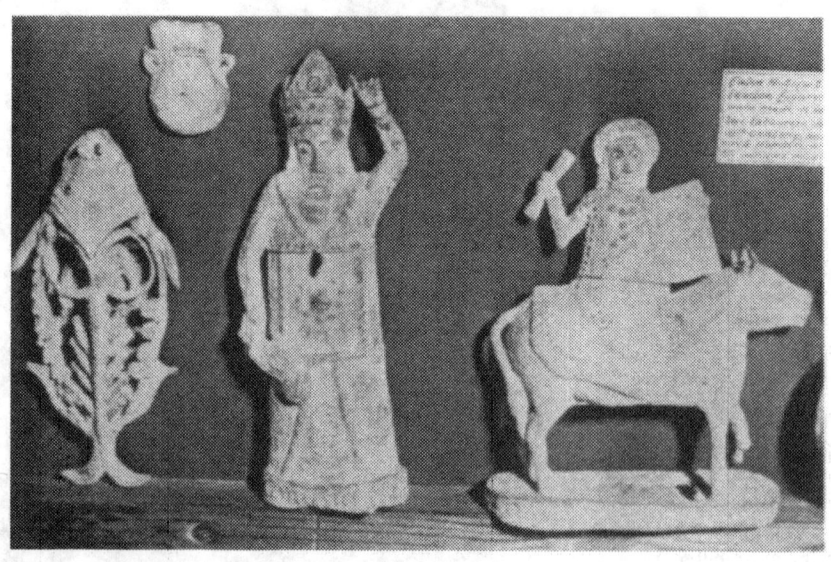

16 Nineteenth-century False Antiquities, " Billy and Charlie " type

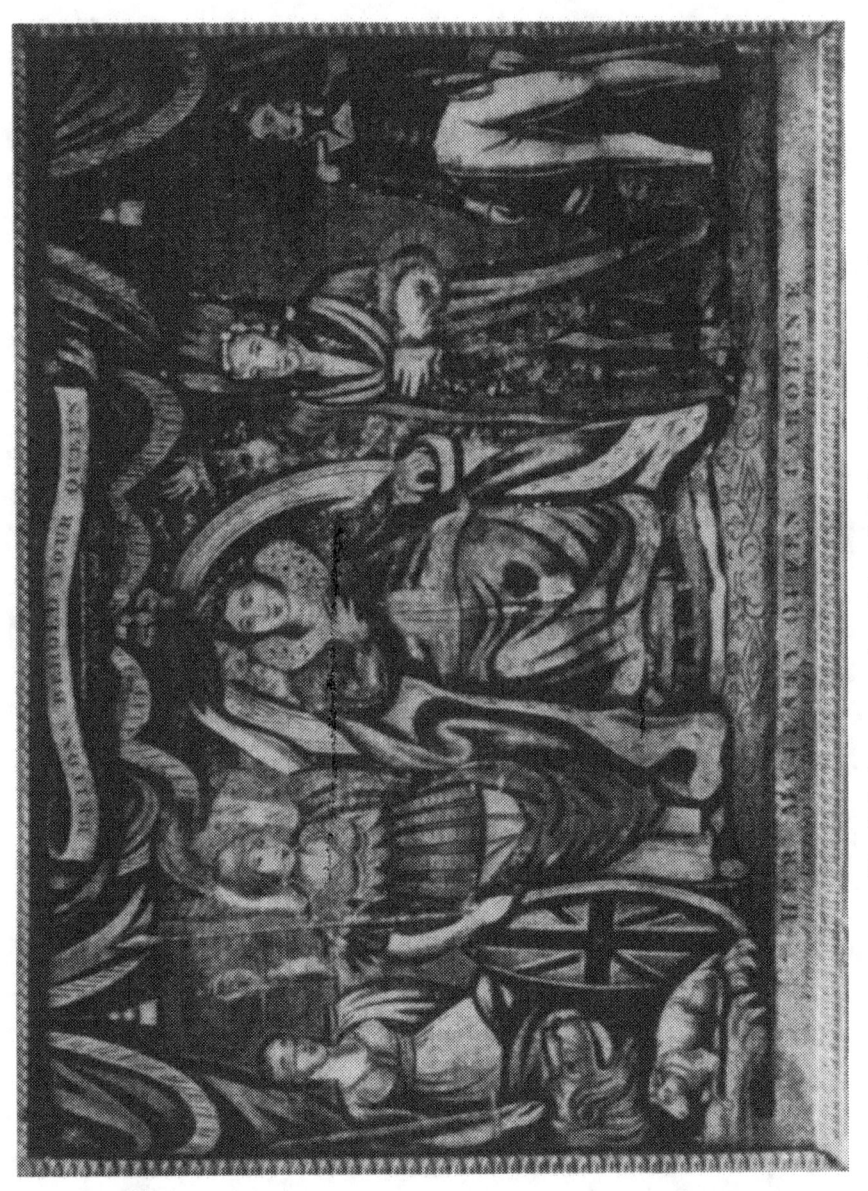

17   Glass Painting, over print: Triumph of Queen Caroline (1820)

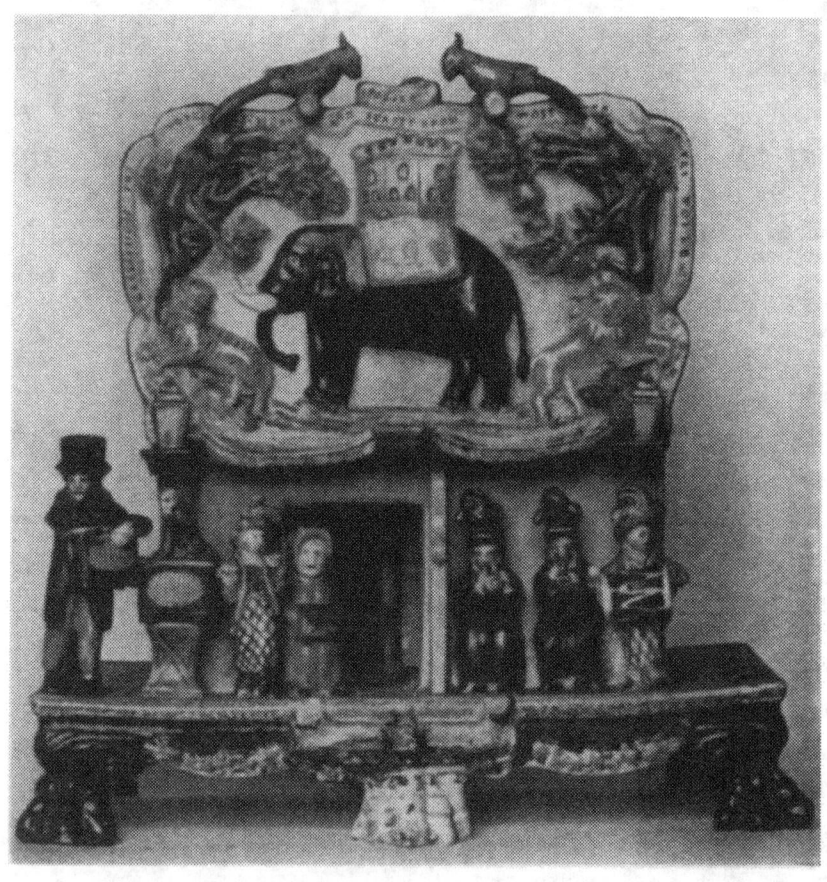

18   Staffordshire Earthenware Group: Polito's " Royal Menagerie "
(early nineteenth century). Height: 12¼ inches

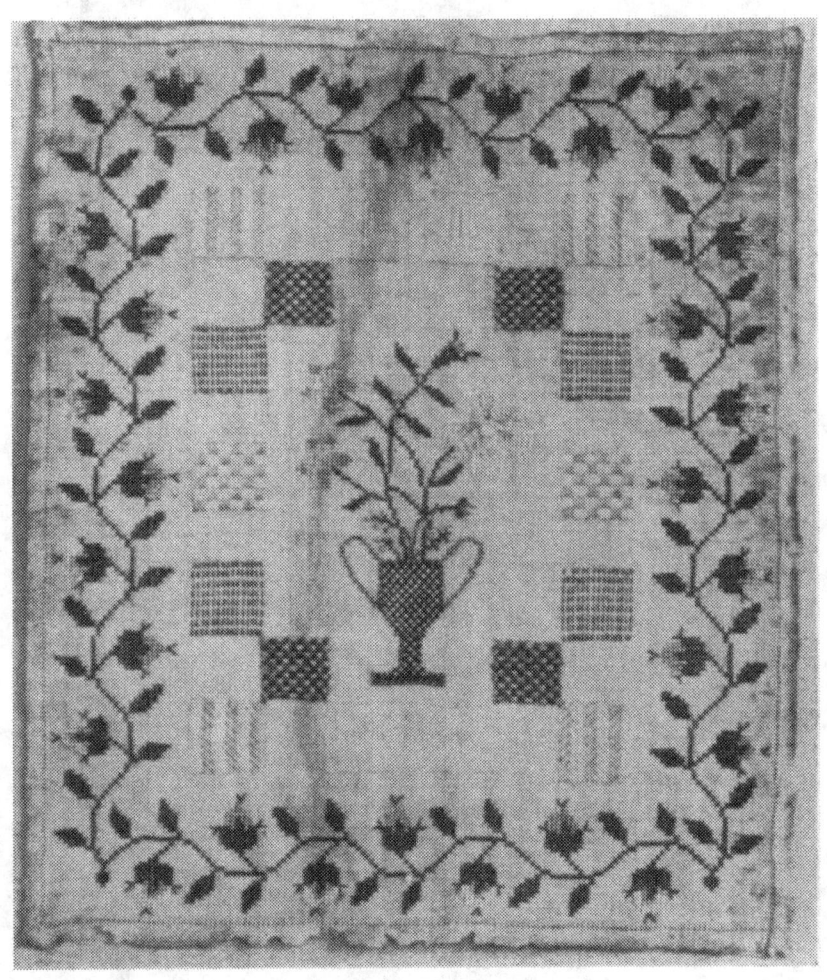

19   A Darning Sampler of 1820

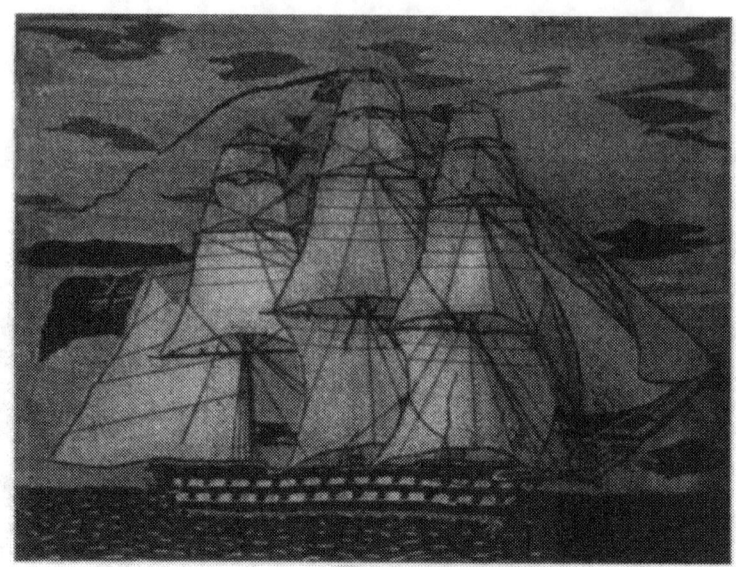

20   Sailor's Embroidered Picture in wool:
"H.M.S. Exmouth 90 Guns"

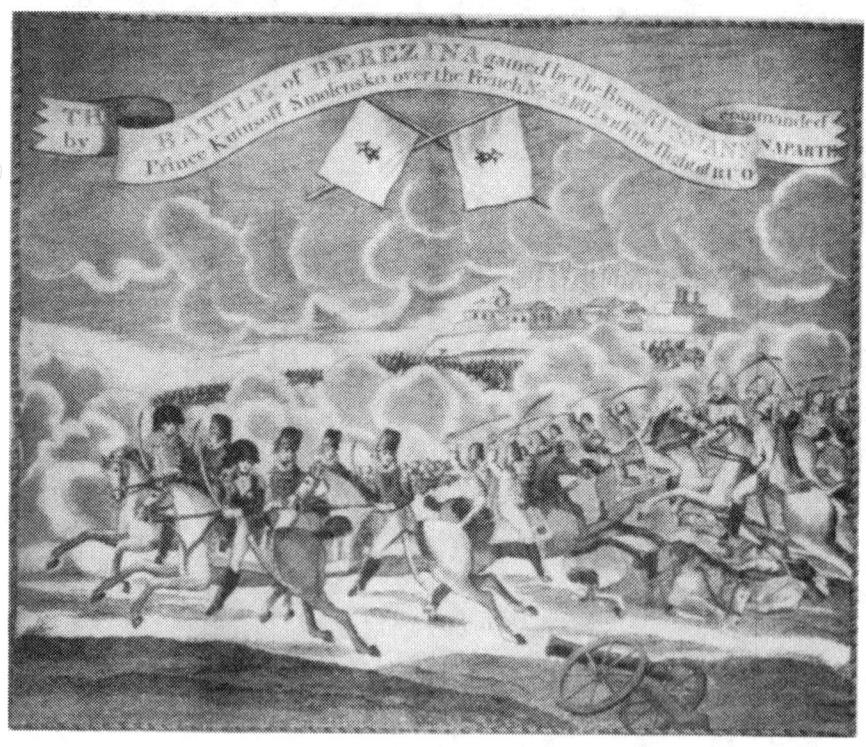

21   Printed Cotton Square, commemorating
"The Battle of Berezina," 1812

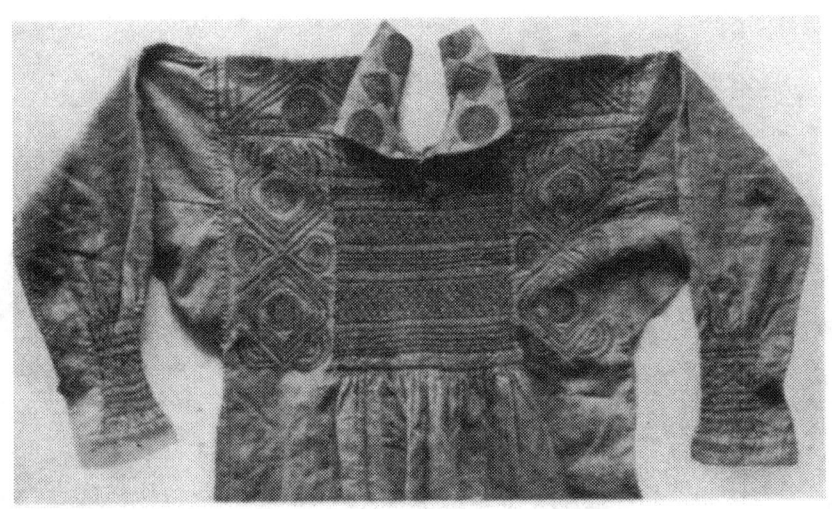

22 Countryman's Smock (nineteenth century)

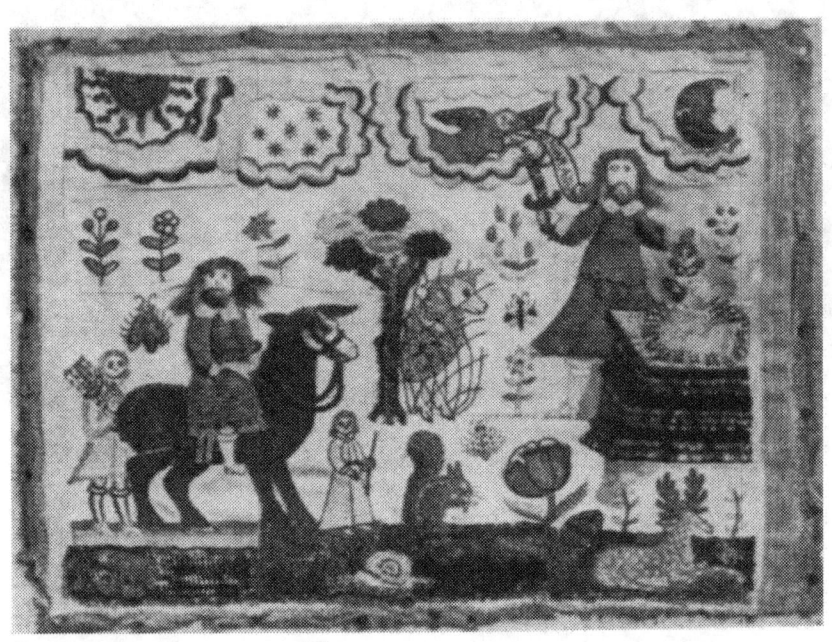

23 Stuart Embroidered Picture: " The Sacrifice of Isaac "

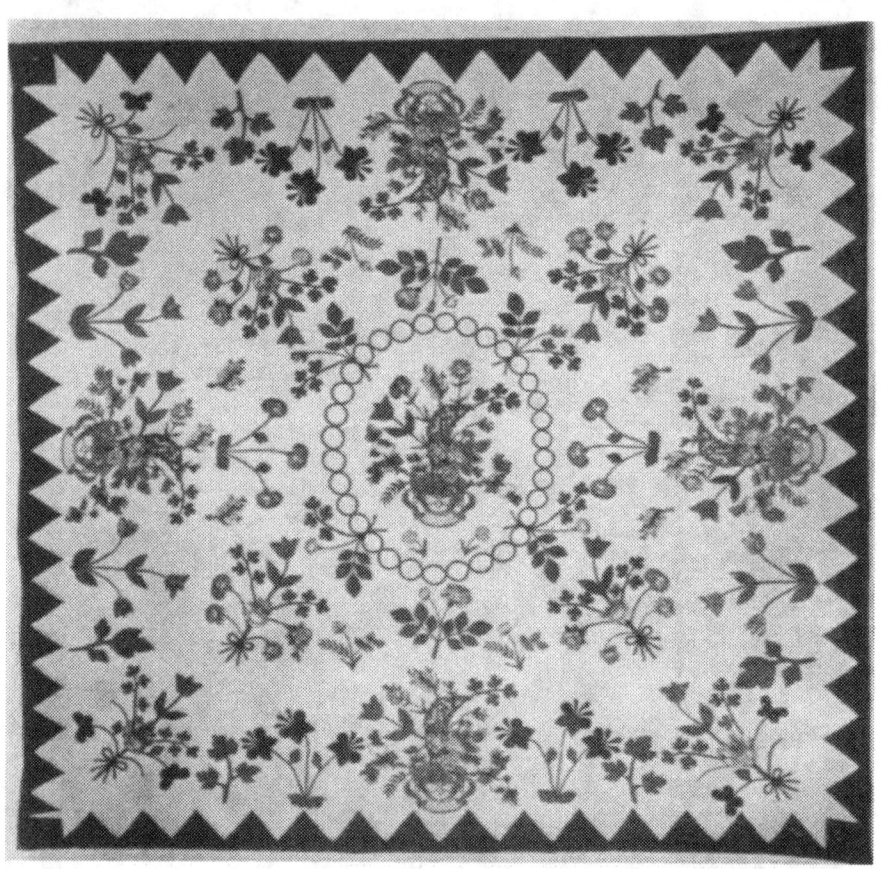

24   Coverlet, appliqué-work on white ground

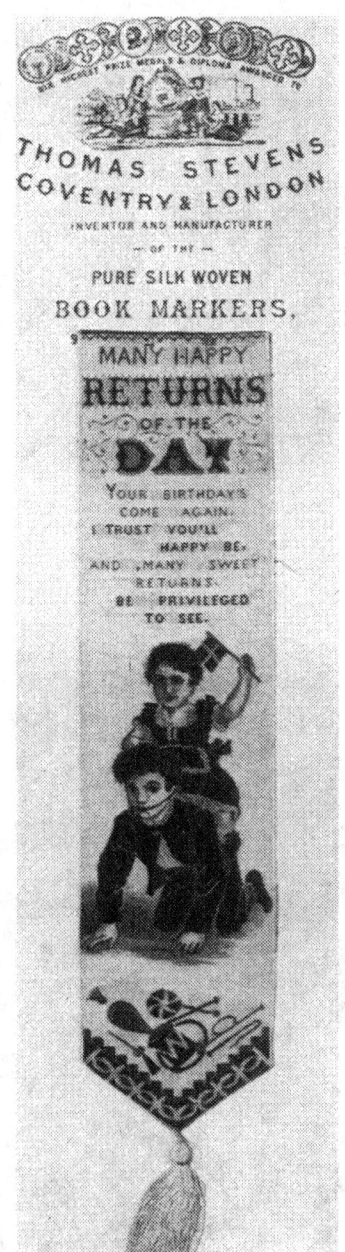

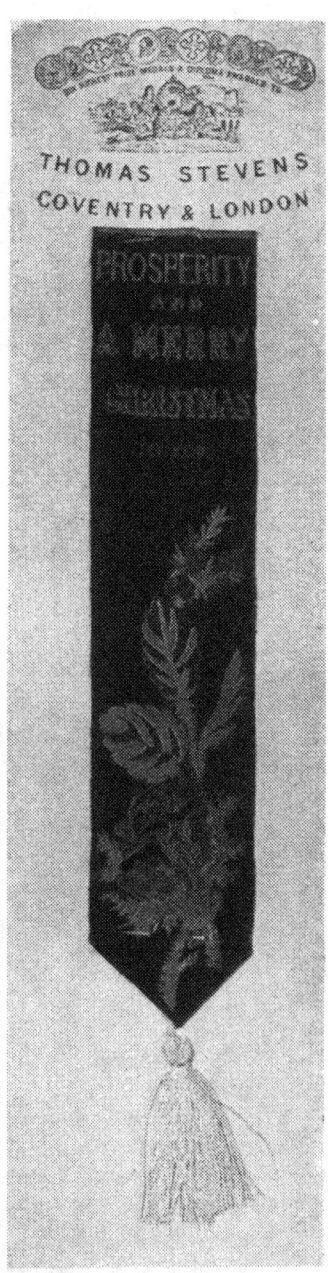

25, 26 Coventry Ribbon Book Marks, as sold on cards

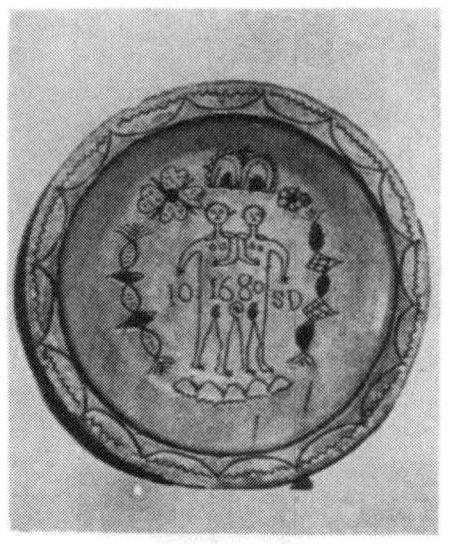

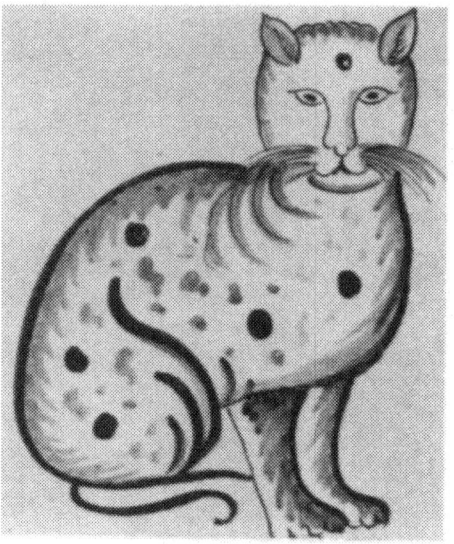

27 Earthenware *sgraffito* Dish (1680), commemorating the birth of Siamese twins and made at Donyatt, Somerset

28 English Bristol Delft Tile

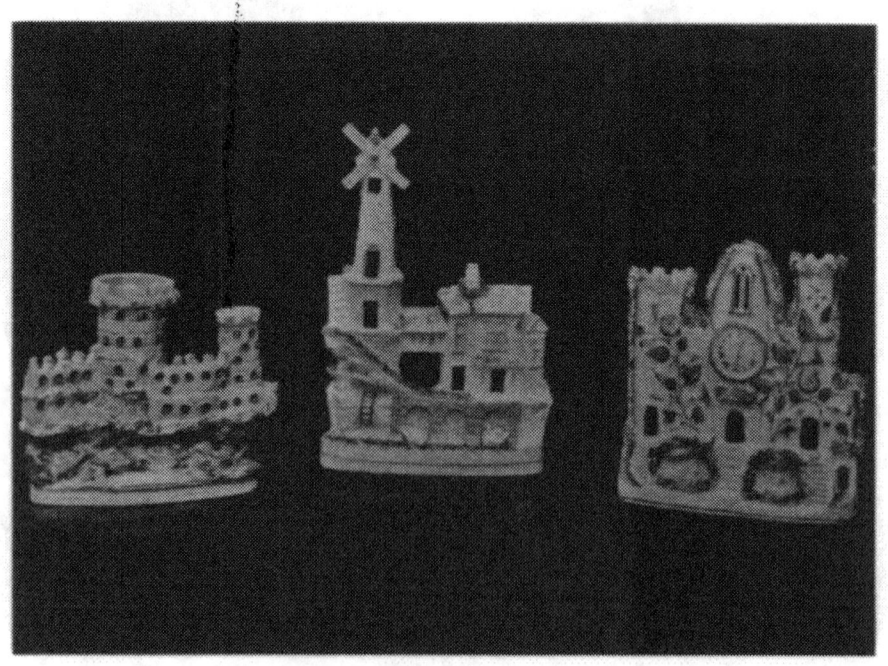

29 Staffordshire Earthenware Castles and Windmill

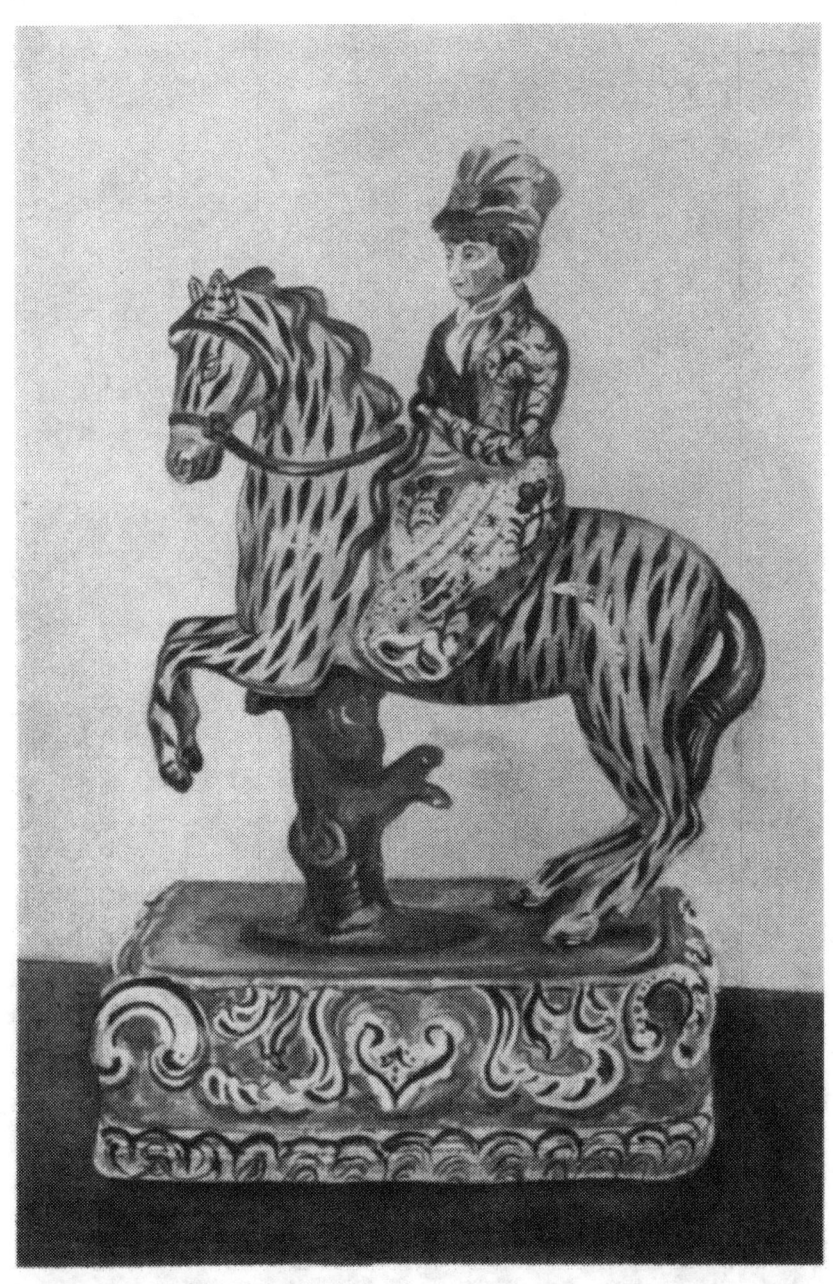

30　Staffordshire Figure (early nineteenth century). Height; 9¼ inches

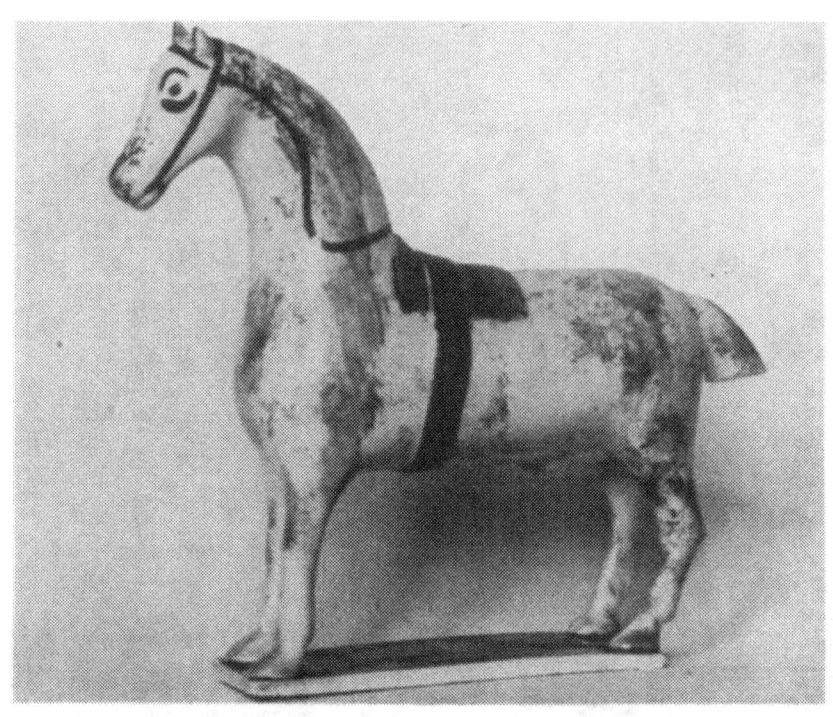

31 Staffordshire Earthenware Horse (early nineteenth century)

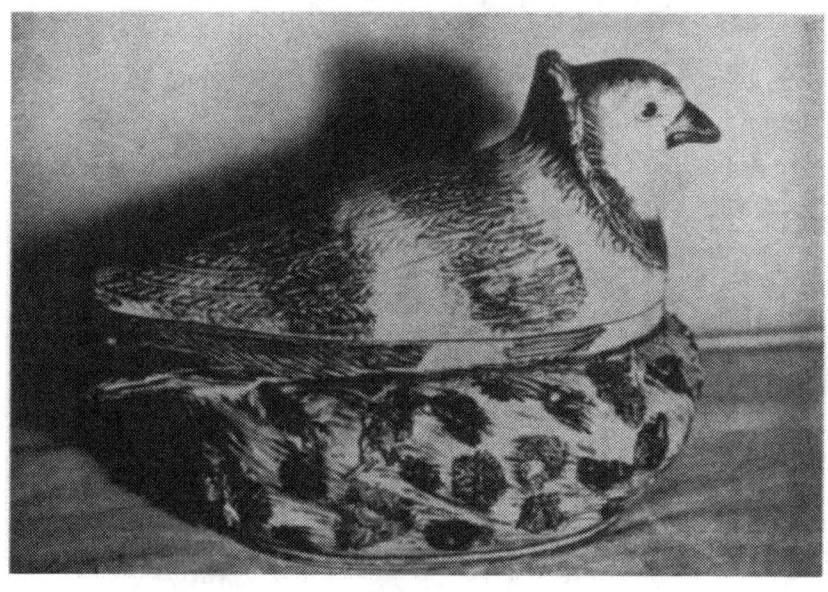

32 Earthenware Nun Pigeon Sauce Boat (probably Staffordshire)

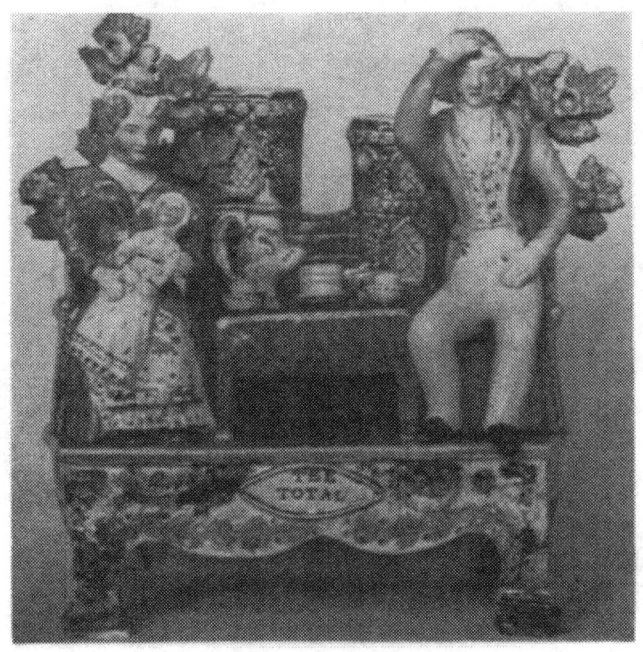

33 " Tee Total." Height: 9 inches

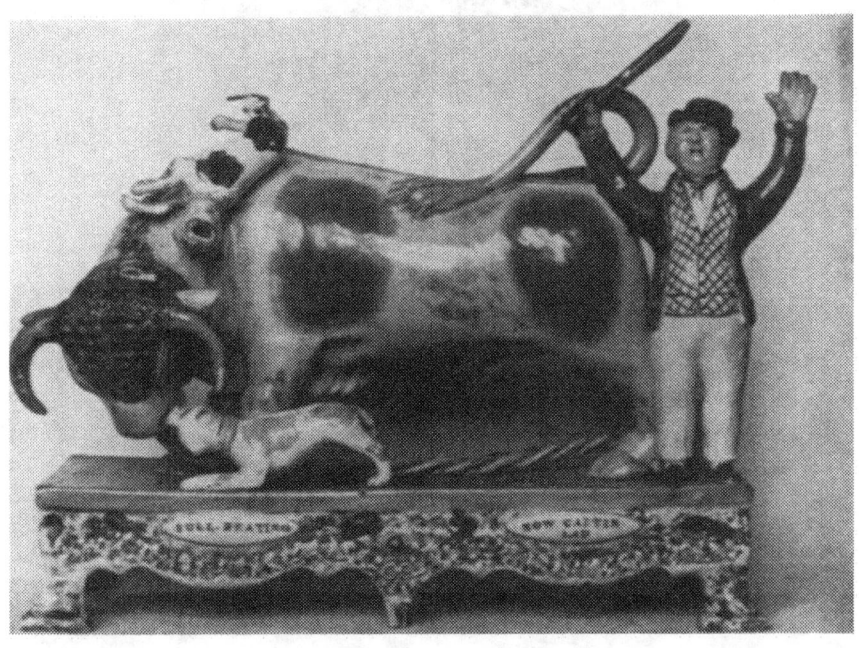

34 " Bull-Beating " (perhaps by Obadiah Sherrett). Height: 11½ inches

STAFFORDSHIRE EARTHENWARE FIGURES

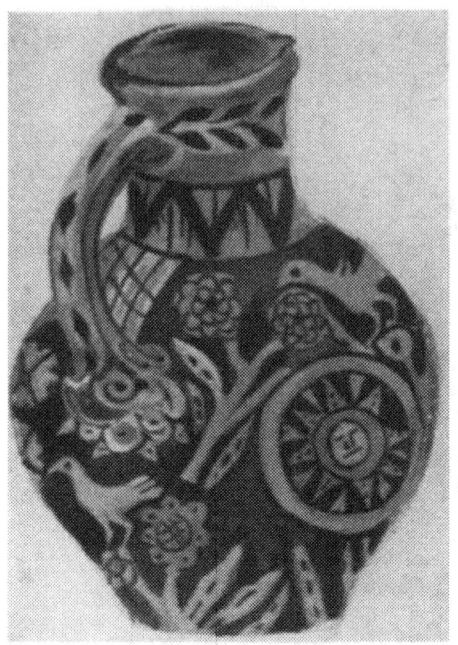
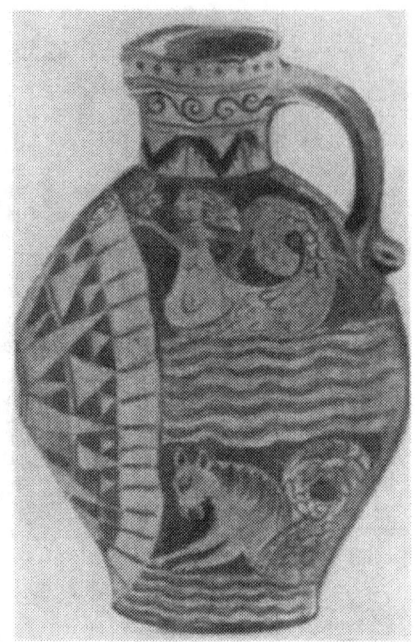
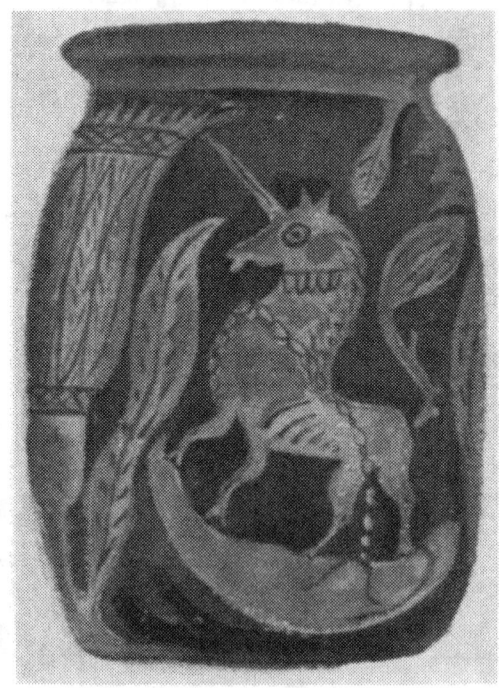

35–37 North Devon Harvest Pottery;
Slipware with *sgraffito* decoration
(eighteenth century)

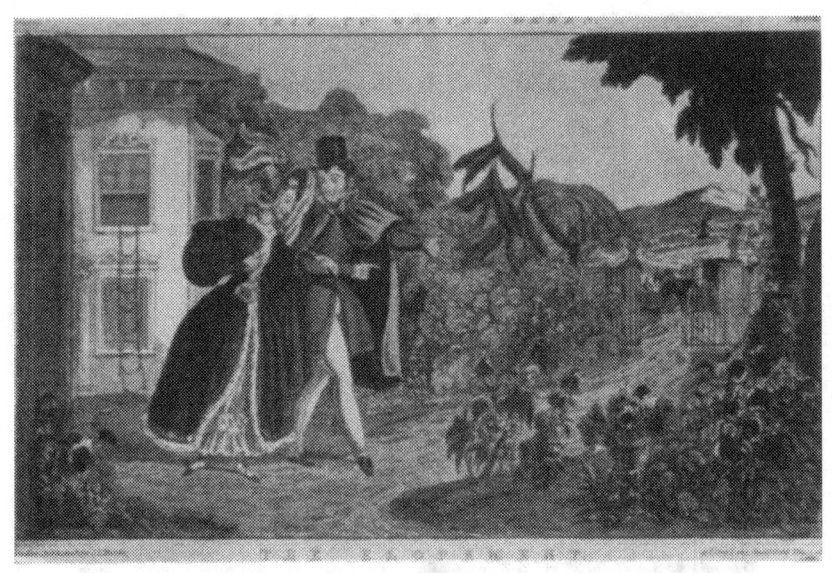

38   " A Trip to Gretna Green: the Elopement."
Published 1 May 1837

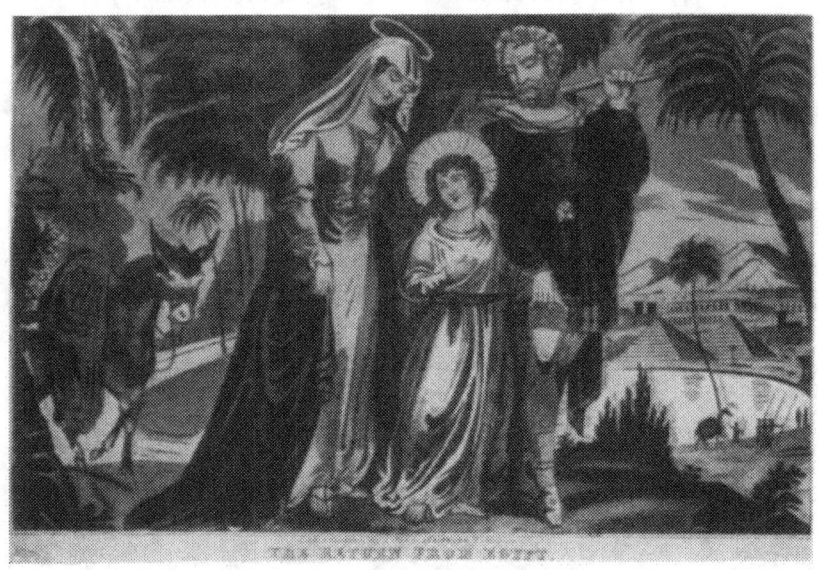

39   " The Return from Egypt."   Published 1 May 1838

HAND-COLOURED PRINTS

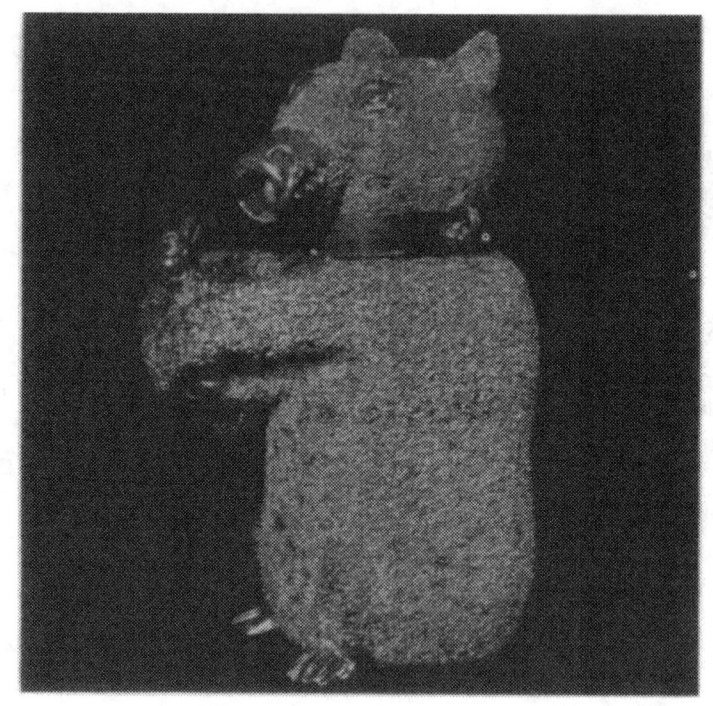

40 Nottingham Stoneware Bear Mug (eighteenth century)

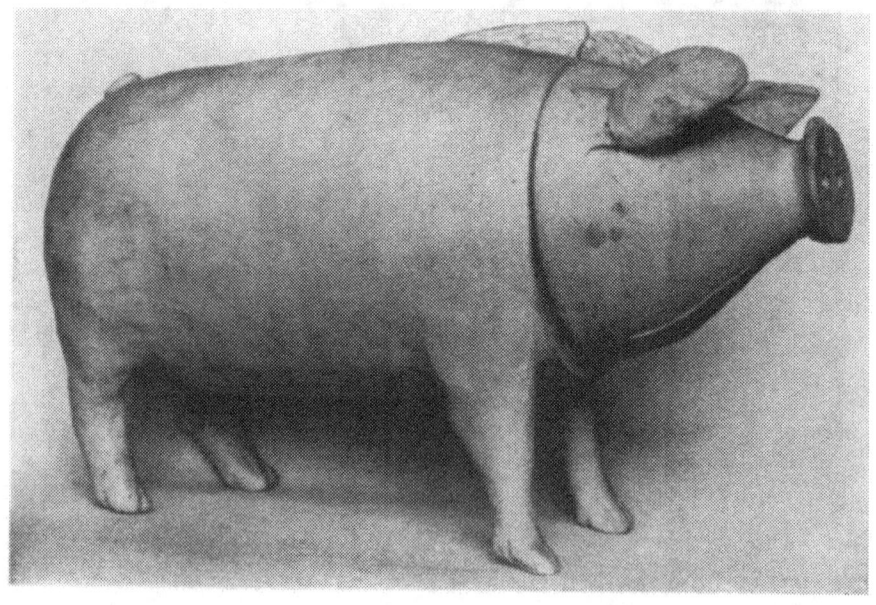

41 "Sussex Pig" Earthenware Jug and Mug

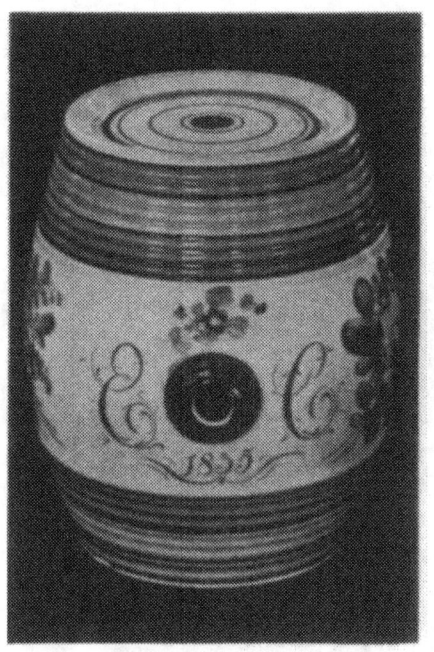

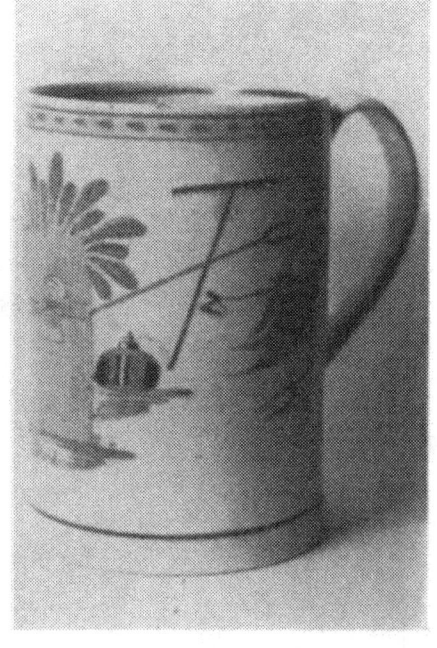

42 Bristol Miniature Earthenware Barrel, painted by William Fifield, 1835

43 Farmer's Mug, Earthenware, hand-painted; Leeds, late eighteenth century

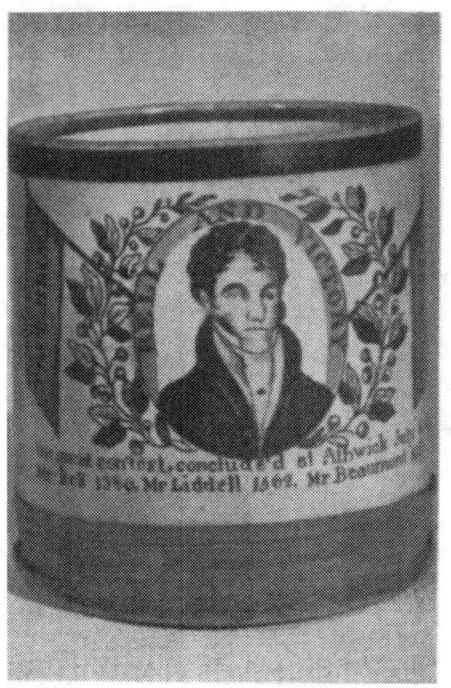

44 (*left*) Election Mug, Earthenware, transfer printed (1826)

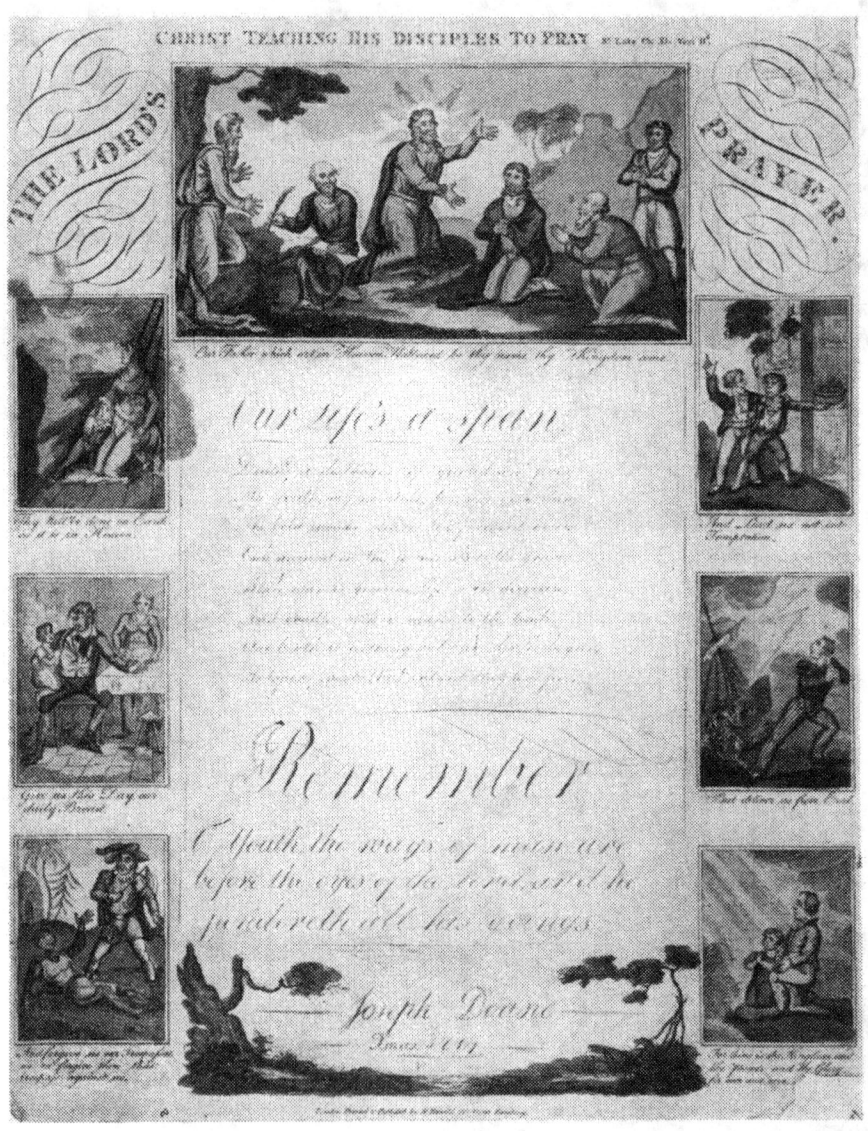

45 Child's Decorated Writing Sheet, with a border of hand-coloured prints.
Script by Joseph Deane, Christmas 1817

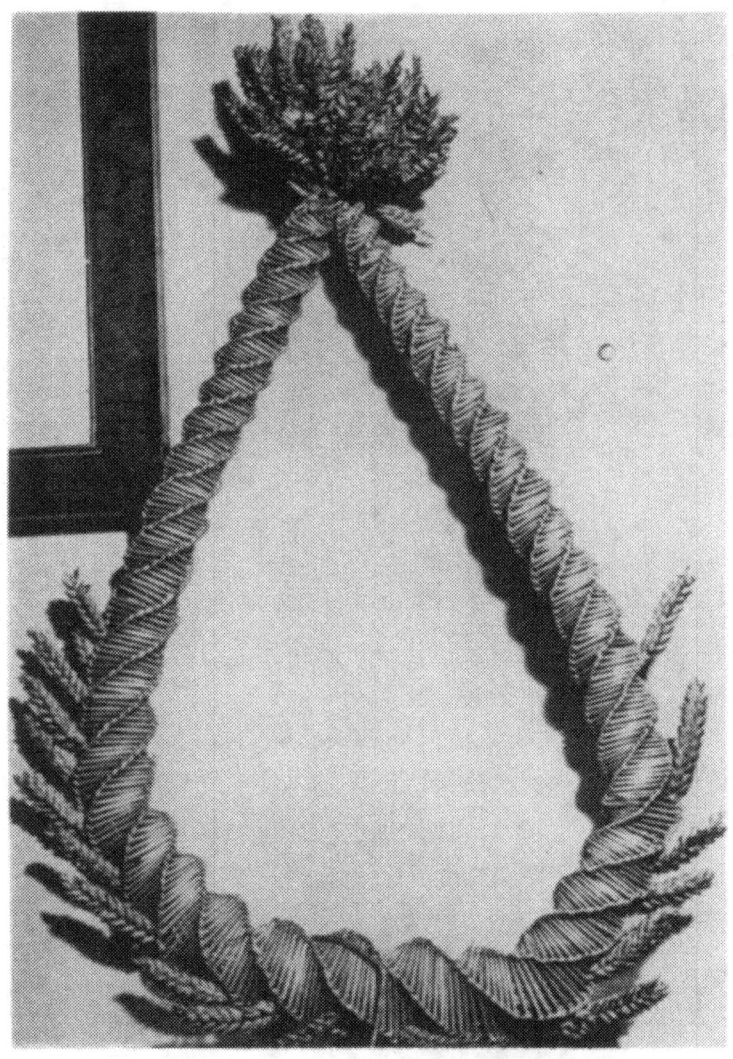

46, 47   Plaited Straw Corn Dollies from Essex

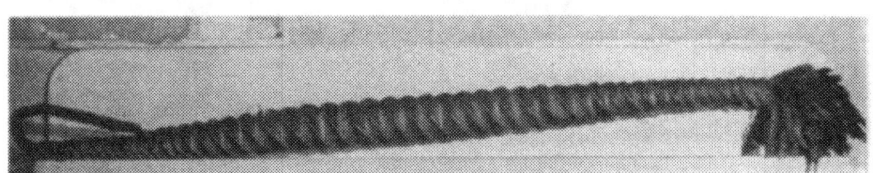

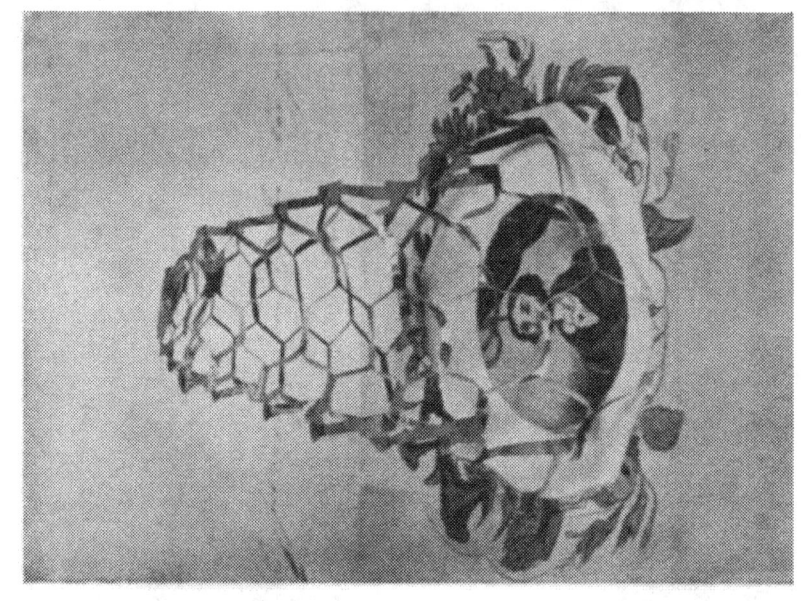

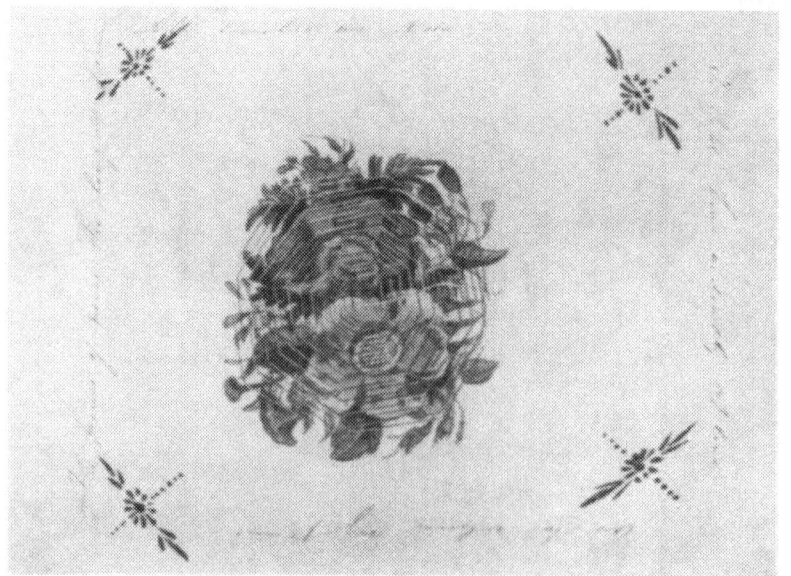

48, 49   Pull-up Valentine: *left*, closed; *right*, pulled-up (mid-nineteenth century)

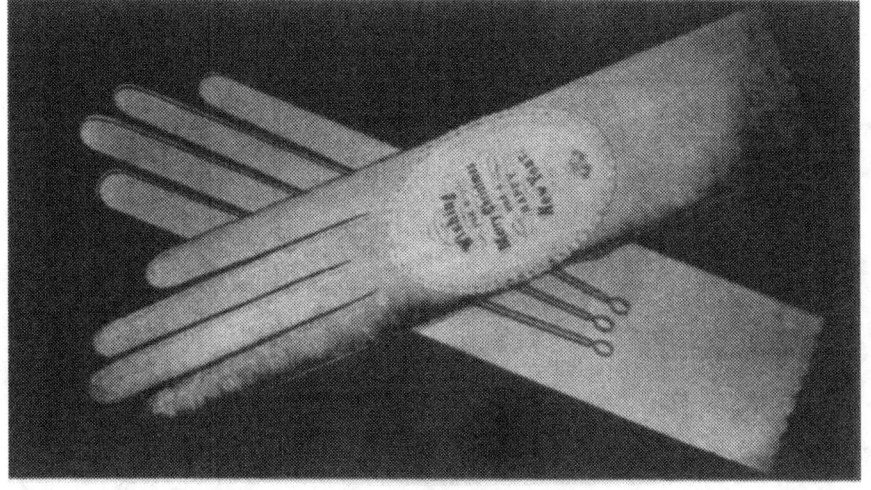
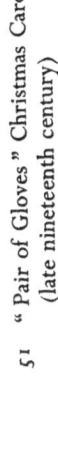

51 " Pair of Gloves " Christmas Card
(late nineteenth century)

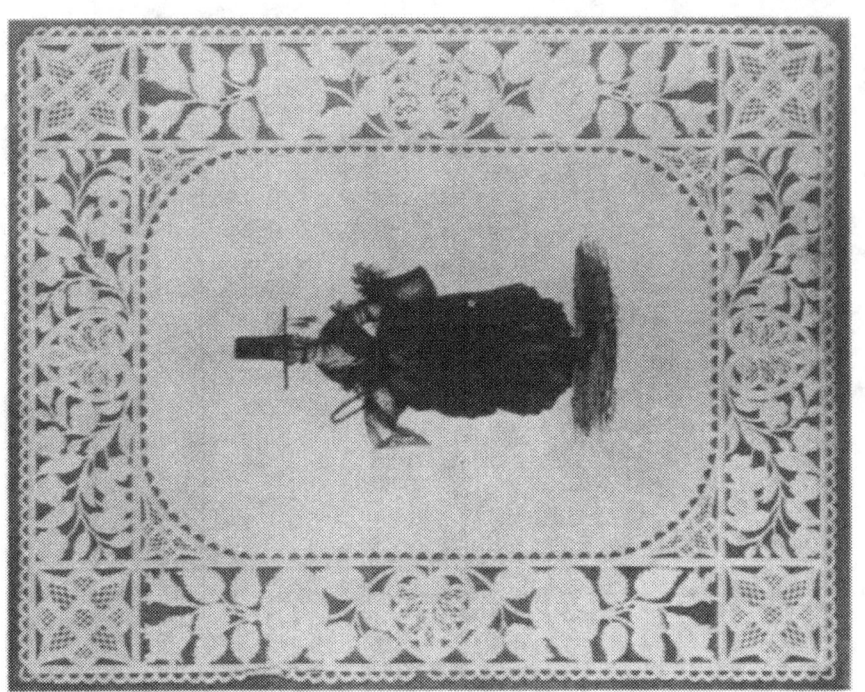

50 Welshwoman: a water-colour painting on embossed paper
(mid-nineteenth century)

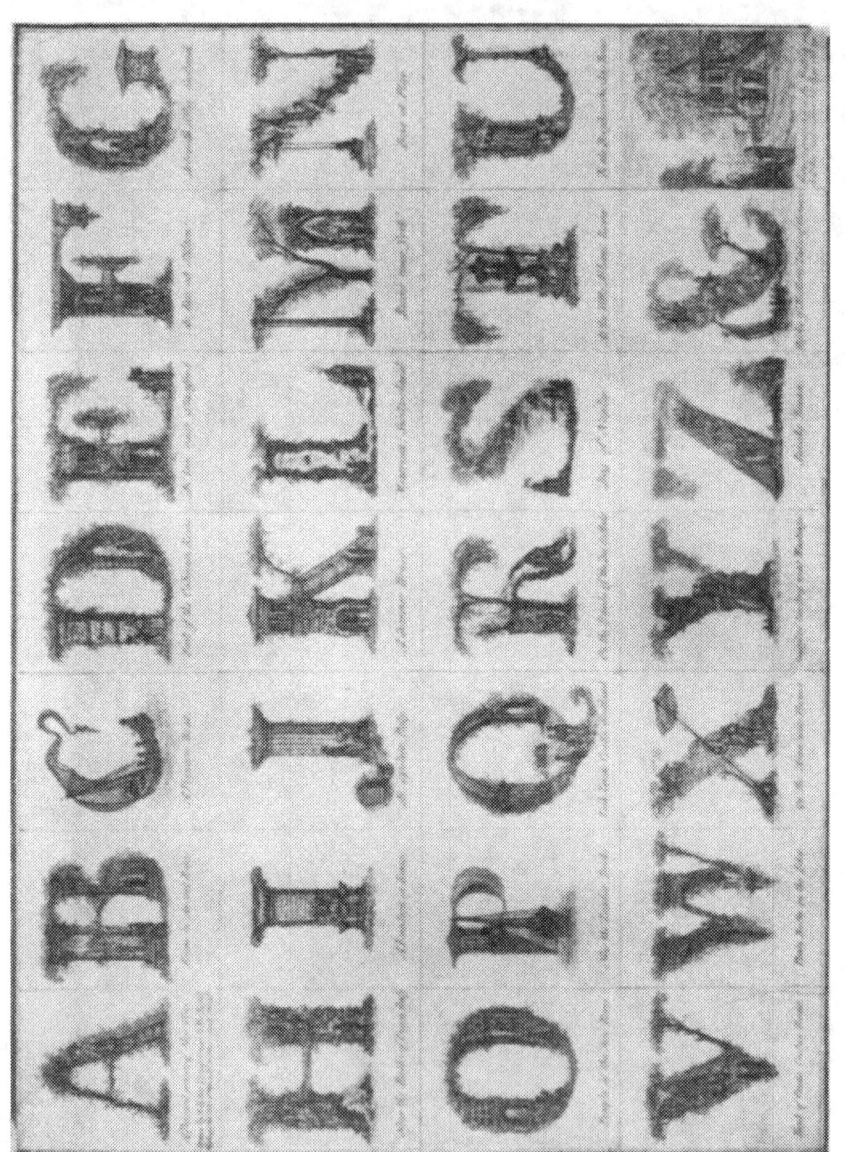

52   Pictorial Alphabet, invented by G. Tytler.   Published 1825

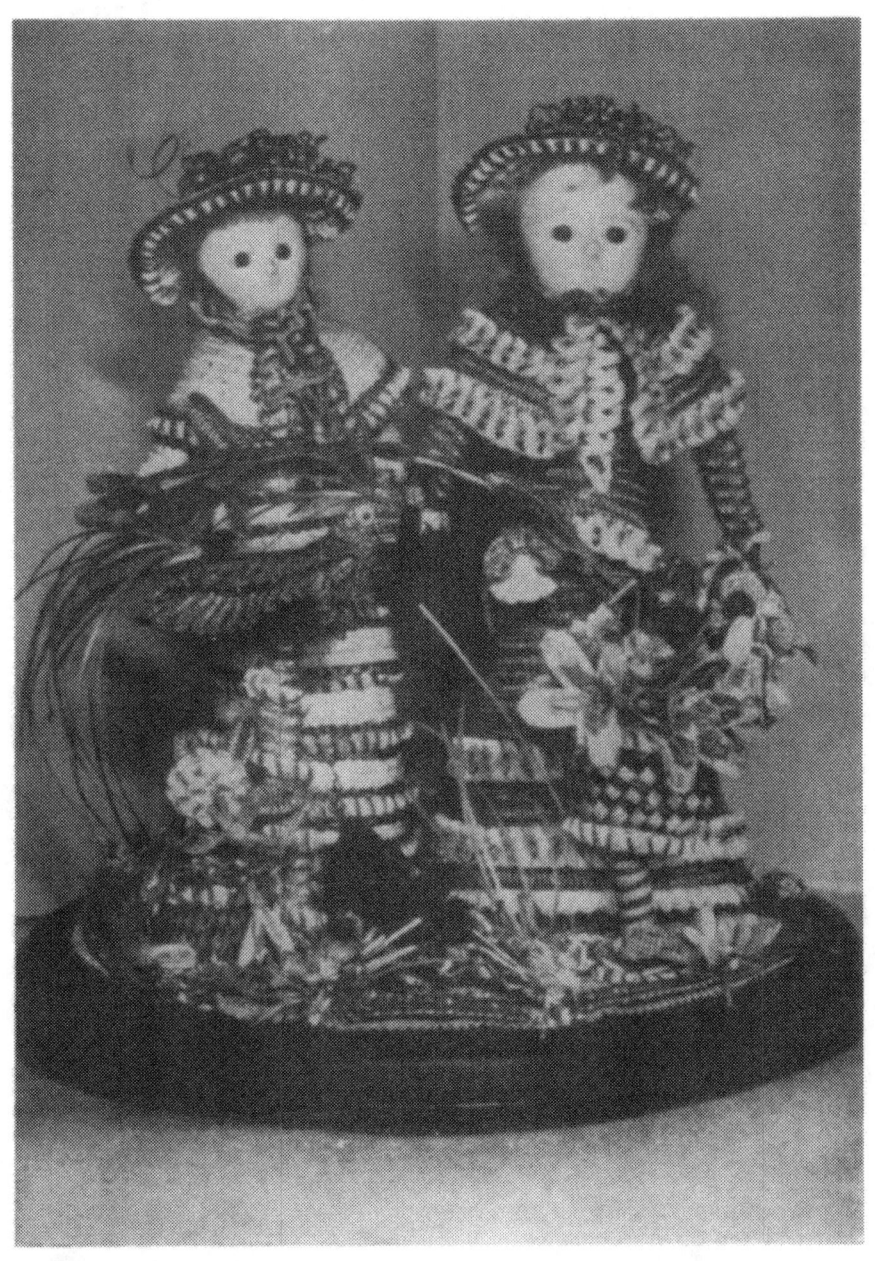

53 Straw-work Group from Luton (nineteenth century)

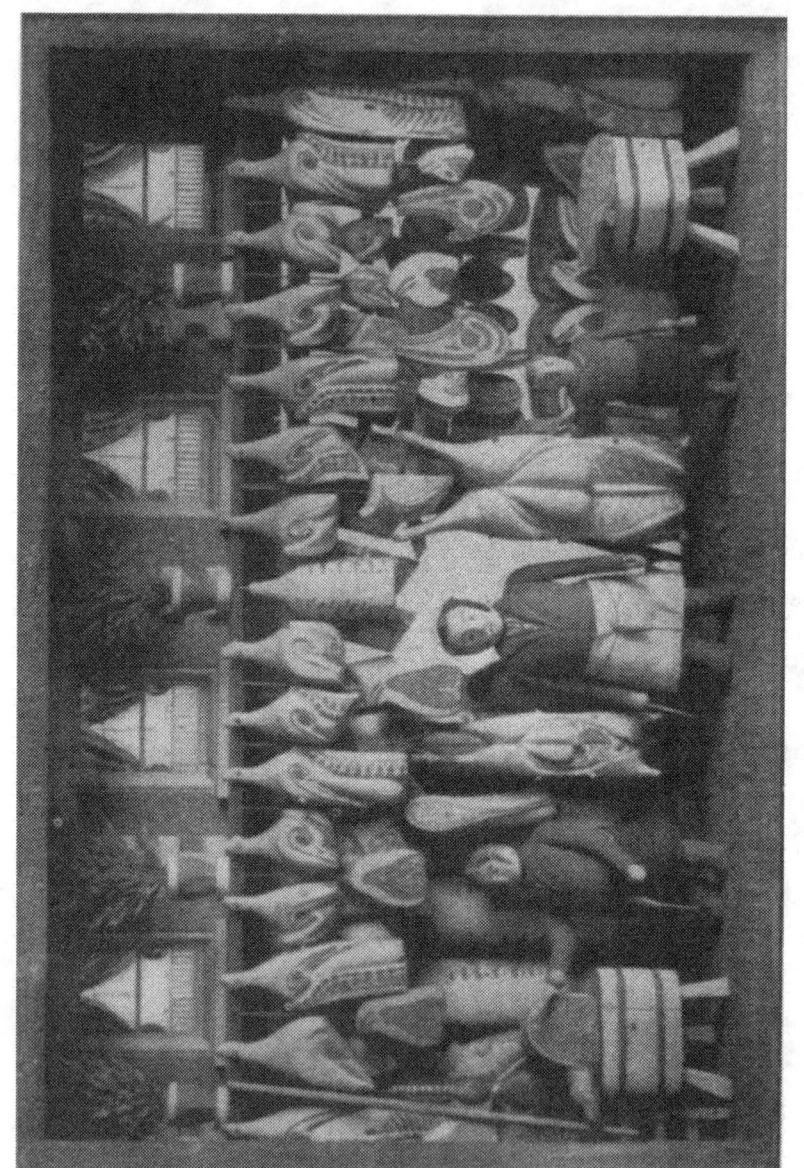

54 Toy Butcher's Shop (early nineteenth century)

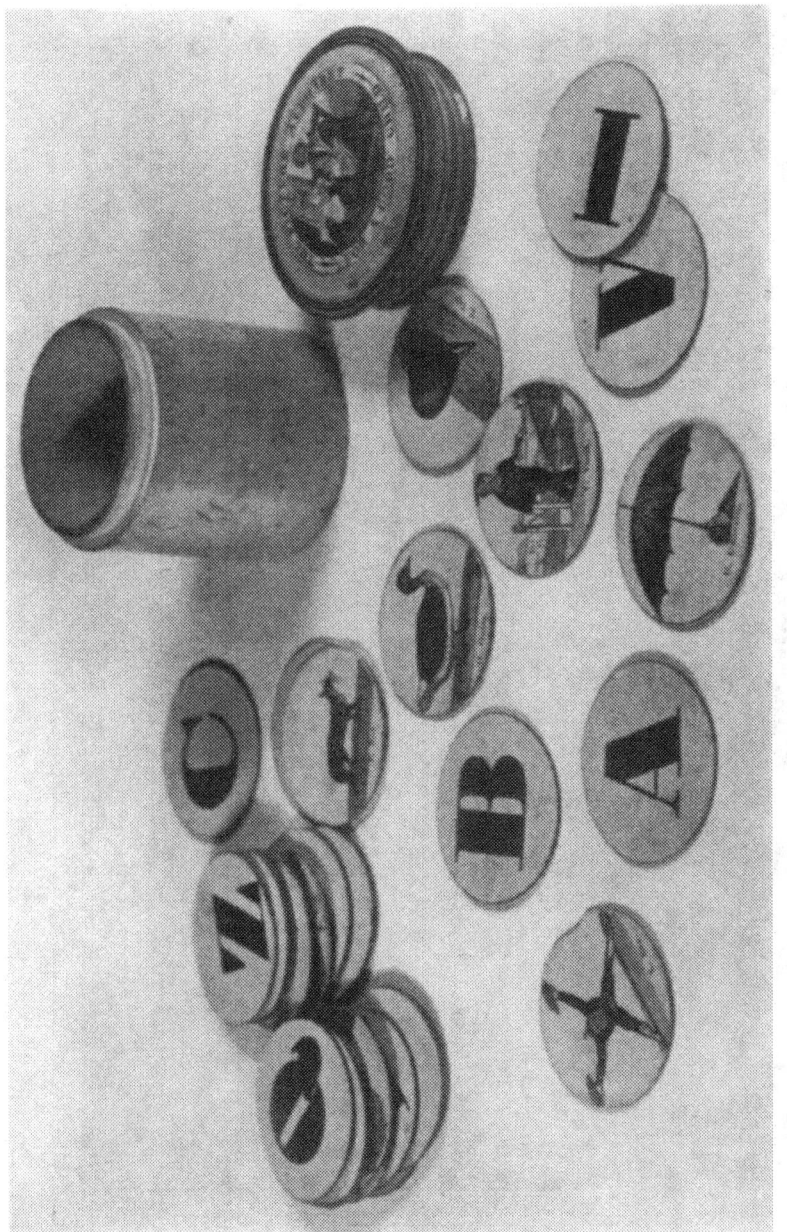

55 " Alphabet Counters " (early nineteenth century)

56 Bristol Blown-glass Dog Jug

it possible to use them for display also, and we
constantly find examples, even in the simplest
wrought iron, where infinite care and patience
have been put into making them useful and ornamental too. Keyhole scutcheons, to take but one
example, in both brass and iron are often most
decorative. The doorknocker is perhaps a borderline case between utility and ornament, and here
too we find a great variety of designs, in iron,
bronze and brass, some abstract in motive, others
pictorial.

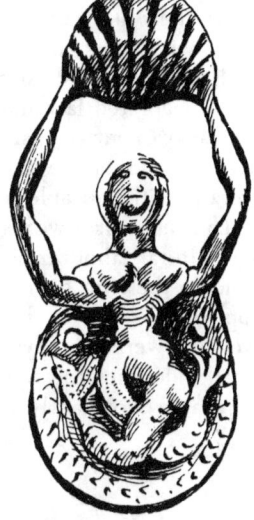

Turning to more purely decorative household
objects, a great many cottage mantelshelf ornaments were made in cast iron, sometimes in the
round, but more often in relief. Akin to them are
the many little figures made for door stops (**10**):
many of sporting subjects, dogs, horses and the
like, others portraits of contemporary celebrities,
like the Duke of Wellington, others grotesques.
We even find little cast iron decorations applied

Brass Doorknocker

to walls or to the ends of gutter spoutings. These little objects deserve more

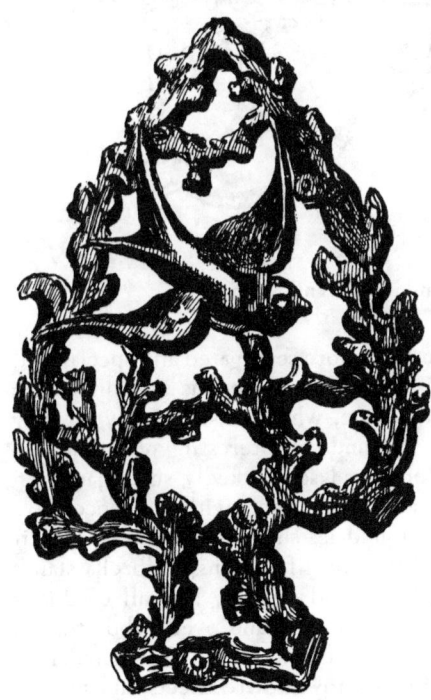

attention than they usually get, but
they have been overshadowed,
particularly in the case of mantelshelf ornaments, by the better-
known earthenware figures.

Doorstops and chimney-piece
ornaments in relief were also extensively made in brass from the
eighteenth century onwards; their
design is rather more sophisticated
than the cast iron, though they
include many of the same subjects.
The brass chimney-piece ornaments were usually made in pairs;
such subjects as a shepherd and
shepherdess reflect eighteenth-
century taste, whilst others, like a
sportsman with gun and a fisherman, or Robinson Crusoe and Man
Friday, look as though they might
have been taken from woodcuts or
engravings. Brass is an extremely
effective medium for such ornaments, which gleam very pleasantly
in the firelight.

Flat-iron Stand in cast iron.

Many miniature objects in brass or iron were made by apprentices to show their skill or as samples. Such are the little cast iron fireplaces, often with brass fire-irons and fender, the little brass chairs, flowerpots with a flower, candlesticks, cups and saucers. Other little brass ornaments often decorated farmhouse clocks and the like. The village band with its odd assortment of instruments, which played in church on Sundays and at fêtes and holidays, would usually include a little brass bird-whistle (p. 43) with movable tongue.

The Sussex ironworks in particular were essentially rural industries; the agricultural labourer would work in the fields in summer, and turn his hand to the iron furnaces in the winter months. Similar conditions often applied in other local ironworks and brass foundries, and even when the workers were employed full time, there were close links between these small industries and the surrounding countryside, so that the traditions of popular art constantly influenced their productions. With the advent of the

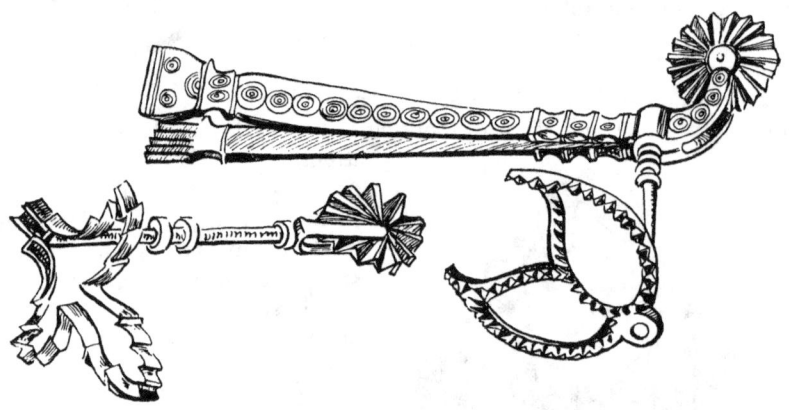

Brass Pastry Cutters, mid-nineteenth century

industrial revolution, metalworks became more segregated and specialised. But in the early nineteenth century fashionable taste was still under the influence of toy Gothic and the Picturesque, which was gradually filtering through to the level of popular art. We find the interesting phenomenon, which had perhaps not previously occurred so markedly since Jacobean times, of fashionable sophisticated taste coinciding with the decorative exuberence of popular art. The iron foundries show signs of this in their productions—the rustic garden furniture, bird fountains, umbrella stands and other fantastically ornamented household objects. Not all of this is admirable, by any means; much is heavily ornate and over-elaborate, but a good deal is full of the old sense of fun and gaiety typical of popular art at its best, such as we associate with the toy theatre sheets and pottery figures. Little domestic objects, such as trivets for flatirons or brass pastrycutters, though often machine-made, still retain some of the qualities of design which we essentially associate with a living tradition of hand craftsmanship. The two techniques, indeed, subsisted side by side, influencing each other. A sense of individuality could still make itself felt even in mass production.

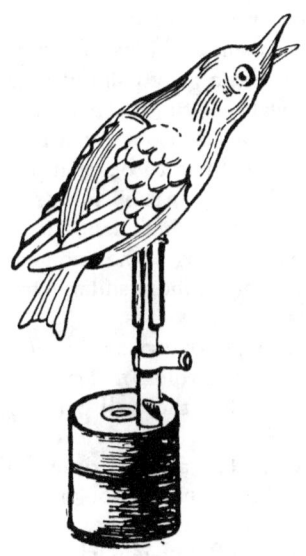

Brass Bird Whistle, from the village band

Chapter Three

PAINTING

Wall Paintings

Wall paintings are very common in and outside peasant houses in many Continental countries, notably in Sweden, Bavaria, the Tyrol and in other parts of central and south-eastern Europe. These paintings are typical manifestations of the popular art in their respective countries, as is also the gaily painted peasant furniture which is even more common than wall paintings in peasant homes all over Europe.

In England, with the exception of our canal barges, caravans and some farm and coster carts, there is little to be seen in the way of this type of unsophisticated painting. The explanation for its absence would seem to be that our native wood is oak, which lends itself naturally to carving, whereas in other European countries the indigenous forests are mainly pine, birch and other whitewoods, more suitable for painting, which helps, too, to preserve these less durable woods.

English church wall paintings have recently received a good deal of attention; through the efforts of Professor Tristram and others much has been done to preserve them, but the wall paintings in houses have been little studied.

We do know, however, that at one time wall paintings in houses and inns were common in this country, though comparatively few of them have survived up to the present time, because, owing to ignorance and changing taste, they have so often been whitewashed or papered over. Sometimes an early painting, like the one recently found at the "Golden Cross Inn" at Oxford, has been partially covered over with panelling in the sixteenth century; later, in the nineteenth century, the panelling too has been covered with wallpaper; in this case, fortunately, the paper was mounted on canvas nailed to wooden battens, so that when it became dilapidated and was removed, the wall paintings were discovered intact. Similarly, one was recently found dating back to the fourteenth century in a house at Longthorpe, near Peterborough; in this case the whitewash had been chipped by the Home Guard during the war, and when the redecorating was being done the owner noticed the painting coming through.

At one time the whole of the Eastern Counties and the West Country were particularly rich in wall paintings. The reason for this may be that in these districts church mural paintings reached a very high aesthetic standard, and this served as an inspiration for the painter craftsmen. It is not uncommon still to find in remote village churches in the West Country paintings on screens and pews.

44

Essex seems to be especially rich in well-preserved wall paintings. For instance, there is a small house not far from Saffron Walden where an entire upstairs room (once the Solar) has all the walls painted with a delightfully free, textile-like floral pattern of tulips and pomegranates, done in several colours with a bold black outline; this design, like so many others of the same kind, has the painting going all over the plaster and beams without a break. One of the peculiarities of this type of wall painting seems to be that whatever the subject, whether abstract or with figures, the painters took no notice of the architectural construction of the rooms

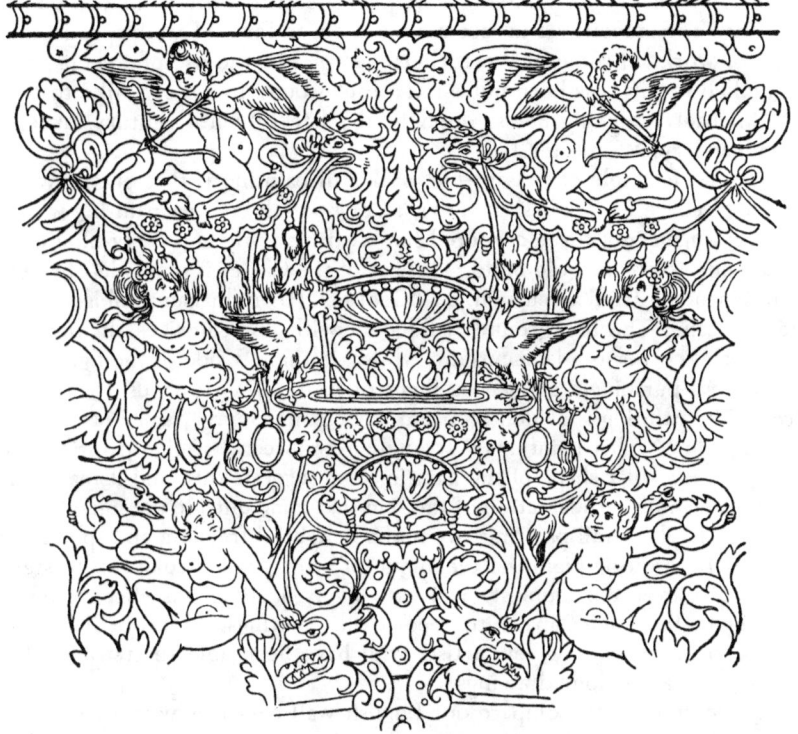

Wall-painting on wall and slope ceiling of attic, Shire Hall, Willington, Kent

but painted across any projections as if on a flat surface; chimney-breasts, beams, the eves of ceilings are all flattened out; doors and windows are treated as unfortunate interruptions. This peculiarity is also to some extent true of the Swedish peasant paintings known as Dalmalningar.

From what we know of them our English wall paintings seem to divide themselves into two groups. First there are those of a type so popular in Tudor times throughout all the arts, a queer fantasy of biblical, mythological and allegorical subjects, into which texts, mottoes and legends are freely introduced; these are done in an Italianate manner and are consequently rather sophisticated. The second type is more purely peasant craftsmanship: many of these have floral motives with textile-like patterns, like the Saffron Walden painting already referred to. Many of this latter type of paintings are drawn in a very vigorous black outline, with pineapples, pomegranates and arabesques, such as were also used in many of the church decorations and on embroideries. Most of the paintings were drawn freehand, but some of them are a mixture of stencil and hand-painting. The stencilled motive became very popular in the eighteenth century. Sometimes, as in No. 5, Market Hill, in Saffron Walden, the motive is a small lozenge repeat spot pattern with a bold floral border, rather in the manner of the block-printed pattern papers that were used for bookbinding. The stencil was in fact used as a cheap form of wallpaper in this type of work. In some of the earlier examples of the use of stencils, the stencilled pattern has been put on as a background to a scene, like that of St. Michael Weighing Souls, done in the late fifteenth century, at The Commandery, Worcester.[1]

Another example of peasant pictorial wall painting is that on the walls of the "George Inn," Chesham (11), an eighteenth century painting which depicts a man in a three-cornered hat wearing a wig and a sky-blue coat with wide skirts and gold braid. The star of the Garter is on his left breast, and depending from a red sash is a "George." His right hand holds a gold-headed cane. The background is filled in with floral devices. In the top right-hand corner is a lace curtain, whilst on the left side of the figure are three dogs pursuing a stag and a flight of birds flying towards a group of trees. The painting is evidently meant to be King George, since it is at the "George Inn." This painting is strongly reminiscent of sign-painting for inns; the irregular shape of the painting also suggests this, and it may well have been an inside adaptation of the sign that hung outside the inn.

In the English wall paintings we find a delightful freedom and spontaneity, partly resulting from the technique of swift brush-strokes on plaster, which give even the simplest motives a lovely quality; this effect is often lacking in the copies made to record the paintings. Professor Tristram seems to be one of the few artists who have been able to translate this quality in watercolour drawings.

It is interesting to compare our English wall paintings with those done by Swedish peasants in the eighteenth and nineteenth centuries; for instance, the story of Tobit has been painted on the wall of the "White Swan Hotel," Stratford-on-Avon, in the sixteenth century, and the same subject has been used by two Swedish peasant artists some two hundred years later. All these paintings, though very different in character, have in common enormous floral motives, out of all proportion to the figures, used to fill in what would have otherwise been empty spaces. Likewise all the artists have dressed their biblical characters in contemporary costume with apparent unself consciousness.

[1] Illustrated in "The Use of the Stencil in Mural Decoration," by Francis W. Reader in the *Archaeological Journal*, Vol. XCV, for 1938, part I.

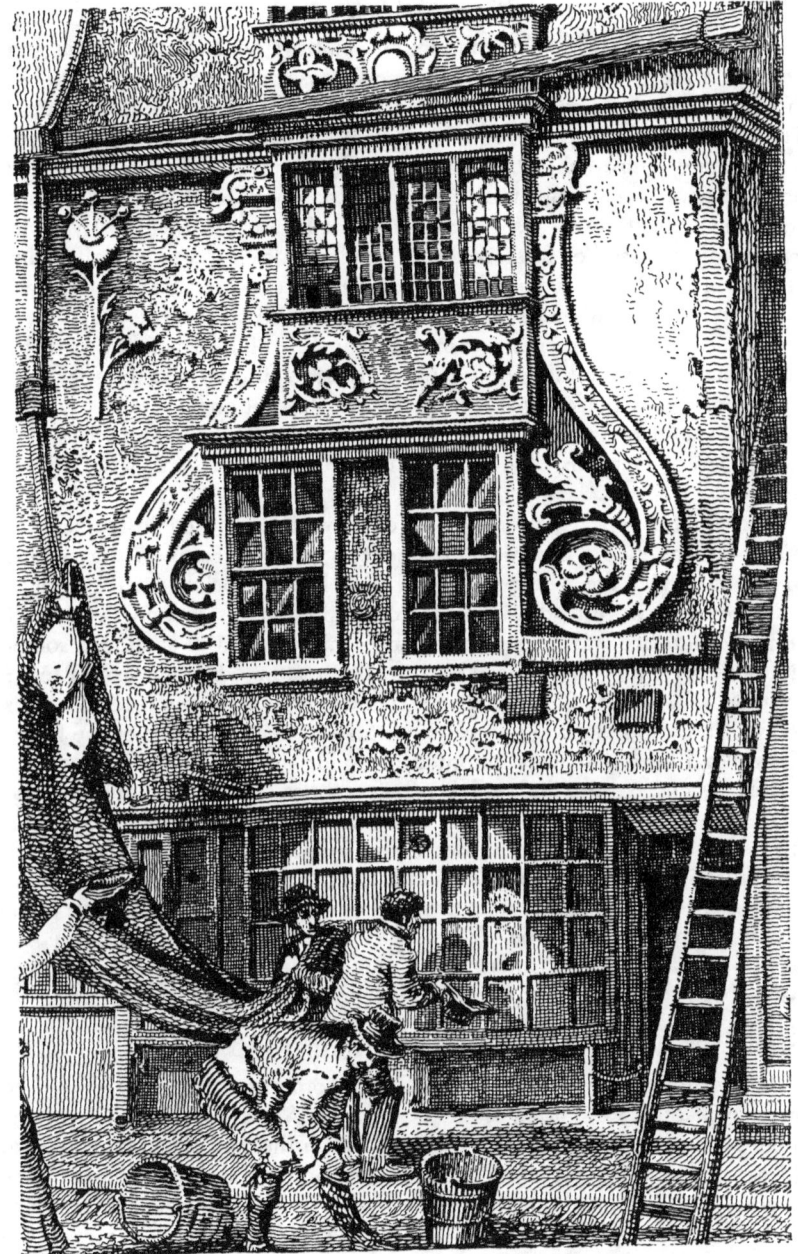

Parge Decoration, Little Moor Fields, London

Wattle-and-Dab and Parge Work

In England there are no outside mural paintings on the walls of inns and houses, as there are on the wayside guest houses in Bavaria, for instance. Instead, we have a great variety of outside decoration in plaster work. These decorations vary from simple patternings on the surface of the plaster to elaborate figure subjects modelled in high relief. This "parge work" ornament was very popular in the sixteenth, seventeenth and eighteenth centuries,. reflecting the fashion of the Great Houses; it was mostly done by the village mason or plasterer, who confined his efforts to a small radius of a few miles. Each plasterer had his own range of patterns and it is interesting to notice how these patterns change from district to district.

Certain places were richer than others in this kind of work. From the old prints we can see that London up to the time of the Great Fire in 1666 had a great many houses with external parge decorations.

Suffolk and Essex are still rich in this kind of work, and in Hertfordshire, Kent, Devon, Hereford, Oxford and York fine examples may also still be seen.

The simpler repeat patterns were done with a pointed instrument or stick. For instance a common ornament in parts of Essex is the zigzag; to get this effect the whole surface of the plaster is pricked with a stick. Some patterns were made with a fan of pointed sticks forming a kind of comb; others are wavy, like water, and some combed in scollops; sometimes the wave lines are crossed horizontally, making a basketwork pattern; another motive is the herrringbone. These simple patterns lead to rather more elaborate designs in low relief with strap work patterns of the formalised floral kind that were common in Tudor times. Besides these rather formal designs, we also find, in low relief, compositions of birds and flowers.

At Ipswich there are numerous examples of external parge decorations from about 1557; the best known is the famous "Sparrow's House." Here the relief is rather high and the subjects of the various panels round the house are representations of figures, buildings and animals; they are commonly supposed to represent Europe, Asia and Africa. Between the figures in panels are scrolled leaves and masks. Heavily moulded swags hang above the figure decorations, under the eaves of the building.

Sign Painting and "Primitive" Painting

In the nineteenth century the pargeter sometimes turned his hand to making plaques for inn signs. In St. John's Wood, the "Knights of St. John's Tavern" has a plaster plaque high up on the wall which is modelled in low relief; it depicts the crusader knights on horseback fighting the Moors. This is picked out in colour; the scene is surrounded by a plaster swag and beneath there is another swag surrounding the name of the tavern, the letters being also in low relief and gilded. But plaster inn signs are comparatively rare. More frequently inn signs are painted on boards and hung from a bracket.

Some of the signs were painted by artists of repute like Hogarth, who did a sign for an ale-house in Oxford Street of the "Man Loaded with Mischief," represented by a man carrying a woman holding a glass of gin, a magpie and a monkey. The artist Crome is also supposed to have painted a sign of the "Barley Mow," and Morland is known to have painted signs ; but the majority of inn signs were painted by local sign painters or itinerant artists.

The limner, or itinerant artist, travelled about the countryside painting anything that came to hand, an inn or shop sign, a portrait of a farmer's wife, his prize cow or fighting cock, or a record of some local event. In Oliver Goldsmith's *Vicar of Wakefield* the limner paints the entire Primrose family, variously costumed, on so vast a scale that the canvas will not go into the house. In remote country districts old people living to-day still remember his visits to their own homes or the local fair.

Signboards are exposed to wind and weather, so few of the earlier ones have survived. We can obtain some idea of the devices painted on them from the engravings on trade cards, bill heads, trade tokens and the like. But these, being interpreted in a different medium, give us only a vague idea of what the paintings actually looked like, and besides are often done in a more sophisticated idiom. For at their best these local painters

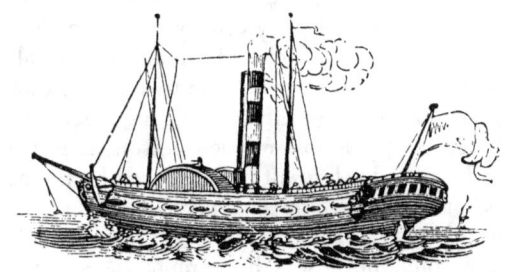

Billhead Ornament

and itinerant artists have a particular character in their work which gives them a special place in popular art. But to find examples of it we usually have to go to paintings that, for some reason or other, have been preserved indoors.

From the evidence of family portraits (**13**) we know that these itinerant artists were at work at least since Holbein made easel portraits fashionable in Tudor times. The early ones painted in oils, but later also used water colour. But whatever the medium, or for that matter the subjects, certain qualities are common to the best of their works of all periods ; it is indeed by these very qualities that we recognise the fact that they are the work of these local or itinerant painters which the Americans more descriptively call "primitive" painters. Perhaps the most noticeable of these qualities is directness of approach, and though such painters are often, from academic standards, inexpert in handling the medium, there is a sort of fearlessness in the forthright way in which they set down what they see and a grasp of the main character of their subjects which might well be the envy of many caricaturists. These qualities they have to some extent in common with children's paintings, but they go further than children, for their work has an adult's assurance in handling the medium, acquired by long practice, and this gives a certain professionalism to their work lacking in children's paintings. They have, however, the same eye for essentials, and though their use of colour may be naïve, it nevertheless always deliberately emphasises whatever mood they wish to express, be it sombre or gay, or something to enhance the character of the sitter (9).

Works of this particular type, though they have aroused great interest in the United States, have received practically no attention in England, so that it is impossible to say to what extent they survive. The most common subjects to be found nowadays are family portraits, treasured and preserved for their sentimental associations. Amongst such family portraits of the unsophisticated type, we may distinguish two groups. The first, borrowing a term from America, may be called "provincial portraits," which indeed exactly describes them. They are painted by professionals more or less in the contemporary idiom, and though they do not have any great technical skill, often possess a good deal of charm. The second type is more purely "primitive" in the sense we have been describing. These vary very much in the amount of skill they display, some being comparatively well executed and others rather rough and crude. But they all have a particular quality of vision, something very definite to express; though the hands of the painter may not always have the skill of a more accomplished craftsman, yet, being himself a very simple-minded person, it suffices to convey what he sees. He does not let himself be hampered by the need for realistic representation or by his ignorance of perspective and proportion, or even anatomy. But his very distortions, though they may be unintentional, invariably serve some purpose: they emphasise some particular point which has caught his eye. The result is saved from being a caricature by a basic seriousness of purpose and a genuinely simple vision.

Silhouettes and Cut Paper

Some of these itinerant artists worked in silhouettes, or cut-out shadow portraits (12) done on black paper, a survival of the elegant eighteenth century art executed so exquisitely by Mrs. Delany and others. Mrs. Nevill Jackson[1] says that this technique, on account of its sobriety and restraint, is particularly suited to English taste. These shadow portraits filled the need for cheap likenesses before the invention of photography, but have their appeal even to-day, possibly because there is an added personal touch. In many of our seaside places, for instance on the pier at Brighton, one can still for a small fee have a silhouette portrait.

Cutting paper to get decorative effects is a development of missal painting. Paper was cut to look like lace, or letters of initials, and sometimes even whole verses of the Bible were cut out, leaving the letters solid, in a technique which is somewhere between needlework and carving. Cut paper ornamentation was ideal for Valentines; it was also used for decorat-

[1] In *The Art of Silhouette,* which deals primarily with the work of sophisticated artists and craftsmen.

ing little memento sketches and for framing mottoes and texts. From hand-made to machine-made lace-papers was a natural step, and some of the early Victorian machine-cut papers are extremely attractive, as too are some of the early machine-pressed papers.

Pin-pricked pictures were, like silhouettes, another development of the decorated missal, and were first introduced into England by religious institutions for decorating votive pictures. Pin-prick pictures were immensely popular for both professionals and amateurs by the end of the eighteenth century. The Young Ladies' Annuals of the 1820's and 30's

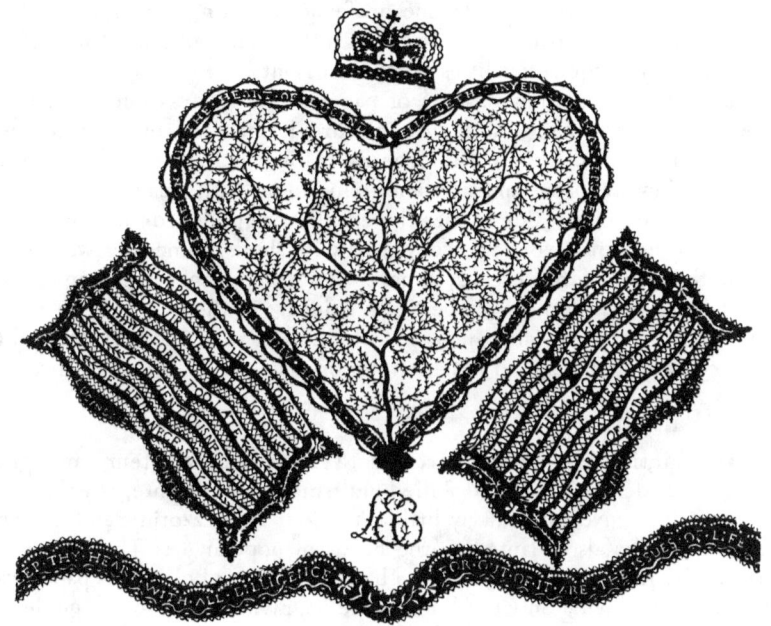

Cut-out Paper

often gave instructions and suggestions for making them. The technique is a strange one, which depends for its effects on the variety of textures that can be obtained by pricking holes of varying sizes in the paper, thus producing an interesting quality of light and shade; combined with this is a certain amount of collage and water-colour drawing. The final effect was of slightly raised work in a sort of low relief on paper.

Parlour Pastimes

It is interesting to note in passing how fashionable it was in the eighteenth and early nineteenth centuries for young ladies to practise as a "parlour pastime" one of these "mock arts." It was evidently not considered *comme il faut* for them to appear capable of serious work. Mary Howitt, writing of her childhood in 1809, speaks of the "elegant arts" of the day, at a Quaker school at Croydon, such as to net, to weave coloured paper into baskets, to plait split straw into patterns: "We soon furnished ourselves with coloured paper for plaiting and straw to split and weave into net," she writes, "and I shall never forget my admiration of a pattern of diamonds woven of strips of gold paper on a black ground. It was my first attempt to do artistic needlework." In fact, they delighted to make all sorts of objects in imitation of something else; hair was twisted and plaited into jewellery, fish bones and scales were painted and made into baskets, and there were a great many variations in paper-work. Nor was this "mock art" confined to amateurs; it might equally be done professionally for souvenirs. But like so many things which start as imitations, in the hands of a naturally gifted person it might acquire qualities in its own right.

One of the interesting variants of paper-work art was cut and rolled paper or vellum work. Teacaddies, picture frames and even firescreens were decorated with this work, done by rolling little strips of vellum or paper of different shapes and sizes and fixing them with a dab of glue edgeways on to the object. Sometimes the edges were gilded or coloured and sometimes the paper work was combined with shells, cameos or waxwork, or, in the case of firescreens, where the rolled paper was sometimes mounted on silk, there might be a silk painting in the centre. The result was a light filigree design which, in conjunction with the graceful eighteenth-century motives, had much charm on account of its great delicacy.

Glass Paintings

Glass painting was another art practised both by amateurs and professionals. It derived from the skilled craftsmen of the eighteenth century, who used it to give particularly brilliant colour to mezzotints and fine engravings; it was also adapted to the needs of popular art. The technique was simple. A print was glued to the back of a sheet of glass, the paper was rubbed away, leaving only the lines of the engraving to serve as a guide for the painting, done in oils on the back of the glass. In the popular art forms, the print is usually of the rather crude broadside type (**17**) and the result is not unlike transfer painting on pottery. The painting is done very freely, paying no great attention to the engraved outline, and transforms what may have been rather a stilted print into something much more primitive and gay.

Fairground Painting

L'Art forain, as the French term not only fairground decoration proper but the whole category of popular art which is akin to it in spirit and execution, may well derive from the earliest fairs and exhibitions of monsters, real and fake, which go back to mediaeval times. Fairground painting ranges from the embellishment of bill-heads stuck on walls to the large, elaborate paintings of forest scenes with wild beasts and the Buffalo Bill cowboys of the Wild West, popular on the booths of nineteenth and early twentieth century circuses, when it reached its zenith. These latter paintings have the qualities of a vast outdoor backcloth and are derived from the types of scenery popular in Regency and early Victorian theatres and music-halls.

From the painting of "A Village Fair," in the eighteenth century, by Joseph Parry,[1] one sees how akin the early fairground paintings were to the inn signs of the same time. In this painting there are two booths: one has six different paintings of wild beasts, and the other a painting of a contortionist; all the paintings are on canvas and hang from poles, rather in the manner of the old type of school map or street banners, so that they could be rolled up and easily transported. In an engraving by Pugin and Rowlandson of an early nineteenth century Bartholomew Fair, we can see in the distance a booth with the more elaborate canvas structure, covered in paintings, that was just coming into vogue. There is a delightful pair of Staffordshire pottery groups in the Willet Collection at the Brighton Museum showing two circus booths (18). In each, the showmen are standing on a platform playing a variety of musical instruments. The booths behind are both ornamented with paintings. One has a forest scene, a vast decoration, with parrots and monkeys in the trees, and a lion and

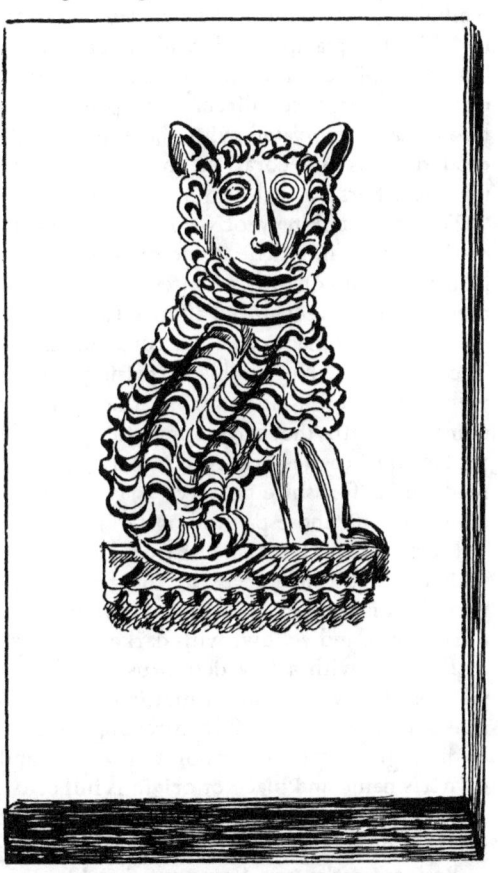

Fairground-type Gingerbread Biscuit Stamp from Horsham in Sussex

leopard; an elephant, carrying a castle on his back, is in the centre.

Nowadays the best examples of fairground decorations are to be found in the old-fashioned merry-go-round, which we have already described. Not content with painted booths and side-shows, the showman delights in gaudily painted caravans, partly, no doubt, because they are such excellent advertisements as they go along the roads through towns and villages, but

[1] Illustrated by Mr. M. Wilson Disher in *Fairs, Circuses and Music-halls.*

also because it is the nature of gipsies all over Europe to delight in brightly coloured things and gipsies have close fairground associations.

The paintings on English canal barges have much in common with fairground decoration. These paintings still persist with their old variety in spite of various attempts, since the nationalisation of the inland waterways, to make state canal boats conform to a uniform pattern of decoration. Several explanations have been advanced to account, in terms of mystic symbolism, for some of the motives traditionally used in canal-boat painting, like the playing-card symbols of hearts, diamonds, clubs and so on, but the subject is a complex one. It is just as possible that the motives may have been taken direct from playing-cards because of the good luck traditionally associated with the symbols. Barge decoration, like all fairground forms of decoration, shows gipsy influence and gipsies are notorious fortune-tellers.

The most striking motives in barge painting are castles and flowers. The castles are set in a little scene on a river or lake. No two pictures may be identical, consequently architectural detail varies quite a bit; nevertheless they all have a recognised affinity to a common ancestor both in style and colour—the romanticised, picturesque castle that we also find in the Toy Theatre sheets. Nor is this surprising if we remember that English canals were being built apace from the 1760's to about the 1830's which coincides with the early romantic phase of the Gothic Revival, when picturesque castles were all the rage. We find a number of them also made in Staffordshire pottery (**29**) and these pottery castles have much in common with those painted on the barges.

Much of the attraction of barge decoration is due to the style of painting, which is extremely free, in the true peasant tradition. Deep green or vermilion is the favourite ground for sprays of roses in contrasting colours of red, pink and yellow, with darker shading. The painter puts on the body of the rose with a few deft brush strokes, adding the shading while the paint is still wet, to get a melting quality. Multi-petalled daisies, yellow, pink, red and blue, with contrasting centres, are set off, as are the roses, by light green foliage, elaborately veined and shaded. The lettering of the owner's name and place of origin is full of twirls, and is shadowed, like the lettering on the fairground and on old-fashioned farm carts, with little garlands of flowers filling in the spaces and corners.

Besides castles and flowers, a bright geometrical pattern of circles and diamonds, known as "Scotch plaid," is also used. Each pattern has its traditional place—the tiller bar, for instance, is banded in contrasting colours like a barber's pole, only wider. Inside the cabin, elaborate bird's-eye graining fills in the background. The equipment is also decorated; blocks and stands for gangplanks, stools, even the large galvanised freshwater cans and washing-bowl. The watercan often has the owner's name inscribed on a scroll. Everything possible is covered with decoration; one boat decorated by Mr. Frank Jones, of Leighton Buzzard, has as many as two hundred flowers painted on various parts of it.

Painted farm carts are unfortunately rapidly disappearing; they had much in common with the barge painting. The painting was chiefly on the front and on the tailboard, and used to consist of panels, painted with the owner's name in shaded lettering embellished with scrolls and curls. Costermongers' and greengrocers' carts are still often prettily picked out in colour; some of them have gaily painted decorations of fruit as well as carved and painted geometrical ornaments on the sides. The spokes of the wheels, too, are usually picked out in red and green paint.

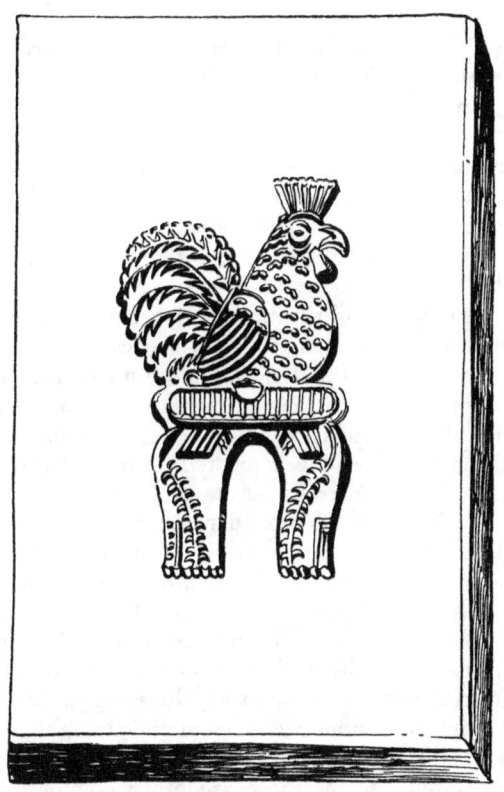

Fairground-type Gingerbread Biscuit Stamp
from Horsham in Sussex

Chapter Four

TEXTILES

Printing

Under the umbrella of textiles there are many manifestations of popular art. They are very varied and range from machine-printed ribbons, neckerchiefs and woven pictures to hand work such as patchwork, quilting, knitting, and various kinds of embroideries, like samplers, smocking and even sailors' embroidered pictures and pincushions.

The printed ribbons and neckerchiefs and the Coventry woven pictures (25, 26) are amongst the most interesting examples. For all they were mass-produced by machinery, they retain the qualities of popular art, showing that it is not the machinery that is to blame for the loss of our native vernacular. The printed neckerchiefs share a great deal in common with the woodcuts and engraved illustrations of the chap-books, both in subject-matter and treatment. So much so as to suggest that the same graphic artists were responsible for the designs in both mediums. This supposition is borne out by the fact that in France, where there has been a good deal of research into the manufacturers of *Imagerie Populaire*, it has been found that certain firms produced printed "dominos" for pattern papers and wallpapers and also printed broadsides and sometimes textiles, turning their hands to whichever was in most demand when trade was slack.

The earliest English examples of this type of printing are the ribbons which were fashionable in the late eighteenth and early nineteenth centuries. In some of the old ribbon pattern-books that were carried about as travellers' samples (one such has been preserved in the museum at Coventry) there are narrow ribbons of various coloured grounds on which are printed, rather crudely from woodblocks, ships and anchors together with inscriptions relating to famous victories of the time, such as those won under Duncan and Nelson.

Besides the printed ribbons there are other commemorative printed stuffs: some made for hangings, but more in squares for neckerchiefs. The designs are usually prints in monochrome from copper-plate engravings.

One design printed on such cotton squares shows the Battle of the Berezina (21); the centre has an engraving of the battle printed in red and an inscription which reads, "The battle of Berezina gained by the brave Russians commanded by Prince Kutusoff, Smolensko over the French November 28th 1812 with the flight of Bonaparte." Another, engraved and printed in red also, shows different scenes from the defeat of the French; this has inscriptions printed in English and German. Yet another on the

same subject shows the conflagration of Moscow, supposedly seen from the
Kremlin, on the entrance of the French Army, on September 14th, 1812;
this one is printed in red and black. There are scenes from other Napoleonic battles also, such as Waterloo, and of earlier ones such as the
Marlborough victories. One design has a map of the war in the Baltic Seas.

In the same period we find similar prints on textiles in other European
countries; both the French and German ones depict the same sort of subjects in a similar treatment, but they differ slightly in character from our
English ones, just as the broadsides of other countries retain their own
indefinable characteristics. The French, for instance, are often more elegant than we are in their engravings, but the English printed squares have
much of the quality of our toy theatre sheets, less elegant perhaps, but
lacking nothing in verve.
The rather wooden figures
retain their stances with
gallant intensity.

Portraits of national
figures and scenes from
historical events were also
depicted on these handkerchief squares, such as a
portrait of Queen Caroline
or one of the Coronation of
Queen Victoria and, later,
one of her Jubilee. The
signing of the Magna Charta
and the Passing of the Reform Bill have a square each
devoted to them. Then
there is a Railway Map of
England, printed in 1846,
when steam travel was still

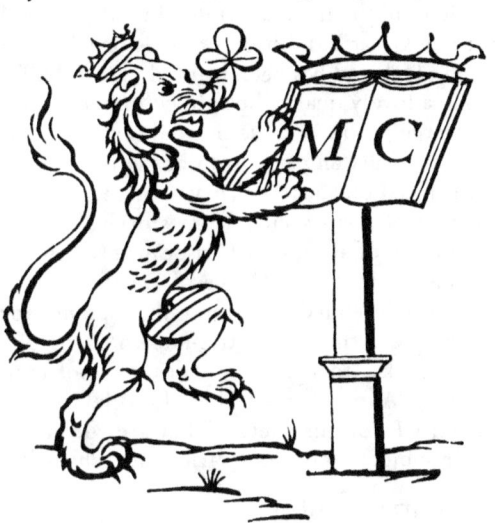

Tillet Block made for marking bales of wool

a novelty, and as a companion there is a Hackney Coach and Cabriolet
Fare Guide. This has in each corner and in the centre a different view
of London; round the centre are the charges and in the border are more
engravings showing four types of carriages and four drivers. There are also
many sporting subjects: scenes and portraits of famous racehorses, grey-
hounds and the like.

Election handkerchiefs form yet another group; these went on being
printed until up to the time of the First World War. In the Victoria and
Albert Museum there is a square showing the Brentford by-election, which
took place in 1768, but the square is printed much later, probably at the
turn of the century.

One of the most interesting political prints on cotton is that depicting
the Manchester Reform Meeting of 1819 on the occasion of the introduction of a Bill by Major Cartwright demanding universal suffrage, annual

parliaments, and election by ballot; this inscription is printed all round the engraving, which is also in red and would appear to have been taken from a drawing done by I. Slack just after the event. The picture shows a large crowd being broken up by the Manchester Yeomanry, who are seen on horseback with drawn swords; in the background are various houses of local political interest. The meeting was, of course, one of many which took place throughout the country during the agitation which culminated in the passing of the Reform Act in 1832, but has been specially commemorated because of the "Peterloo Massacre" which ensued.

As one would expect, there are many different squares showing the Great Exhibition of 1851. One, a very fine engraving printed in manganese, shows in the centre the Crystal Palace and, round the border, the flags and emblems of the nations printed in full colour. Possibly the most interesting of these Great Exhibition prints is one done for curtains and glazed; it is a wood block and has been printed in iron buff, madder red and indigo blue, giving a lovely quality both in colour and design.

A large group in these printed textiles are the prints made for children; they are really an early form of rag book, only they are not in book form, but printed on squares. They are generally in one colour, mostly with engravings of strip scenes from stories; there is one, for instance, of the adventures of Robinson Crusoe printed in red. A more macabre one has a sequence from the Dance of Death; it is not clear for what use it was originally intended—we can only hope not for childern.

An interesting and little-known form of printing is that done from tillet blocks, to mark the bales of wool exported during the eighteenth century. A number of the old tillet blocks are still preserved in St. Nicholas Priory in Exeter. They are cut in wood and have metal pin spots. Their subjects represent various merchants' trade signs.

Coventry Ribbons

Just as the majority of the printed textiles mentioned are commemorative in character, so were the Coventry woven ribbons (25, 26). These little pictures and scenes were woven in silk on a jacquard loom; they vary in size from 2 × 1 inches to 6 × 8 inches. They were made from about the middle of the nineteenth century to create new markets when times were bad for the ribbon weavers, and there are still people living in Coventry who remember seeing them sold off barrows in the streets at sixpence a piece. Thomas Stevens' of Coventry is the most famous firm associated with them, though they were made elsewhere also, both in England and abroad. The Stevens woven ribbons, however, display a character and individuality which distinguish them completely from any other woven ribbon pictures.

Many of these pictures were made as companion pairs, to be framed by their purchasers and hung on the walls of cottages. There is also a large group made as book-marks; many of these must have been intended for the use of children, for there are so many nursery rhyme subjects amongst them. Another considerable group consists of sporting subjects, obviously taken from prints which were popular at the time, such as "The Meet" and the companion piece "Full Cry." Later comes a bicycle-racing scene called "The Last Lap"; "Are you Ready?" shows the start of the Oxford and Cambridge Boat Race. The "Good Old Days" represents a Royal Mail coach; its pair, "The Present Time," has an early railway. A large number are portraits of Queen Victoria or Prince Albert, the Royal Family, or the Great Exhibition, and of famous contemporaries such as Mr. Disraeli and Mr. Gladstone. National heroes and heroines are also included, such as Grace Darling rowing through a storm in her father's lifeboat to save sailors from shipwreck. And as they were made in Coventry, Lady Godiva is also there. Many of these little pictures have an inscription or verse woven underneath; they are woven with very gay colours on different coloured grounds. Black seems to have been a favourite background colour, not only in the mourning pictures, such as those on the death of Prince Albert or Lord Beaconsfield, but also in many of the nursery rhyme book-marks. Coventry ribbons were even woven in small roundels to be stuck on notepaper as decoration and for Valentines.[1]

Quilting and Patchwork

So far we have been dealing with machine-made textiles in the popular art tradition. But there are, of course, a much greater number of handicraft types, some purely decorative, others combining utility with ornament. A painting of a quilting party done by an unknown artist in 1840–50, and now in the Bettman Archives,[2] shows American country people quilting, but they might easily have been English or Welsh, for the same sort of parties were held all over this country, too; indeed, there are still people to-day who can recall being taken to them when young. This particular painting shows a domestic scene with several ladies, young and old, seated round a large quilting frame, with gentlemen handing round refreshments. In one corner sits an elderly gentleman dandling a baby which has just been handed to him by a lady standing beside him; a dog and a cat are fighting under his chair. In the background more gentlemen are being handed refreshments by the lady of the house. The room has a beamed ceiling and on the walls are two framed embroideries besides a gun and a pair of antlers. The quilt, the centre of all this activity, is composed of large patches arranged like a chess-board.

In the past quilting in England was carried on in most homes, great and small, but in the nineteenth century was mainly a cottage industry, though still done in most parts of the country; nowadays, in spite of the efforts of the Rural Industries Bureau to keep the industry alive, there are only a few places in Wales, Durham and Devon where it still survives. Various districts seem to specialise in different types of patterns: in Wales, for instance, the designs are usually rather geometrical; in Northumberland

---

[1] A fuller account of the types and subjects is given in an article on Coventry ribbons in the *Rayon Design Journal*, September 1950, by Enid Marx.

[2] Reproduced in *American Quilts and Coverlets*, by Mrs. Florence Peto.

and Durham the patterns are rather formalised, with arrangements of waves, cords, feathers, tassels and fans; while the Devonshire quilters use somewhat similar motives as well as floral ones in a rather freer way. Though the quilters are influenced by their local traditions in the type of patterns, they make their own designs. This is indeed a very considerable achievement when we realise the large scale of quilt designs, how beautifully the weight and mass of the centres and borders are balanced, and how successful are the corners and borders themselves, always difficult parts of a design to manage. In Devon especially, quilters would appear to have taken their motives direct from nature. Mrs. Elizabeth Hake [1] recalls an old lady telling her that she could remember her mother and her grandmother picking sprays of oak leaves, ivy and clover, and even thistles, bringing them home to study in the evenings before making the great decision as to which should form the basis of the design for the new quilt. If oak was the final choice, it was usual to combine it with ivy, as they grow together.

One side of the quilts, the showy side, was often either a patchwork, or *appliqué* (**24**); sometimes, particularly in the *appliqué* quilts, the quilting pattern is worked as part of the general scheme, but more often, especially with the patchworks, the quilting pattern ignores the patchwork design. Many of the old patchwork designs, both quilted and unquilted, show the greatest ingenuity and taste in the arrangements of colour and patterns and especially in the use of light and dark patches of colour, yet they could scarcely be made from simpler materials. So, too, many of the *appliqué* designs are exquisite arrangements of formalised floral motives. Much more attention has been given to collections of old quilts in America than here, though many of their designers were of English origin and the craft seems to have been brought by English settlers.

Knitting

Not only quilting but also knitting had its parties. William Howitt in *The Rural Life of England*, written in 1837, describes the knitting parties which he found in Lancashire and Yorkshire. "The most characteristic custom of the Dales is what is called their Sitting, or 'going-a-sitting.' Knitting is a great practice in the dales. Men, women and children all knit. Formerly you might have met the wagoners knitting as they went along with their teams; but this is now rare; for the great number of visitors, and their wonder expressed at this, has made them rather ashamed, and shy of strangers observing them. But the men still knit a great deal in the house, and the women knit incessantly. They have knitting schools, where the children are taught; and where they sit in chorus knitting songs. . . . These songs are sung not only by the children in the schools, but also by the people at their sittings, which are social assemblies of the neighbourhood."

He adds that at the end of the day "they set out with their knitting to

1 Mrs. Elizabeth Hake in *English Quilting, Old and New* (Batsford, London, 1937).

the house of the neighbour, where the sitting falls in rotation, for it is a regular circulating assembly from house to house through the particular neighbourhood. The whole troup of neighbours being collected, they sit and knit, sing knitting-songs, and tell knitting stories. Here all the old stories and traditions of the dale come up, and they often get so excited that they say, 'Neighbours, we'll not part to-night,' that is, till after twelve o'clock. All this time knitting goes on with unremitting speed. They sit rocking to and fro like so many weird wizards. They burn no candle, but knit by the light of the peat fire. And this rocking motion is connected with a mode of knitting peculiar to the place, called swaving; which is difficult to describe. Ordinary knitting is performed by a variety of little motions, but this is a uniform tossing motion of both the hands at once, and the body often accompanies it with a sort of sympathetic action.

The knitting produced is just the same as by the ordinary method. They knit with crooked pins called pricks and use a knitting-sheath consisting commonly of a hollow sheath or dagger, curved to the side, and fixed in a belt called the cowband. The women of the north, in fact, often sport very curious

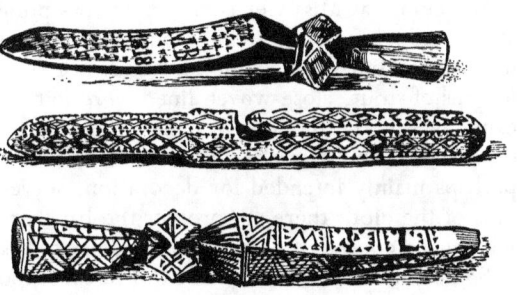

Knitting-sticks

knitting-sheaths. We have seen a wisp of straw tied up pretty tightly, into which they stick their needles; and sometimes a bunch of quills at least half a hundred in number. The sheaths and cowbands are often presents from their lovers. . . . Upon the band there is a hook, upon which the long end of the knitting is suspended that it may not dangle. In this manner they knit for Kendal market, stockings, jackets, nightcaps, and a kind of cap worn by the negroes, called bump-caps. These are made of very coarse worsted, and knit a yard in length, one half of which is turned into the other, before it has the appearance of a cap . . . the price for knitting one of these caps is threepence. At Garsdale, the old men sit in companies round the fire and because they get so intent on knitting and telling stories, they pin cloths on their shins to prevent themselves from getting burnt."

Being mainly utilitarian, little of this traditional knitting has survived in England, unlike the Scottish islands, where it is still a living craft with its own distinctive patterns. But at least one interesting survival in England is the fisherman's jersey or guernsey as knitted on the Yorkshire coast. Here the design varies according to the village from which the wearer comes, allegedly so that, in case of shipwreck, the bodies washed ashore can be more easily identified, but probably local pride and tradition also form part of the explanation.

Smocking

Smocks were once worn by countrymen all over England; the smock is, in fact, our national peasant costume (**22**). William Howitt, writing in 1831, says: "In the counties round London, eastward and westward through Berkshire, Hampshire, Wiltshire, etc., the English peasant, shepherd and drover is the white-smocked man of the London prints. In Herefordshire and in that direction, he sports the olive-green smock. In the Midland counties, especially Leicestershire, Derby, Nottingham, Warwick and Staffordshire, he dons a blue smock called the 'Newark frock,' which is finely gathered, in a square piece of parchment on the back and breast, on the shoulders and at the wrists; is adorned also in those parts with flourishes of white thread, and as invariably has a little white heart stitched in at the bottom of the slit in the neck. . . ."

Smocking, as Miss Gertrude Jekyll [1] has pointed out, is not only decorative but highly practical. A smock is simply a garment with a hole that a head can be put through; neither body nor sleeves are cut into shape. The lengths of stout, close-woven linen were left full width, and the smocking came where the fullness was drawn up into close gathers. These were decorated with various devices in embroidery. The close gathering, though perhaps mainly intended for decoration, served through the extra thickness of the cloth there, to protect the back or chest. The whole garment will turn a good deal of wet and the smocked parts are almost rainproof.

Some authorities believe that the various smocking devices signified the trade of the wearer, conventional symbols of which were embroidered on the front, with the object, apparently, that at country hirings the farmer could more easily recognise the type of skill he required—ploughman, shepherd, dairymaid, and so on, though no doubt professional pride will also have played a part, as with other uniforms.

Miss Alice Armes [2] gives this list of the emblems on smocks and attributions to the different occupations: *wagoners or carters:* cart wheels, whip lashes, reins and bits; *woodmen:* trees and leaves; *gardeners:* flowers and leaves; *shepherds:* crooks, sheep-pens, hurdles and sheep; *milkmaids:* churns, butterpats, hearts; *gravediggers:* crosses; *butchers,* in Shropshire, seem to have had chopping-blocks, saws and joints of meat. It is not, however, always possible to identify the different devices, and other authorities are inclined to attribute them to local traditions in decoration. Whatever the explanation of their origin, we find a large number of interesting and different designs on the old countrymen's smocks that have been preserved.

Embroidered Pictures and Samplers

Smocks are primarily utilitarian. But another form of embroidery, more purely decorative in purpose and once common all over England, is the embroidered picture (**20, 23**) and the sampler (**19**).

[1] In *Old English Household Life* (London, 1925), which also contains several illustrations of smocks in use.

[2] Alice Armes, *English Smocks* (London, 1928).

Chaucer uses the word "ensampler" to mean pattern, and the earliest dated samplers which have come down to us, some three hundred years old, are just this: they are notes of motives made by the embroiderers for future use. It is always interesting looking through a designer's notebook, and these early samplers are no exception. From the many references to samplers in early literature, we can see that they were being made some while before the earliest ones we possess. For instance, the poet Skelton (1469–1529) refers to "the saumpler to sew on, the lacis to embraid." We also know that from mediaeval times onwards decoration of personal attire and the home was one of the main occupations of women, so that embroidery was widely practised. Pattern books for such needlework were also available from an early date. Perhaps the two most famous English ones are Shorleyker's *Schole-house for the Needle*, published in 1624, and *The Needle's Excellency*, the twelfth edition of which appeared in 1640, with a preface in verse by John Taylor, the Water Poet. He tells us, though perhaps with a little pardonable exaggeration, that the designs in it were derived from all over the known world:

From the remotest parts of Christendome.
Collected with much praise and industrie,
From scorching *Spaine* and freezing *Muscovie*,
From fertile *France* and pleasant *Italie*,
From *Poland, Sweden, Denmarke, Germanie*,
And some of these rare patterns have been set
Beyond the bounds of faithless Mahomet,
From spacious *China* and those Kingdomes East,
And from great *Mexico*, the Indies West.
Thus are these works far fetch'd and dearly bought,
And consequently good for ladyes thought.

He also gives us an idea of favourite motives:

Flowers, Plants and Fishes; Beasts, Birds, Flyes and Bees,
Hills, Dales, Plains, Pastures; Skies, Seas, Rivers, Trees,
There's nothing ne'er at hand or farthest sought,
But with the needle may be shap'd or wrought.

Pattern books, however, were scarce; their life was limited, since the designs were traced by pricking through the page on to the cloth, and then rubbing charcoal or some coloured powder through the holes; they were also expensive, so that few people had the chance of using them. Hence the samplers. These samplers were in their turn copied and re-copied until ultimately the adaptations evolved into new designs. This accounts for our so often finding certain motives—for instance, the carnation, taken from Persian designs—again and again in different versions.[1]

Samplers can be divided into several groups according to the different

[1] Mr. Marcus B. Huish in *Samplers and Tapestry Embroideries* (London, 1913) gives many details of the early history of samplers, together with the different types of ornament and their origins.

types of ornament, but these groups do not necessarily bear much relation to the date, for many of the different kinds were popular at more or less the same time.

The earliest ones were, as we have said, notes of motives, grouped rather haphazardly. Then came coherent designs, at first usually embroidered on long, narrow strips of linen, bleached or unbleached, the length some three times the width, and worked in bands, many with drawn and cut thread work, some of the patterns being taken from lace. These long-banded samplers were made for about a hundred years, from the middle of the seventeenth century onwards.

Some of these banded samplers have letters and numbers worked on them, useful for those who had the task of marking household linen. Some also had little pictures embroidered on them. A lovely sampler (dated 1656) from Mrs. Charles Longman's collection,[1] has two scenes of the sacrifice of Isaac; it is headed with the maker's name and the date, then comes the alphabet, then the two biblical scenes, and below them four bands of varying depth each containing a row of formalised flowers; it is worked on cream linen in red, blue and green silks.

Texts and mottoes as well as biblical scenes were very popular in the seventeenth century samplers. We find them also in the little embroidered pictures (23) raised in relief, the "stump" or stamp work, which was also extensively worked in the seventeenth century, but, unlike the samplers, quickly went out of fashion. These little English embroidered pictures have been severely criticised as lacking in sophistication when compared with the high-relief embroidery done abroad, in France, Germany, Italy and Spain, at the same period. But we may find in their very simplicity and *naiveté*, the stiff stances of the figures, odd perspective and immense pre-occupation with the details of costume and accessories, no lack of character and charm. They are essentially English. The subjects are usually biblical or mythological scenes or figures of royal personages. The background is filled in with a large number of often incongruous motives, birds, butterflies, beasts, flowers, trees, castles, with no regard to proportionate size. So odd are some of these objects that various surmises have been advanced to account for them symbolically. But such speculations do not appear to make sufficient allowance for the English mentality. The aim of the embroiderer was to make these little pictures look rich and sumptuous, and what better way of doing so than by putting in as much as possible? The fantastic effect is enhanced by the attempts at realistic detail, such as the real hair that is sometimes used, the seed pearls to decorate costume, bits of paste, glass or metal spangles, and beads for eyes, or the knot stitches used to give the fleece of sheep a particularly curly appearance. It is perhaps not surprising that these little embroideries did not survive in the rational atmosphere of the eighteenth century.

The samplers, however, persisted right down to the middle of the last century. In the eighteenth they were being extensively worked by chil-

[1] Illustrated by Sir Leigh Ashton in *Samplers* (London, 1926).

dren, mostly between the ages of seven and twelve, in all parts of the country. As part of their educational value they acquired improving verses; some were maps, useful for learning geography as well as needlework. It is these children's samplers that mainly concern us here, for they too have the qualities of popular art. We do not know how far the children were allowed to select their own motives, though the prevalence of spelling mistakes suggests that they had a fairly free hand in working them out. The extent to which the personality of the embroiderer can influence even the most ordinary patterns is markedly shown in three text samplers made by the Brontë sisters during childhood and illustrated by Mr. Marcus B. Huish.[1] All three follow the same main design and even use the same motive for the borders, and yet each shows a very different character, both in the design as a whole and also in the choice of verses. Emily has embroidered a mystical passage of divine revelation with many references to the natural elements, from the thirtieth chapter of the Book of Proverbs. Anne's verse from the same book is much simpler and more direct, as, indeed, is her whole design. Charlotte's sampler begins with the words, "A house divided against itself cant stand"; her design is efficient and competent. All three are rather sombrely embroidered in black silk on coarse canvas.

Children's samplers are indeed some of the most interesting from the point of view of design; at times they are quite outstanding. A very remarkable one, made by E. Philips[2] in 1761 at the tender age of seven, is an extraordinary achievement both from the aesthetic and narrative points of view. In the centre she has worked her father in a blue coat, white stockings and buckled shoes; he points to her mother in a hooped costume; round them are the five girls, of various ages and, in the top corner, the boy with his tutor; in the other top corner are two servants, one coloured; a little negro boy is in charge of the dog; the house too is shown, surrounded by trees, butterflies and birds. Below is the far-away land to which the father must have gone, with the ship shown sailing across seas infested by mermaids and alligators, where black swans and other rare birds live.

Another child's sampler, of quite outstanding design, is one made by Mary Young in 1811, when she was eleven years old.[3] The centre has a panel representing Jacob's Vision; Jacob, in a pink sheet, lies sleeping in a bottle-green sleeping bag, flanked by trees going up into the sky; above him, in two rows, are bottle-green angels with yellow wings, with a ladder behind them. On the two sides of this sampler are the names and dates of birth of all the rest of Mary Young's sisters and brothers, with spaces filled in with verses and designs; one illustrates a text from Genesis, "And the water was spent in the bottle and she cast the child under one of the shrubs," by a large baby lying under a tree with its mother in white pointing with one hand to the baby and with the other to a bottle as big as the baby under another tree.

[1] In *Samplers and Tapestry Embroideries.*
[2] From Mr. Huish's own collection and illustrated in his book.
[3] Illustrated in Sir Leigh Ashton's *Samplers.*

These are two famous samplers of exceptional merit. Yet we can find hundreds of others examples of samplers worked by young children showing a remarkable if sometimes rather naïve sense of pattern in the choice and arrangement of pictures and letters. Nor should we overlook the simpler form of darning samplers (**19**), when the variously coloured darning stitches are generally arranged round some central motive, often with very considerable decorative sense.

Sailors' Embroideries

Embroidery is usually considered a feminine occupation, but both soldiers and sailors have turned their hands to it on occasion and have produced some very characteristic work, usually in the form of love tokens.

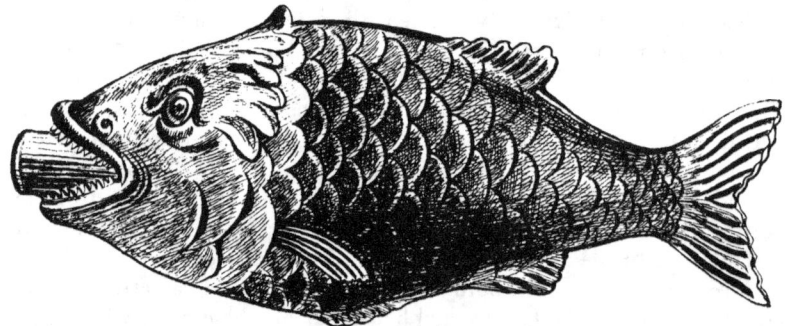

Sailor's Flask, Lambeth stone ware

The long voyages on sailing-ships provided plenty of leisure for such work, as did rest periods in camp and hospital. One of their chief specialities during the nineteenth century was the fat, betasselled pincushions, some are heart-shaped and all lavishly decorated with buttons, bead; pinheads and bits of looking-glass; many have regimental emblems worked into the design. They are full of exuberant fancy. Another form is the embroidered pictures, in wool and even silk. These are specially noticeable for their gay colours and strong, if sometimes ornate, designs; many of them are of sailing-ships (**20**).

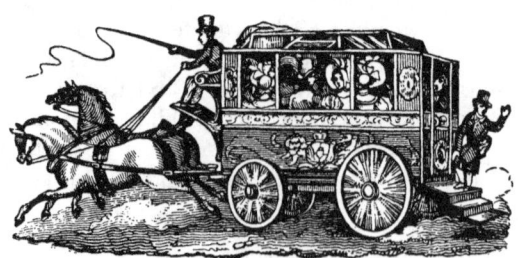

Printer's Ornament

Chapter Five

POTTERY

Slipwares

The country potter was once common all over England, playing an essential part in each rural community. Village potters often inherited their craft, and sometimes exercised it on so small a scale that they might be part-time farmers as well. The great bulk of their work was done for purely utilitarian local needs, and because earthenware is cheap and easily broken, little of this everyday output has survived. Indeed, if we remember the rough usage it got—how the pots would be carried to market on a packhorse perhaps, to be exposed on the rough cobbles of a village street market or hawked round the countryside on the backs of pedlars, and were then put to hard wear—it is surprising that anything remains. This ordinary pottery had little if any decoration. But for festive occasions, holy days, harvest, wedding or christening celebrations or to commemorate some remarkable event, the potters would make special pieces, using all their skill. These things have been treasured by many generations of owners, and amongst them we can find some of the most characteristic and delightful forms of English popular art, ranging from mediaeval times to the present century.

Slipware is one of the simplest ways of decorating pottery, and as such has been, and still is, used by peasant potters all over the world. The basic technique consists in taking a different coloured clay from the body of the ware, mixing it with water to the consistency of cream, and then applying it as a slip, either all over the body or in patches to make a pattern.

There are many different ways of applying the slip as decoration. It can be dotted, dropped or trailed on to the ware from a spout or pipette, as in icing a cake. Trailed slip is the favourite technique of Thomas Toft, greatest of English slipware potters, and his many followers; or bands of differently coloured slips can be laid side by side and brushed or combed through each other to get a marbled or feathered effect. In a thicker consistency, the slip can be used for relief decoration, by sticking on little pads, stamped with various shapes, as in the old Wrotham wares. The reverse method is to stamp the body of the ware or press it in a mould, perhaps leaving a raised edge, so that the depressions can be filled in with slip, like an inlay; this technique has been used for tiles since mediaeval times. Or a coating of slip can be laid all over the body and then cut away in parts to make a pattern against the darker background, or scratched through to give an effect of incised lines. The wares is then given a lead glaze.

In these simple techniques, the English slipware potters produced a great variety of "special" pieces. Some, like the miniature cradles given at christenings, were only ornamental. Others, like the large dishes and plates decorated with pictures and inscriptions, were scarcely suited to regular use. Others again, like the many, sometimes oddly shaped, drinking vessels, were primarily for convivial gatherings; such are the tygs, or multi-handled loving cups, which enabled each guest by holding a different handle to put his lips to a clean place on the rim. Posset pots, percursors of the punch bowl, have a lid, and a spout to drink by. Two-eared porringers recall our ancestors' liking for sloppy foods. Puzzle jugs, with hollow handles to draw away the liquid from an unwary drinker, or nests of fuddling cups linked together by a central tube so that, as one siphoned into another, he was forced to drink too much, are well-known examples of potters' tricks.

The great age of English slipware was from the early seventeenth to the end of the eighteenth centuries. Some of this work was very richly and elaborately decorated, in harmony with contemporary fashions. We recognise distinctive styles and techniques at different times and in different centres, such as Wrotham in Kent, in and around London and, above all, in Staffordshire.

All these groups of early English slipwares are deservedly famous. Less widely recognised, perhaps, is the high level of artistic achievement reached by many small potters, often anonymous, working in remote rural areas, far removed from the influence of the great pottery centres like Staffordshire or even from the trends of fashions in the big cities. One such group of little local potters, possessed of no great technical skill, but with an attractive individual style in shape, colour and decoration, flourished in North Devon (35–37) from at least the seventeenth century onwards, grouped round the Fremington clay-bed, which lies between Barnstaple and Bideford. This provided clay for the body of the ware, whilst the white pipeclay for slip was also close at hand. The ordinary output of these potters would be utilitarian. Decorated pieces were only occasionally made; some of the best are associated with the Fishley family, who were at work from the eighteenth century until a few years ago. For special pieces the usual decoration in North Devon (as at Donyat in Somerset (27) and on many Welsh harvest jugs) was a coating of white slip, cut away in parts or scratched through to show the darker body. The motives were mostly taken from everyday life and treated naturalistically: such things as flowers, especially tulips and butterflies; or agricultural themes, a ploughman at work or ears of wheat; or, reflecting the seafaring interests of the district, compasses, sailing-ships, even mermaids and seahorses. This sea decoration often occurs on the great harvest pitchers, made mainly at Bideford. The lion and unicorn was another popular motive. Reminiscent of ships' figureheads are the moulded heads sometimes set beneath the spout and handle of a jug; they were used by the eighteenth century George Fishley, who, to judge by his signed pieces, was an exceptionally gifted potter.

Another typical North Devon characteristic is a coil, like a twist of rope, at the base of the handle; this may sometimes be seen also on Welsh harvest jugs. A written inscription enclosed in a border often forms part of the decorative scheme.

The most interesting glaze is a rich greenish yellow (lead tinged with copper), through which the body shows as an ochreous brown and the slip honey-coloured. On well-fired pieces this glaze gives extremely subtle effects, more so than the deep clear yellow which was also used. The potters tried their hands at all sorts of ornamental objects—candlesticks, chimneypiece ornaments, even portrait busts, besides the more usual pitchers, jugs, mugs and honey-pots. More durable are tiles, sometimes with embossed relief patterns, sometimes stamped and inlaid with slip, which were extensively made in North Devon, as in other potteries. These earthenware tiles provide a direct link with mediaeval work, as we can see by the motives which persist unchanged through the centuries. They may often be found in churches near potteries. In Staffordshire earthenware has even been used for headstones.

It is interesting to compare with North Devon work that of another little group of West Country potters, established throughout the seventeenth and eighteenth centuries at Donyatt, near Ilminster, and at the nearby hamlet of Crock Street. The "sgraffito" technique of scratching through a coating of slip is the same, but the style very different, being much more abstract and formal, even for flower and bird motives, depending on the effect of incised lines instead of, as in the Devon work, setting mass against mass. Possibly this Somerset tradition of linear decoration contributed to the great success of the delftware brush-stroke technique at Bristol and Wincanton. Two extremely sophisticated examples of Donyat linear design (if such they be, for their precise place of origin is not known) are now in the Taunton Museum. One, a large dish with serpentine border, represents a lady and two smaller figures (perhaps her daughters), with wasp waists, curious coiffures and hands raised; it is dated 1685. The other, a smaller dish, is in more bucolic style: it commemorates the birth in 1680 of twins joined together (27), just such a local marvel as the broadside writers delighted to record.[1] The children appear under a crown, with a lively border of fruits and flowers. These two pieces are exceptional, and show the heights that could be reached; the general level is not so subtle in design, though very pleasant. The glaze is a deeper yellow than in North Devon, sometimes flecked with copper green.

A different type of slip technique was used by the many little groups of potters working in Sussex, some of which still survive. Here the design is usually inlaid, by incising or stamping the body and filling in with white

[1] These twins evidently caused quite a sensation, for Mr. F. H. Garner in *English Delftware* refers to their appearance on a delft charger of about 1680, when they are held aloft by two male figures, with the inscription: "Behould to parsons (two persons) that are reconsild to rob the parents and to keep the child," in reference to an attempt by two of the local gentry to exploit the children for profit.

slip. The decoration is slight and has a rather precise and formal appearance. Motives include sprays of leaves, or stars and circles, or printed lettering stamped on as though with printer's type, or drawn with a slip-filled quill. Possibly this choice of stamped decoration in Sussex slipwares was influenced by the local cast-iron work, where the pattern is stamped in sand. Sussex potters showed great ingenuity and fun in devising money-boxes, such as a hen and chicks or fir cone, but as these must be broken to serve their purpose, few have survived. The Sussex pig (**41**) is a delightful piece of potter's wit. It stands on four legs, but can be set on its haunches to form a jug, whilst the head, which is attached to the body by a piece of string or a peg, lifts off and stands on its broad flat snout to make a cup. Guests could thus drink a "hogshead" of liquor without undue effects. Old Sussex glazes are often pleasantly flecked with black, caused by traces of iron oxide in the local clay. The colour of the ware varies from rich dark browns and reds to buff, according to the district.

Such are but a few examples of the many lesser-known local English slipwares. Each district had its own favourite shapes, technique and style of decoration. But curiously enough, in the sentiments with which they inscribed their wares the potters showed little originality. We find the same rustic apophthegms, sometimes in identical words, occurring again and again. For instance, a very common verse runs:

> When this you see remember me
> And keep me in your mind
> Let all the world say what they will
> Speak of me as you find.

Or there are many variants of these lines, from a Bideford harvest pitcher dated April 28th, 1775:

> Harvest is come all by itself
> Now in macking of your barley mow
> When men do labour hard and sweat
> Good ale is better for their meat.

Common to many seafaring districts is:

> From rocks and sands and every ill
> May God protect the sailor still.

Two inscriptions from North Devon contain a sort of potter's philosophy. A jug decorated with flowers and butterflies says:

> The tulip and the butterfly
> Appear in gayer coats
> Than I at ome be dresst
> Fine as those worms
> Excell me still.

A big harvest pitcher says:

> When I was in my native place
> I was a lump of clay
> And digged was from out the earth
> And brought from thence away.
> But now I am a jug become
> By potters art and skill
> And now your servant am become
> And carry ale I will.

English Delft

The slipware potters only had a limited range of colours at their disposal. Brighter colours needed a white ground to show them up. One way of getting this was by using a glaze made white and opaque with oxide of tin, the so-called delft or tin-enamelled wares (**28**). Delft technique came to us from Holland in the sixteenth century, the Dutch having themselves taken it from the maiolica of the Italian potters, who derived it from the East. Delftware needs a clay that will give a porous body when fired to absorb the water from the wash of enamel; this clay was first thrown or turned in the ordinary way, then fired, then dipped in the tinglaze, and decorated by painting in colours on this white, unfired surface. The painting must be quick and deft, as the unfired glaze is absorbent, rather like painting on blotting-paper, which gives delft brush-work a lovely free-flowing line.

Delftware flourished during the seventeenth and eighteenth centuries; a little was still being produced in the early years of the nineteenth. A great variety of objects were produced in delftware, much of it for every-day use, like mugs, cups, plates, dishes, porringers, candlesticks, apothecaries' drug-jars or pill-rolling slabs, bleeding cups, even specially shaped barbars' dishes with appropriate pictures. A story current about these last says that any customer mentioning an unsuitable subject like cut throats had to put a coin in the barber's dish. Other delftware objects were mainly ornamental, like the big chargers or large dishes as much as eighteen inches across, painted in very free and bold brush-work drawing. Some of the very large plates, painted with flowers and birds, made in Bristol during the eighteenth century, were used in West Country farm-houses for ornaments during most of the year, but taken down to serve as plum-pudding or cake dishes on feast days. Delftware was not primarily made for the wealthy classes, who could afford imported and, later, English porcelains; it catered for lower and wider social strata: yet in its development we can trace the great change that came over English manners, from the directness, even crudity, of the seventeenth century towards an increasing refinement as the eighteenth progressed. This shows not only in elegant shapes and more delicate painting, but even in the softened colours of the potter's palette.

An attractive use of delftware is for tiles (**28**). Each tile may have its own motive or a set may build up a picture. A cat and a dog give a domestic note to hearth tiles.

Staffordshire Figures and Chimneypiece Ornaments

Unlike the Dutch, the English did not make much use of delft for chimneypiece ornaments, though we sometimes find cats. These little "image toys," as one of their most famous makers called them, are some of the most delightful products of English potters (30, 31). Until recently, when the interest of collectors sent up prices, no cottage mantelshelf was complete without its row of brightly coloured little earthenware images, watchstands, spillholders or just ornaments.

Most of these little "Staffordshire" figures, as they are generally called, though by no means all were made there, still to be seen in the positions they were intended to occupy, date from the late eighteenth or early nineteenth century. Earlier ones survive in special collections and are much sought after. But even these only go back to the seventeenth century, when they were beginning to be produced in two distinct ceramic processes—saltglazed stoneware and coloured earthenware.

Stoneware, like delftware, originally came to us from abroad; it is, as its name implies, very hard and non-porous; it is made of plastic clay and sand fired at high temperatures. The famous saltglaze is produced by common salt thrown into the kiln at the height of the firing; it gives the ware a glassy surface, finely granulated and pitted like an orange skin.

The earliest group of stoneware figures made by John Dwight (whether or not he actually modelled them) are some of the most exquisite productions of British ceramics, but can hardly be termed popular art. The stoneware technique, however, soon spread to the Midlands, to Nottingham and Staffordshire, where it flourished exceedingly during the eighteenth century and was adapted to the popular idiom. The little bear mugs (40), chiefly associated with Nottingham but also made in Staffordshire, are full of fun; the head lifts off for a cup, and the body serves as a jug. Both Stafford and Nottingham were bear-baiting centres, so the bear sometimes hugs a dog. Owl jugs were also made with detachable heads; details of face and plumage were picked out in brown, often giving them very amusing expressions. Most wittily observed are the famous pew groups, which have two figures seated on a pew or in an arbour, sometimes a boy and girl, but more often an elderly couple ogling each other.

Such was the rage for porcelain, however, that the Staffordshire potters eventually abandoned their saltglaze figures for the newer and more sophisticated material.

Earthenware figures, also made mainly in Staffordshire, developed at the same time and along lines parallel to the saltglaze ones, but, unlike saltglaze, held their own against porcelain. Earthenware being the coarser and cheaper material lent itself to the robust, vigorous style of popular art, as opposed to the greater elegance and delicacy of porcelain figurines; it became, in fact, the poor man's porcelain (32). Indeed, the potters often copied or, rather, freely translated porcelain models into earthenware, and sometimes these imitations, in their own broad and primitive idiom, give quaint results almost like deliberate caricatures. We get some idea of the people for whom these figures were made from Rowlandson's picture of the image-seller going round a country town and hawking his wares from a tray to the farmers and their wives.

The earliest of these earthenware figures were decorated by using differently coloured clays under a translucent lead glaze. These are the "Astbury"-type figures, called after the famous Staffordshire potter John Astbury (1688–1743), though of course not all were made by him. Then came the use of variously coloured glazes, by mixing metallic oxides with the lead glaze. Manganese gave a brown mottling, the "tortoise-shell" specially associated with the name of another famous Staffordshire potter, Thomas Whieldon (d. 1789,) though again other people also used the "Whieldon"-type glazes. They have a lovely translucent, melting quality; applied to the little, simply modelled figures a few inches high, the "image toys" as Whieldon himself called them, they are extraordinarily effective.

Not all eighteenth century earthenware figures have this primitive charm. Some of the later ones, produced for instance by the famous Wood family, are sometimes as sophisticated in their own way as the porcelain of Chelsea or Bow, and show the influence of fashionable foreign models. They have a different appeal from the *naïveté* and humour of the popular tradition. But the St. George of the younger Ralph Wood and the Toby Filpot jugs of the elder are in the old tradition. Toby of the jugs, that typical English eighteenth-century figure, is now known to be descended, not from Tristram Shandy's uncle, but from a mid-eighteenth century drinking song, the "Brown Jug," a free adaptation of the Latin verses of an Italian author.

Such was the attraction of these little earthenware figures that by the beginning of the nineteenth century a host of potters, some known, some unknown to us to-day, were making them. Plaster moulds had cheapened production; enamel colours, painted on after glazing and fired at a low temperature, provided bright decoration at little extra cost. Some have their makers' names on the back, but the majority are anonymous, and attribution based on tricks of style and the like is a chancy business, for the potters constantly and flagrantly copied each other.

The early nineteenth century earthenware figures were still modelled and painted in the round (30). But about the 1830's there developed a simpler and cheaper style; a rather flattened shape with the figures only fully modelled and painted in front, and the back left white (33). Such figures were produced in large quantities right down to the end of the nineteenth century. For all their simplified style, they have the old qualities of robustness and humour, though degenerating towards the end into much weaker and coarser forms. They are the equivalent in pottery of the broadsides and "catchpennies" of the street literature which the ballad-mongers hawked, and are the more interesting as the type was developed during the full tide of the industrial revolution, affording yet another illustration that it was not mass production in itself which has led to the vulgarity of so much of the cheap gift pottery of to-day, but rather a change in tastes, perhaps associated in some way with changing social habits.

Again like the street literature, the subjects covered by these little figures range very widely, and afford us an insight into the popular interests and tastes of their times. Many of them show the same qualities of "primitive vision" that we find in the work of itinerant painters and the like, concentrating as they do on presenting the essence of their subject as they see it, without being hampered by ideas of naturalistic representation or lack of technical skill in modelling. Tastes in colour change too: with the later types the colours become brighter, though sometimes they are only dabbed on in vivid patches. A very deep cobalt blue comes into vogue on these flattened type of figures, possibly because, during the Napoleonic wars, cobalt had been unobtainable, and when it came back public opinion liked it to be lavishly used.

Popular heroes change with the times, but royalty always ranks high. Reflected in these little figures we can see the change that comes over public opinion towards the throne. With George IV loyalty is at its lowest ebb; popular sympathies are all for the Reformers. The tide turns decisively with the accession of the young Queen Victoria. Figures of her appear, sometimes on horseback and later with Prince Albert, in magnificent state robes of deep blue, red and gold. The royal children soon come on the scene; the Willett collection at Brighton has a group of the first two sleeping in their coroneted beds, whilst above them a large white-robed angel spreads protecting hands.

The wars are reflected in the many naval and military heroes (some on horseback), with Nelson and Wellington having pride of place. Even Tsar Alexander and Marshal Bluecher find their niche; for the retreat from Moscow the bear of the jugs has become a Russian one; he hugs a miniature French grenadier labelled "Boney." But Napoleon is not always treated so irreverently. In spite of the stout patriotism which pervades these figures, he is sometimes presented as sympathetically as Wellington, whom indeed he often narrowly resembles. Mr. Wooliscroft Rhead vouches for the fact that, to economise in moulds, figures of Wellington and Napoleon were sometimes interchanged, with a few suitable modifications of detail, as Nelson and Wellington frequently were. This was the same trick that the street ballad-mongers and purveyors of cheap prints used, unhesitatingly touching up an old block for service as a new portrait. It seems quite possible that the potters took their portraits from such sources. That this practice was beset with pitfalls is amusingly illustrated by a figure in the collection of Mr. T. Balstone. It represents Pope Pius IX, standing full length, wearing his papal robes for three quarters of the way down, but with the rest of his legs encased in white Victorian gentleman's trousers. In this pre-photographic age no one bothered about literal accuracy; details of military and naval uniform were cheerfully mixed together, and the results gave a brave show of martial valour.

Political struggles are likewise recorded. Abroad, sympathies ran with the cause of nationalism and democracy; Garibaldi was particularly popular in a magnificent red shirt, though, being overglaze painting, this garment tends to flake off with the years. At home, in the big political issues of the nineteenth century—Reform Bill, Corn Laws, Ireland and the rest—the predominant feeling is liberal and radical, from the portraits of Sir Francis Burdett, Radical M.P. for Westminster, to Mr. Gladstone.

In this time of religious revival, biblical and religious subjects are frequent. There are portraits of great preachers from Dr. Sacheverell (in saltglaze) to Moody and Sankey, but Wesley is the most popular. Sometimes there are anticlerical gibes, like the group of the farmer and his wife presenting the parson with their tenth child as well as the tithe pig. Biblical scenes form the subject of many figure groups, especially the earlier ones. In costume these personages wear a modification of what then passed for classical, but often charmingly decorated with motives from contemporary cotton prints—little sprigs, sprays, stripes and spots. So do the ladies representing various virtues, Prudence or Faith, Hope and Charity, and the many characters from mythology.

Personifications, like the virtues, the seasons (in Arcadian garb), the four elements and classical divinities, are often taken from porcelain originals, but translated into more homely terms. We cannot help wondering what their owners may have made of some of these personages, though we must not forget that the "March of Mind" was well under way and that this is the age of Hone's popular tracts, the Society for the Diffusion of Popular Knowledge and the Penny Cyclopaedia. Literature, the arts and sciences have their heroes too: Shakespeare and Milton or Sir Isaac Newton with globe and telescope. Stage celebrities appear in the same vivid colours and heroic stances as in tinsel pictures; Kean as Richard III wards off the ghosts (*1*); Lister, Macready, Kemble, Jenny Lind the singer, Fanny Elssler the dancer, are some of the stars in earthenware. There is also the circus. "Wombwell's Royal Menagerie of the Wonderful Burds and Beasts from most parts of the World" shows the front entrance with little figures summoning the public in; a companion group shows Polito's Royal Menagerie.

Crime too had its public. From the Whieldon plaque (done from a Hogarth engraving) of Sarah Malcolm, executed for a triple murder in 1733, onwards we find a galaxy of criminal celebrities. A pair of idyllic cottages are inscribed "Potash Farm" and "Stansfield Hall," one the home of Rush, the murderer, and the other the scene of the crime.

Sport is represented in many forms, bull-baiting (**34**), bear-baiting, cock-fighting, prize fighting, coursing, shooting, racing, with a whole gallery of bygone champions, from Tom Cribb, the "Black Diamond" of the prize ring, to the unbeaten racehorse Eclipse. Conviviality has naturally close associations with pottery, and drunkenness is an age-old joke. Now and then a little temperance reform creeps in: of a pair of groups, the one inscribed "Tee Total" (**33**) shows a husband drinking tea with his wife and child; the other, inscribed "Alehouse," shows a married couple in a brawl outside an inn, with furniture and mugs flying. Many domestic groups and scenes provide a vivid insight into the everyday life of the times—lovers meeting or parting, children at play, a fortune teller, and many more.

Then there is a large class of architectural subjects (**29**), not necessarily associated with any real building: romantic cottages, battlemented castles —some semi-utilitarian, like pastille burners, watchstands, inkwells, some purely ornamental. They were also made in porcelain, but more delicately and exotically; the earthenware ones are solidly foursquare, with good, substantial flowers climbing up the front. Many reflect the romantic and picturesque fashions in architecture of the early nineteenth century, the toy Gothic of St. John's Wood or the Houses of Parliament: octagonal houses with perhaps a little turret, such as J. C. Loudon or P. F. Robinson delighted to design. These fashions persisted in earthenware long after Ruskin and the Gothic revival had substituted morality for gaiety in English building. The castles have the same shapes that still appear in the painted decorations of canal barges.

Such are some of the many subjects represented by these little image toys, reflecting as they do not only the tastes but also the passing interests, aspirations and views of many generations of ordinary English people. Yet some of the most attractive record nothing special: the multitude of animals and birds, many with oddly human and sentimental expressions; the grave dogs with gilt chains that sit sentinelwise on either side the shelf, cats, cows, sheep, and little human personages. Homely models have sat for exotic beasts; lions have an agreeable resemblance to the domestic cat; the airy baroque flourishes of Meissen, Chelsea or Bow have been transmuted into fantasy of a more stolid and substantial kind. Often these little figures hit off perfectly some characteristic of their subject, so that we can well understand their popularity, and not in England only, for in most of the seafaring countries of Western Europe—Belgium, Holland and Scandinavia—they have acquired the same traditional place in peasant homes that they have in their own country.

These "Staffordshire" figures are all miniatures, as befits mantelshelf ornaments. But we may sometimes find large pottery figures also, which may perhaps have sometimes served as shop signs, like the wooden Highlander of the tobacconists. One such figure in painted terracotta, some two feet high, is now in the Willet Collection at Brighton (*VI*). It represents a comic, Baron Munchausen sort of bravo, fiercely mustachioed, with cocked hat, top boots, hand on sword and a fine strutting stance. Nothing is known of its place of origin, but it appears to date from perhaps the early years of the nineteenth century, whilst the shape and base suggest that it was used as a shop or inn sign.

Stoneware Bottles and Flasks

The idea of making vessels in grotesque human or animal shapes must be one of the oldest of potters' fantasies. English mediaeval potter made them, and the "Bellarmines," stoneware bottles with a quaint human mask, were known long before the unpopular Cardinal from whom they got

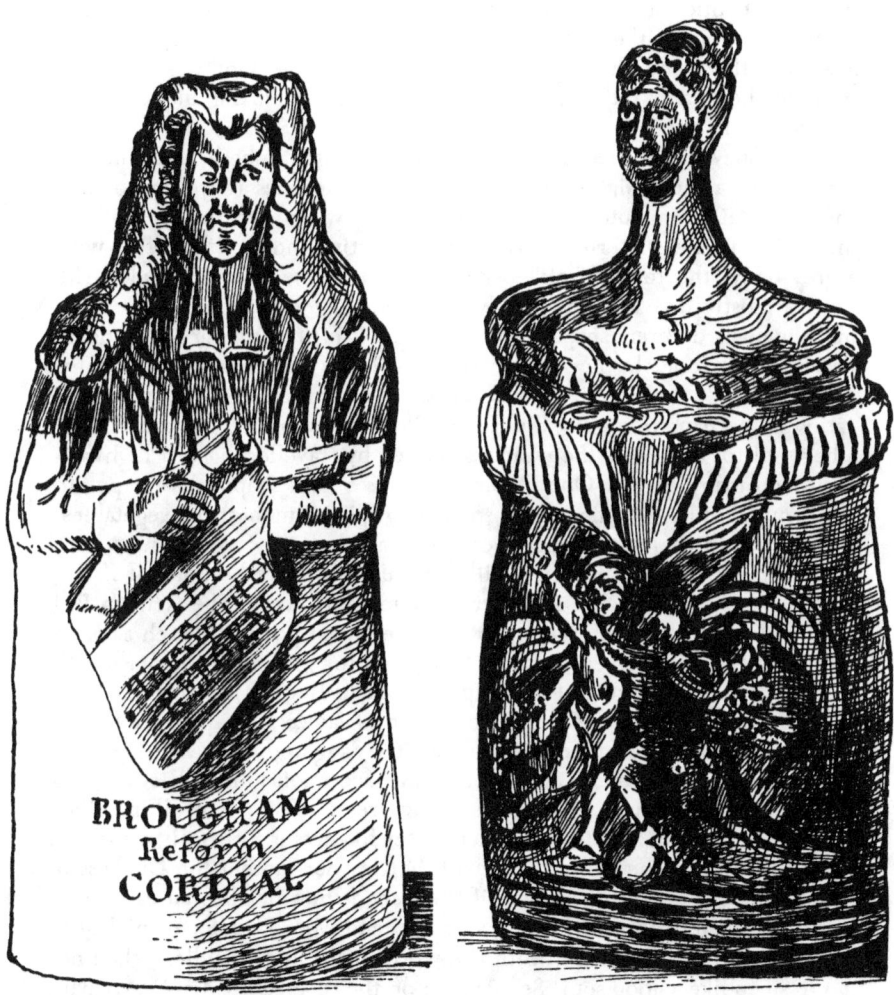

Stoneware Reform Bill Bottle   Stoneware Bottle: Queen Victoria

their name. Descendants of the Bellarmines are the earthenware and stoneware flasks and bottles, ancestors of the modern gingerbeer bottle, which were produced in all sorts of odd and grotesque forms.

The Mermaid, earthenware made at Rockingham, is glazed a rich chocolate brown like the teapots, and is evidently meant to lie in a basket, as her scaley tail curves round so that she cannot be stood upright. These mermaids have various faces, but all are extremely *décolleté*. They were probably meant as sailors' flasks, like the Oakwreath, a flat ring bottle embossed with a patriotic garland. There are Rockingham Tobies, both jugs and bottles; a variant is the Toper, an old gentleman astride a barrel, holding a glass in either hand; his top-hat holds the cork. The Boot was probably made for hot water rather than spirits, and used for putting in jack boots to dry them.

The stoneware bottles, made most of them at Lambeth, Fulham and Denby, are a much lighter brown, ranging sometimes to yellow ochre, and the details come out more incisively. They were preceded by jugs and mugs with a relief pattern of little scenes, sporting and the like, often with a grey body, the top half glazed dark brown; these are still made. The bottles mostly date from the early nineteenth century, when they were made in many different shapes. The Lambeth Fish (p. 66) is very handsome; nearly a foot long, he lies on his side and holds the cork in his mouth. There are book, barrel, railway-clock flasks, a police truncheon, commemorating or perhaps ridiculing Sir Robert Peel's new police force of 1829; a horse pistol flask, like the weapons carried by travellers against highwaymen, and many others. One of the oddest is a flask shaped like a potato and reputed to have been used for smuggling spirits amongst the vegetables, especially into the new workhouses where alcohol was forbidden.

More practical, because they will stand upright, are the portrait flasks, representing the head and shoulders of some personage. The Reform Bill controversy produced a great crop of these bottle portraits, such as King William IV and the Reformers, Lord Brougham (p. 77) or Lord John Russell, holding scrolls with suitable inscriptions: "The Reform Cordial" or "The True Spirit of Reform." Oddly enough, royal ladies were popular figures for flasks, the injured Queen Caroline, her daughter Princess Charlotte, Good Queen Bess and Queen Anne. At her accession Queen Victoria was portrayed wearing her crown and evening dress, holding a scroll inscribed "My Trust is in my People." A rather better likeness is a portrait medallion of the Queen on the side of a squarish bottle; her mother the Duchess of Kent's picture is on the other. Of these medallion bottles, an early Victorian favourite showed the heads of Mr. and Mrs. Caudle, in night-cap and curling-pins, and underneath the words: "No, Mr. Caudle, I shall not go to sleep like a good soul! See *Punch*"; on the reverse is "Miss Prettyman" in bonnet and parasol. Douglas Jerrold's "Mrs. Caudle's Curtain Lectures" were appearing in *Punch* at the time.

Painting and Transfer Printing

These portrait flasks are perhaps more ornamental than strictly practical. But there is an immense field of popular art in pottery where the decoration is painted or transfer printed on to more utilitarian forms, jugs, mugs and the like. So vast is this field that we can only pick out, more or less arbitrarily, a few examples.

When in 1762 Josiah Wedgwood presented a breakfast service of cream-coloured earthenware to Queen Charlotte, this comparatively new material was well launched into fashionable society, where, for tableware, it gradually ousted white stone ware, being kinder to cutlery. The discovery of how to get a white body for both stoneware and earthenware, made in the early years of the eighteenth century, was indeed a considerable achievement in ceramic technique. As the potteries became increasingly industrialised, production cheapened, and we find cream-coloured earthenware filtering down to the popular art level for domestic use, besides, of course, for the Staffordshire figures. Jugs and mugs, even miniature barrels, were gaily painted, often in the broad, sweeping brush-strokes still used for flower motives on canal barges, or perhaps with agricultural implements (**42, 43**) or a host of other motives.

Transfer printing, often combined with painting, offered an excellent medium for cheap decoration, being easily multiplied, and yet, as the engraving is hand cut, capable of retaining individual qualities even when mass produced. Curiously enough, though the technique is so simple and akin to printing, no one seems to have thought of using it for pottery till as late as the mid-eighteenth century. As in ordinary engraving, the design is cut (or etched) on a metal plate; from this a print in colour is taken on tissue paper, and then transferred to the ware by laying it on and rubbing

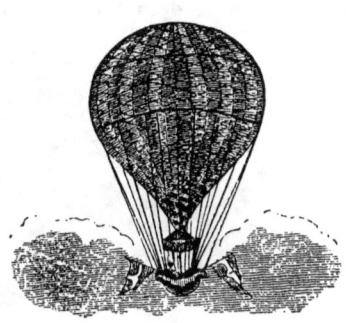

Engraved Ornament

it down. Some of the most famous English pottery decoration has been done by transfer printing, including the Willow Pattern. A good deal of the effect depends on how the engraving is placed on the ware, and indeed we notice the decline in standards not so much in the print, as the old plates could be used over and over again, but in careless placing. As the technique involves a double transfer, very fine engraving cannot be used, but this is no disadvantage, particularly for popular art. Transfer printing is particularly suited to written inscriptions and so we find it much used for "presents from places," keepsakes and motto pottery.

Naturally when woodcuts and engravings for the street broadside literature were at their height, their style much influenced the popular art forms of transfer pottery. We find a large group of pieces looking as though a broadside cut had been put straight on them and coloured by hand: little scenes perhaps satirising some political event or pointing a moral—the evils of card playing or drunkenness. One very popular piece of wit, taken apparently from an actual broadside, was the Tythe Pig, showing a fierce sow chasing the parson, while the farmer and his wife look on in high glee.

A large number of mugs, especially, were decorated with imaginary arms of various trades, possibly derived from inn signs. During the nineteenth century all the big pottery centres, Staffordshire, Liverpool, Leeds, Sunderland, Newcastle and many smaller ones were making them. For instance, the Mariners' Arms has two sailors, in old-fashioned dress (for the old plates were used right through the century), supporting a panel with verses, whilst ships, anchors and other nautical symbols fill the background. The Masons' Arms uses a free adaptation of the symbols of the Freemasons, often giving rather startlingly *surréalist* results. Very popular was the Farmers' Arms, with the farmer and his wife supporting a device composed of farm implements, plough, harrow, flail, butter churn, scythe.

The advent of railways produced a whole crop of railway decoration on cups, mugs, jugs and so on, with pictures of the Rocket and other famous railway events. Looking at them we can recapture something of the excitement which this new mode of travel, with its hitherto unbelievable speeds, produced in the ordinary public. Indeed, the whole history of

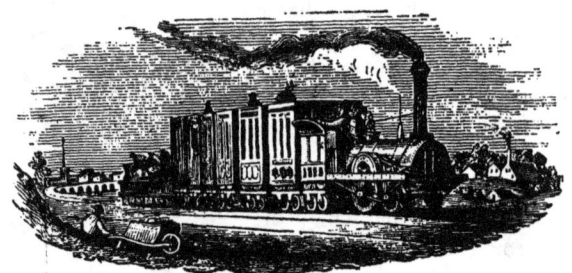

Early Railway Print

early British railways can be followed in these simple wares, whilst the old patterns are still repeated on modern products, though with a certain loss of quality due to over-hasty production.

Transfer printing also made possible reasonably recognisable if sometimes rather crude portraits. Political elections offered abundant opportunity for likenesses of the various candidates with suitable inscriptions (44). So, too, did great national controversies, like the anti-Corn Law campaign, or important events, victories or coronations or jubilees; whilst portraits of popular heroes, and even great religious leaders like John Wesley, were constantly repeated.

Some of the most attractive effects were obtained by combining transfer prints with painting and banding in lustre. Lustred earthenware had been in vogue in England from the last decades of the eighteenth century, and no doubt the intention, when the wares are silver or copper lustred all over, was to supply a cheap substitute for metal. But as so often happens, these imitations soon began to develop their own aesthetic qualities. Pattern painting or banding in differently coloured lustres, or lustre resists which leave the pattern white against a lustre background, gave very lovely results. Some of the most characteristic popular art pottery with lustre decoration is to be found amongst the many gift and souvenir pieces made mainly at Newcastle and Sunderland. These are all the more typically English for being so often associated with the sea. In a seafaring country, where partings are frequent and may be long, mementoes and keepsakes take on special significance. These Sunderland and Newcastle lustre wares were often designed as sailors' gifts. They were made from about the 1780's to well on in the nineteenth century. Technically they leave much to be desired. The larger pieces are usually decorated with untidy wavings and marblings of pink lustre, especially round the rims of mugs or jugs, and framing white panels on the front and sides, within which are pictures and verses, transfer-printed underglaze in black or perhaps blue. These prints are decorated by hand painting in overglaze colours, in vivid splashes and sweeps of red, green and yellow, making little attempt to keep within the outlines. The lustre too is unstable and apt to wear off. But if anything these imperfections enhance the feeling of freedom in the painting, which, combined with a lovely sense of colour, gives these things their special charm.

Smaller pieces, cups and saucers, jugs, mugs and plates, often have bands of pink or silver lustre. Sometimes the picture itself is not a transfer, but hand-painted in lustre. For some reason houses seem to have been much used, ranging from imposing country mansions to rough impressionistic sketches of cottages, rather like a child's drawing.

Characteristically English is the attention paid to religion and morality. Faith, Hope and Charity appear charmingly on teacups. More severe are the text plaques, shaped like a picture in a frame, with holes to hang them up. They bear an admonitory text in bold letters: "Prepare to Meet Thy God" and "Thou God Seest Me" form one such pair; "Praise Ye the Lord" and "Rejoice in the Lord" make another. Round the main text is a brightly coloured garland, with, as clasp at the top, a trumpeting angel perhaps or an all-seeing eye, and yet another line from Scripture in minute print. A broad band of pink lustre marbling forms the surround, whilst the frame is painted dark brown to resemble carved wood. Sometimes these plaques have portraits, such as Wesley, and occasionally they break away from religion altogether and have pictures of sailing-ships.

An old potters' joke often found in the Newcastle and Sunderland lustre mugs is a model of a toad or lizard set on the bottom to give the drinker a surprise, as well as the various tricks with hollow handles and the like to make the liquor disappear.

As the nineteenth century advanced, the manufacture of porcelain was cheapened, and so we find the increasingly popular "presents from places" and motto pottery made in cheap china, but with the old decorative traditions persisting. Unfortunately the decline in taste coincided with the introduction from abroad of cheap, crudely coloured lithographs for transfer printing; it is this process which has made some of the worst modern atrocities feasible.

Giant Teapots

But whilst aesthetic standards were declining throughout Europe, there were times when the old tradition reasserted itself. One such example of a return to popular art is the giant teapots (*VIII*), some three feet high and with a little model teapot forming the lid, made during the 'eighties and 'nineties, and very popular among the canal boatmen. Cups and saucers were also made of the same ware and were so heavy that they were often used as domestic missiles, whence they got the nickname of "clout cups." They are glazed a rich dark brown, like the traditional Rockingham teapot, and gaily decorated with stamped pads of white relief ornament, sprays and baskets of flowers and birds, roughly picked out with dabs of green, purple and blue. Many of them have inscribed on a rough scroll the names of donor and recipient with a date. These particular teapots were made, apparently, by a potter named Mason, who had a small factory at Midway near Burton-on-Trent, somewhere about 1885–96; he had previously been at Church Gresley.[1] He was therefore working during the full tide of industrialism, yet these giant teapots show all the old qualities of gaiety and humour which we associate with popular art at its best.

[1] We are indebted to Mr. Bemrose, Curator of the Hanley Museum, for this information.

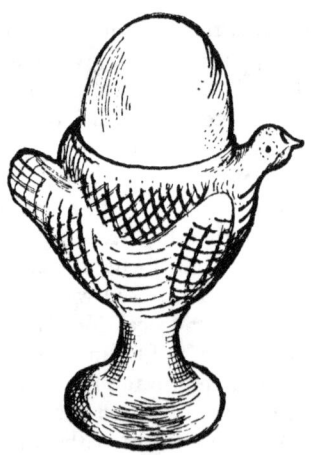

Unglazed Earthenware Egg-cup
with incised lines

Chapter Six

GLASS AND MISCELLANEOUS

Nailsea Special Pieces

Glass is a medium admirably suited to popular art, for it can be spun, blown and twisted into the most varied shapes, giving great scope to individual dexterity and fancy. But as glass is even more fragile than earthenware, even fewer examples of early popular art in it have survived.

Many of the glass objects we usually think of as "Nailsea" (though probably many pieces were made elsewhere too) did not form part of the regular output of glassworks, but were made as *tours de force* by individual glassworkers in their spare time. Some of these pieces have been treasured for generations in their maker's family, some were presents, and others were intended to be sold for private profit. The Nailsea glass works themselves were founded in 1788 and survived till 1873, but there have been glass works at Bristol and the neighbourhood for much longer. At Nailsea the main production was utilitarian, such things as sheet glass for glazing, but each glassworker would be given a quota of glass for the day's work, and could use up any that was left over as he pleased. Skilled glassworkers from other parts of England, such as Birmingham, were employed at Nailsea, as were also a number of Frenchmen. These foreign workers introduced new techniques, such as the Venetian *latticino*, the gaily coloured ribboning which is so characteristic of Nailsea, as also perhaps the equally typical flecking in different colours. The French workers also brought with them the Gallic habit of eating snails, which were supposed to be a specific against chest diseases, to which glassworkers were particularly prone owing to the heat of the works.

A great variety of these individual pieces were made at Nailsea; there are bottles, jugs and mugs of all sorts of sizes and shapes, some in plain glass, some flecked or ribboned with a different colour. The common dark-green bottle glass might be flecked with opaque white or milky blue; or the bottle itself might be in clear glass with brilliant spottings and stripings, such as claret red and royal blue. The *latticino* stripings are very attractive on the many little flasks, varying in size from about three to ten inches high, which are said to have been in demand among the ladies and gentlemen taking the Bath waters. These flasks show a wide range of colours, ranging through clear or opaque whites, yellows, pale golden browns, dark ruby reds, pinks, dark and light blues, and greens. *Latticino* decoration was also much used for ornamental tobacco pipes (p. 84), bells and rolling-pins, all typical Nailsea products. The pipes are, some of them, over three feet long, with gracefully curving stems and giant bowls rimmed in a different colour; or with miniature bowls and elaborately interlaced stems. Whether they were actually smoked seems doubtful, though some have the mouthpiece tipped with red sealing wax like the clay pipes of the time. More practical are the little cigar holders (p. 91), a few inches long, often with a coloured bird perched on top, and so are the tobacco stoppers. The handbells, which really ring, were also sometimes made in giant sizes; often with the handle and clapper in different colours. The hunting and coach horns, which really blow a note, are some straight, as much as three feet or more in length, others twisted like the horns used by stage coaches. The rolling-pins are hollow, with one end open to take a cork, and can be filled with flour; some are also engraved with a name and date. Twisted glass toasting-forks were also made; so were glass stamps for biscuits.

A curious use for glass is in the polehead emblems for the village clubs, which flourished in the West Country, though these insignia were normally made in metal. But at least two *latticino* glass poleheads have been

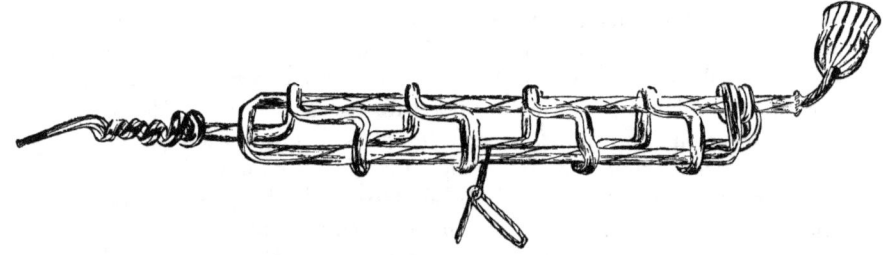

Nailsea Glass Pipe

found, belonging to the old Nailsea Glassmakers' Guild which used to meet at the local Glass Makers' Arms. The twisted glass rods, some as long as eight feet, with handles curved like a walking stick, also had a curious special use; they would be set up in West Country cottages to keep away diseases, which were supposed to collect on the rod, whence they could be wiped away; to break a rod was most unlucky. The hollow glass balls, painted inside with bright colours, kept off witches and the evil eye.

Besides these quasi-utilitarian things, a great many intricate little ornaments were made, like the miniature glass bellows, a few inches long, or the little top-hats, with their old-fashioned upcurved brims, both characteristically Nailsea, or paper weights, and the many little glass birds and beasts in which all glassmakers delight.

Spun and Twisted Glass

This "Nailsea" type work represents the high water-mark in glass, with its exquisite sense of shape and colours. But there are also a great many other glass ornaments, not particularly associated with any one district, which, if not perhaps quite as subtle as Nailsea, yet have great vitality and charm. Not so many years ago no fair would have seemed complete without its glassworkers displaying their amazing skill, as they may still be found in Continental fairs. The shapes seem to have been mostly traditional, and we find the designs, both here and on the Continent, repeated again and again, with individual variations. Such are the sailing-ships made of interlacing strips of glass, with, on the larger models, little sailors running up the rigging, two smaller boats alongside, and a lighthouse set behind. Or there are the many groups of birds, with spun glass tails, perching on branches with large brightly coloured flowers, or sometimes on a fountain. An exquisite example of a glass fountain with birds is now in the Victoria and Albert Museum. These twisted glass ornaments look remarkably like spun sugar, and indeed it seems likely that they were originally derived from confectioners' decorations. More substantial are the partially blown glass

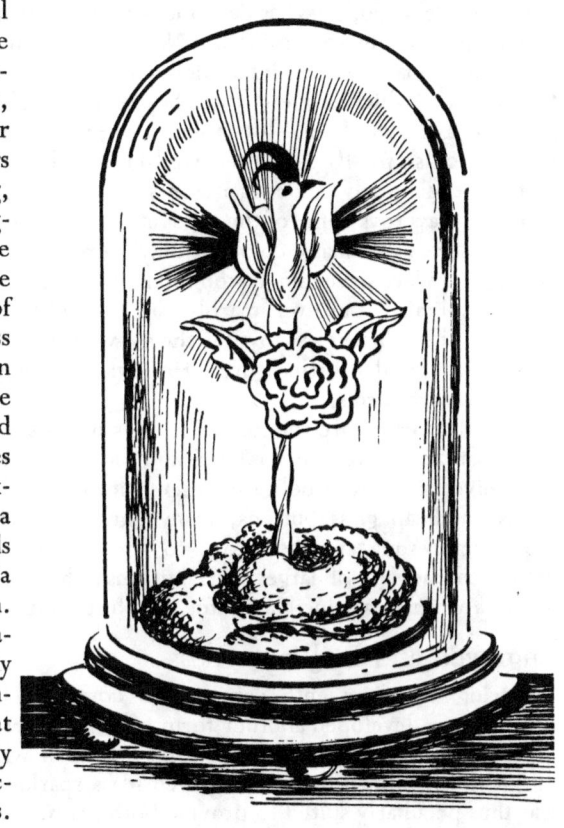

Bird in Coloured Spun Glass

figures of horses, dogs (**56**) and the like, with hollow bodies; for some reason the body of the horse is often coloured blue.

Lustred Glass

Glass can also be silvered and lustred like earthenware, and it too was often used as a cheap substitute for silver. At one time churches in the poorer parishes used altar vessels of silvered glass, which proved attractive for secular use also, as inexpensive vases, candlesticks and similar ornaments, gaily painted on the outside with bands of colour and groups of flowers. Their glitter and cheapness gave them a special fairground appeal, where they were often used as prizes in the sideshows, as well as for general decoration. In the same tradition are the little coloured balls, birds with spun glass tails, and other shapes, used for Christmas trees; the modern ones are usually foreign.

Love Tokens in Glass

Like pottery too, glass has been much used for keepsakes and love tokens. Hollow glass rolling-pins, like the Nailsea ones, but in plain opaque white or coloured glass, with painted pictures on the outside, are found all over the country, which suggests that they were widely made. Many of them seem to have been sailors' love tokens, to judge by the inscriptions and the pictures of ships, flags or even well-known landmarks. Tradition has it that these seemingly innocent presents were also used for smuggling spirits. Amongst glass toys some of the most attractive are the marbles, with their twisted threads of many colours; they were sold for a penny and a half-penny, and were exceedingly common a few years ago; the very small size was for solitaire. But even marbles, in the old forms, are now becoming rare. Another cheap glass toy was the snowstorm; the older ones often had very well modelled little figures. Here glass tends to be ousted by plastic in the modern forms.

Akin to marbles are the many varieties of glass beads, of which some of the most attractive are to be found on the old lacemakers' bobbins, themselves often most delicately carved in wood. Then there are the many forms of cheap glass buttons, many extremely decorative; perhaps the most picturesque are the "Road to Ruin" sets worn by costermongers before the advent of large pearl buttons; they have little pictures of a horse, a woman, a wine glass, etc., to illustrate their title.

Engraved and Brilliant Glass

During the nineteenth century, to correspond with changing social needs, there developed another form of popular art in glass, the engraved or blasted glass screen or window, examples of which may still be found in Victorian public-houses. Engraved glass sparkles but also obscures. It was thus peculiarly suited to provide both privacy and also a festive feeling of glitter and gaiety, the two prerequisites of the urban public-house, when, on the one hand, the growing cult of respectability made drinking a slightly furtive business, where the social classes must be rigidly segregated and patrons barred from prying eyes, and, on the other, the glitter of the gin palaces was all the more inviting by contrast to the surrounding murk and grime. Long after the bad old days of "drunk for a penny, dead drunk for twopence" had passed away, the pleasantly fantastic traditions of shine and sparkle persisted, though the traditional public-house interior is now giving way to the streamlining and chromium plate of the modern road-house.

The patterns of these engraved glass screens are often very decorative, with their scrolls, festoons, and groups of fruit and flowers. The public-house sign, a swan perhaps or a ship, is sometimes brought in. Often the lower half of the glass is frosted and the upper half left clear, which throws up the patterns in contrasting textures. For interior decoration engraved mirrors in so-called "brilliant" glass were much used, and, indeed, at one time such "brilliant" glass was made in the Nailsea works. Set in pairs, these mirrors reflect each other, giving an illusion of light and space. They were much used for the interior of early Victorian theatres, and, indeed, there is a close affinity between the theatre and public-house decoration of the time, as also with the traditional fairground where we still find "brilliant glass" used. These engraved mirrors were also much used in shops, and we may still sometimes come upon an old-fashioned grocer's shop, perhaps with "brilliant" cut mirrors engraved with various herbs, like tea and cocoa; alongside the painted tins and jars they create an impression of oriental opulence.

The decorative themes most usually found on this engraved glass derive from the early Victorian riot of styles and periods which reached its zenith at the Great Exhibition of 1851. Extremely naturalistic fruit and flowers or maybe a swan-lake scene are surrounded by highly stylised swags and twirls derived from rococco or pseudo-Gothic, with, perhaps, for good measure, a Pugin ironwork grille motive filling in any empty spaces. As the century progresses the falling aesthetic standards make themselves felt; the curves lose their spring, growing pinched and stiff, the general design becomes more stereotyped, with sharp angular Gothic motives more obtrusive, and taking on a machine-made, poverty-stricken look, not because it is machine-made, but because the gaiety and spontaneity of the Romantic Movement have been swept away by the flowing tide of the Gothic Revival.

Straw Marquetry

In the museum at Luton is a delightful pair of dolls (53), dressed entirely in plaited straw, with straw baskets and straw flowers. As Luton is the centre of the straw-plaiting industry, it is likely that this exhibit was made as a *tour de force* by one of the straw plaiters, in the same way that many of the apprentices in other trades made toys and miniatures, such as the shoe snuff-boxes, and the doll's furniture made by cabinet-makers.

One of the best examples of the skilful use of straw for decorative purposes is straw marquetry. This was very fashionable in England in the eighteenth century, when straw plaiting was an industry at Stilton and Yaxley. Arthur Young, writing in 1768, says on visiting Dunstable that it was a centre of the straw industry, and that they manufactured various articles of different coloured straw, as well as boxes, baskets and hats.

This industry suffered severely when, at the time of the Napoleonic wars, the French prisoners confined in the prison at Norman Cross, near Peterborough, and at other places began making and selling straw marquetry at much lower prices. The English workers complained, but the French work continued, so much so that most of the examples in private collections to-day are commonly attributed to French prisoners.

Straw marquetry is a miniature inlay work done in straw, not unlike the little wood mosaics of Tunbridge ware which were influenced by it. The best-quality straws were selected and split to an average length of ten inches with a sharp instrument; the older ones were made of bone; some had a set of blades radiating from a central core. The split straw was tied in bundles and dyed with vegetable dyes, then pressed flat; it was then cut again into the minute pieces needed for the design and glued in position on to whatever surface was being decorated. All sorts of boxes were ornamented with straw marquetry; tea caddies, hand screens, pin and needle poppets, toys, and even furniture was decorated in this way.

Corn Dollies

By far the oldest surviving forms of traditional straw decorations in England are the kern-maidens or corn-dollies (**46, 47**), made at harvest time with the last sheaf of corn. According to Sir James Frazer in the *Golden Bough,* this custom is a relic that has come down to us from very early religious beliefs; it is associated with myths like that of the Goddess Demeter, mother of Persophene, and is a ritual to ensure the continuance of the crops and seasons.

The shapes of kern-maidens, as well as the names given to them, varied from district to district; nowadays there are not many country places left where they are still made. In Essex a few people can still make them; here the most common form is a long twist, called a "neck," of barley. Near Tewkesbury the straw is plaited in a triangular shape with little triangles at the corners hanging like tassels. In Devon, a later development is straw ornaments for church decoration, sometimes in the form of a cross. It was also once customary to finish off the thatching on ricks and roofs with straw ornaments, and as the style of thatching varies from one English district to another, so did these decorations. In the West Country straw "crowns of the rick" might be most elaborate, or straw figures in the shape of a bird or animal would add the final flourish. In the West Country, too, little twists of straw braided in twos or fives were worn as buttonhole favours. The straw ornaments might also be hung in the churches at harvest. Even to-day the decorations in many country churches at Harvest Festival, Easter and Christmas are still a delight, with their posies of wild flowers and big garden bunches, garlands of evergreens and great still-life groups of fruit and vegetables. They come as a constant reminder that popular art in England is still a living tradition.

Easter Eggs

Easter eggs are still made in the traditional way in some parts of the country, particularly in the North. Here they are generally called "paste eggs," a corruption of Pasque. The shells are coloured by boiling them with various homely ingredients, such as onion skins; they may be mottled or striped, by skilful wrapping, or be patterned in white with ferns or little

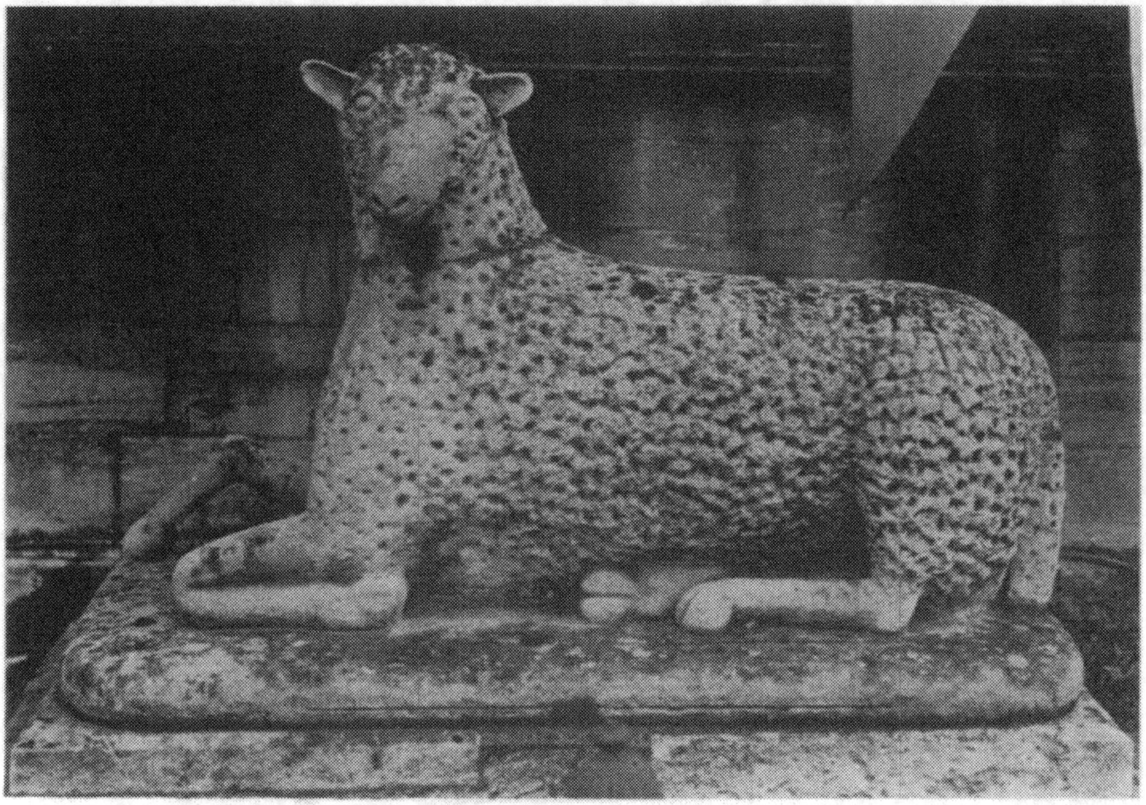

57. Stone carving: the Lamb at Trowbridge, Wiltshire.

58. Wiltshire wood carving: the Bear at Devizes.

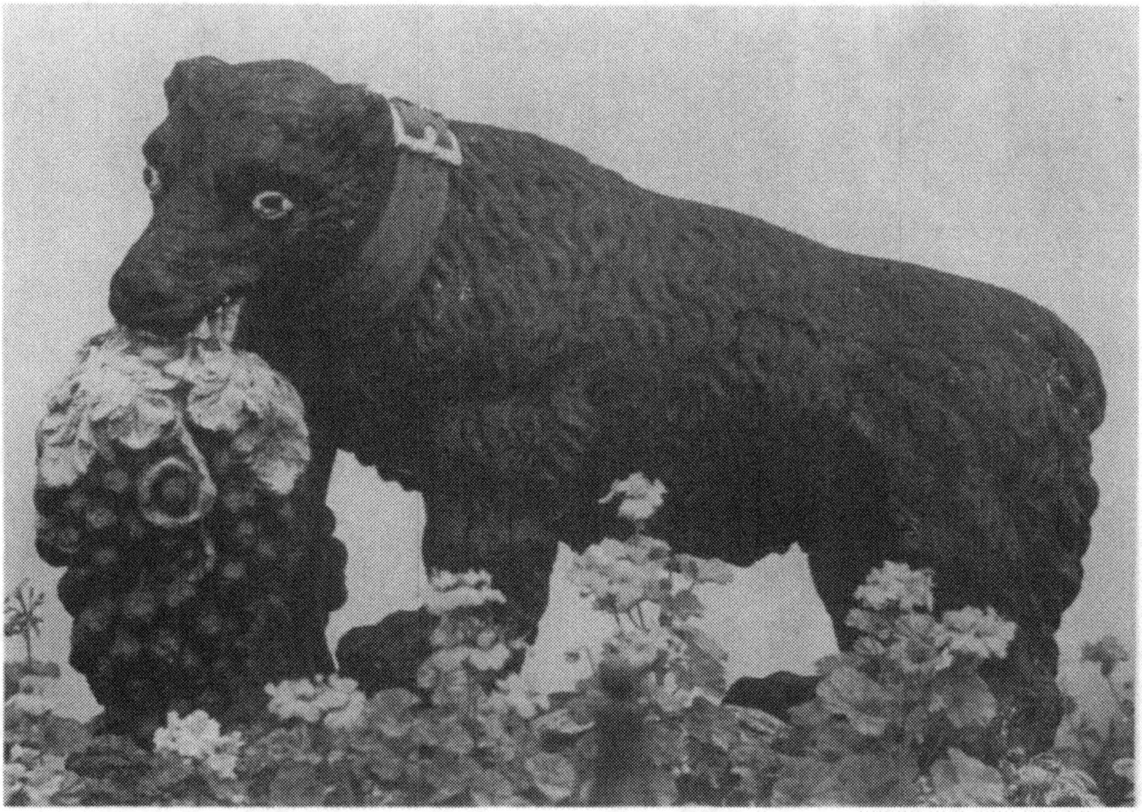

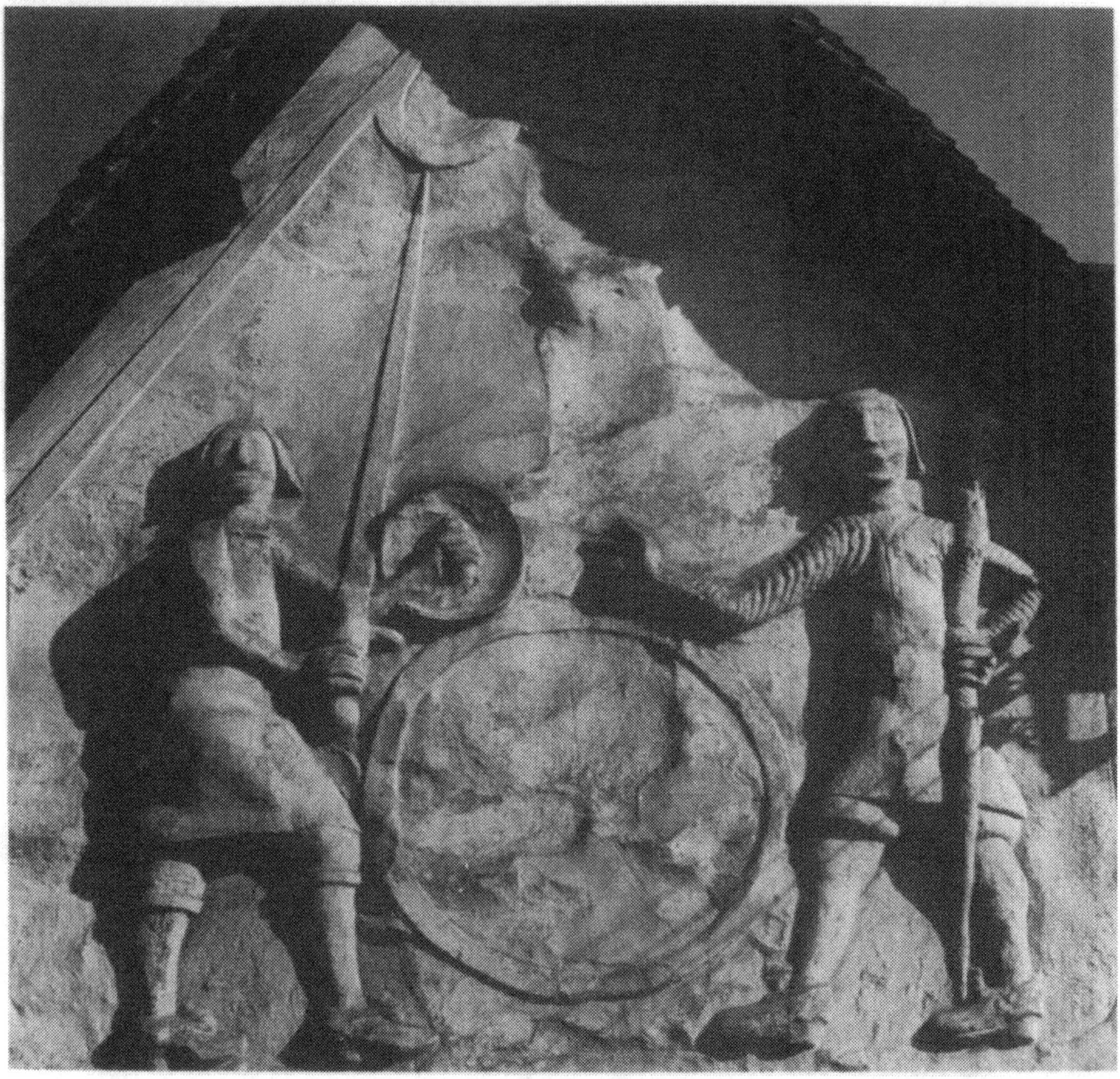

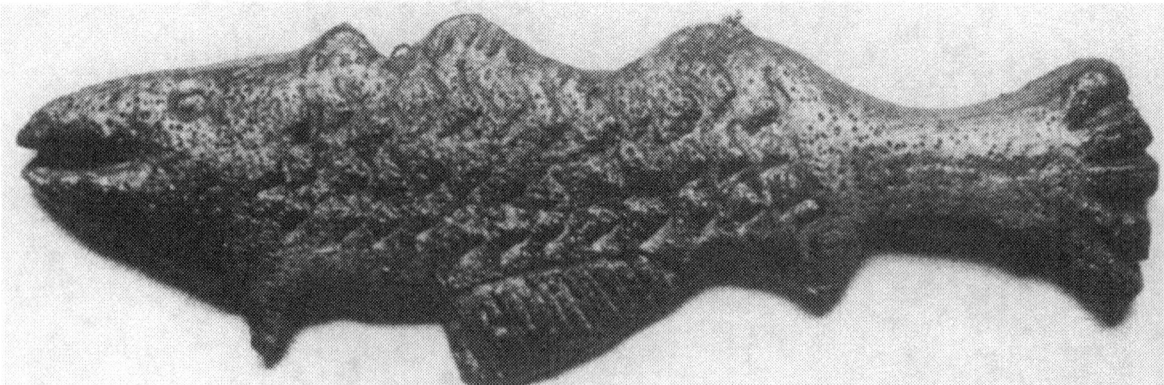

59. Parge figures from the Old Sun Inn, Saffron Walden, Essex. *Photograph Edwin Smith.*

60. Fish formed from bread or dough for Easter festival. 2 foot in length.

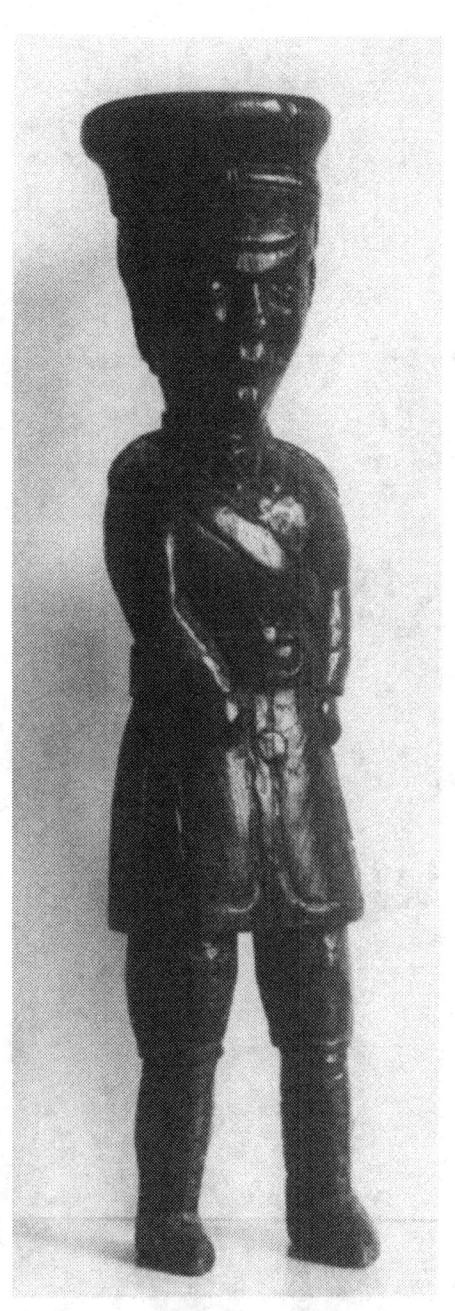

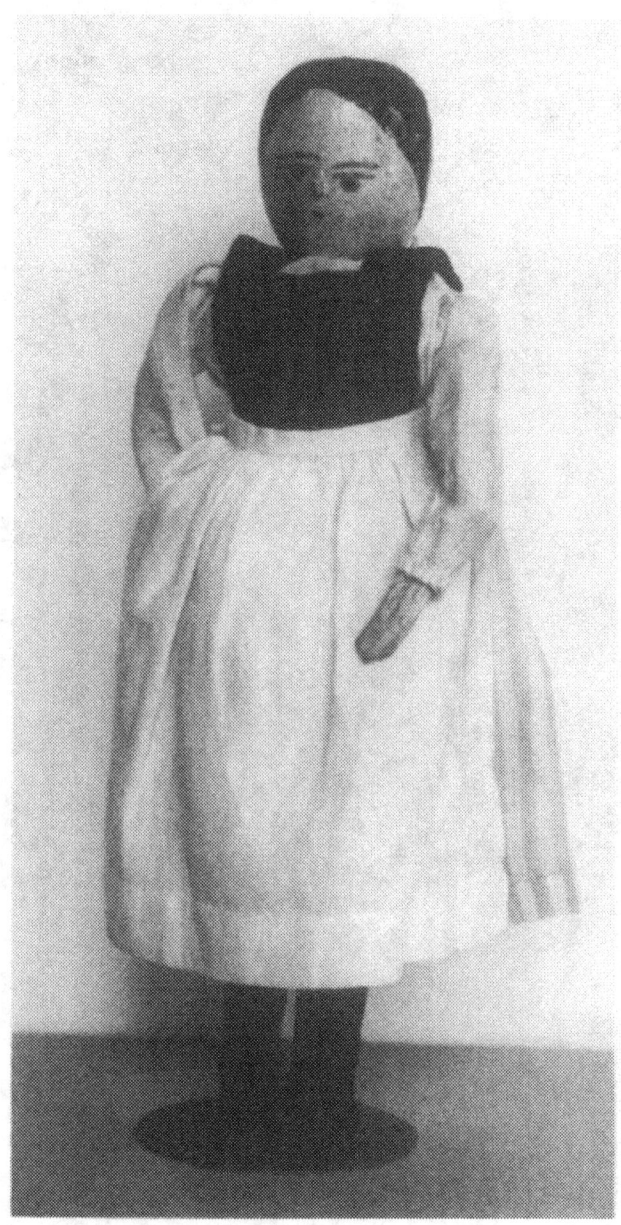

62. Dutch Doll.

61. Carved figure of a Boer War
soldier, 20″ high.

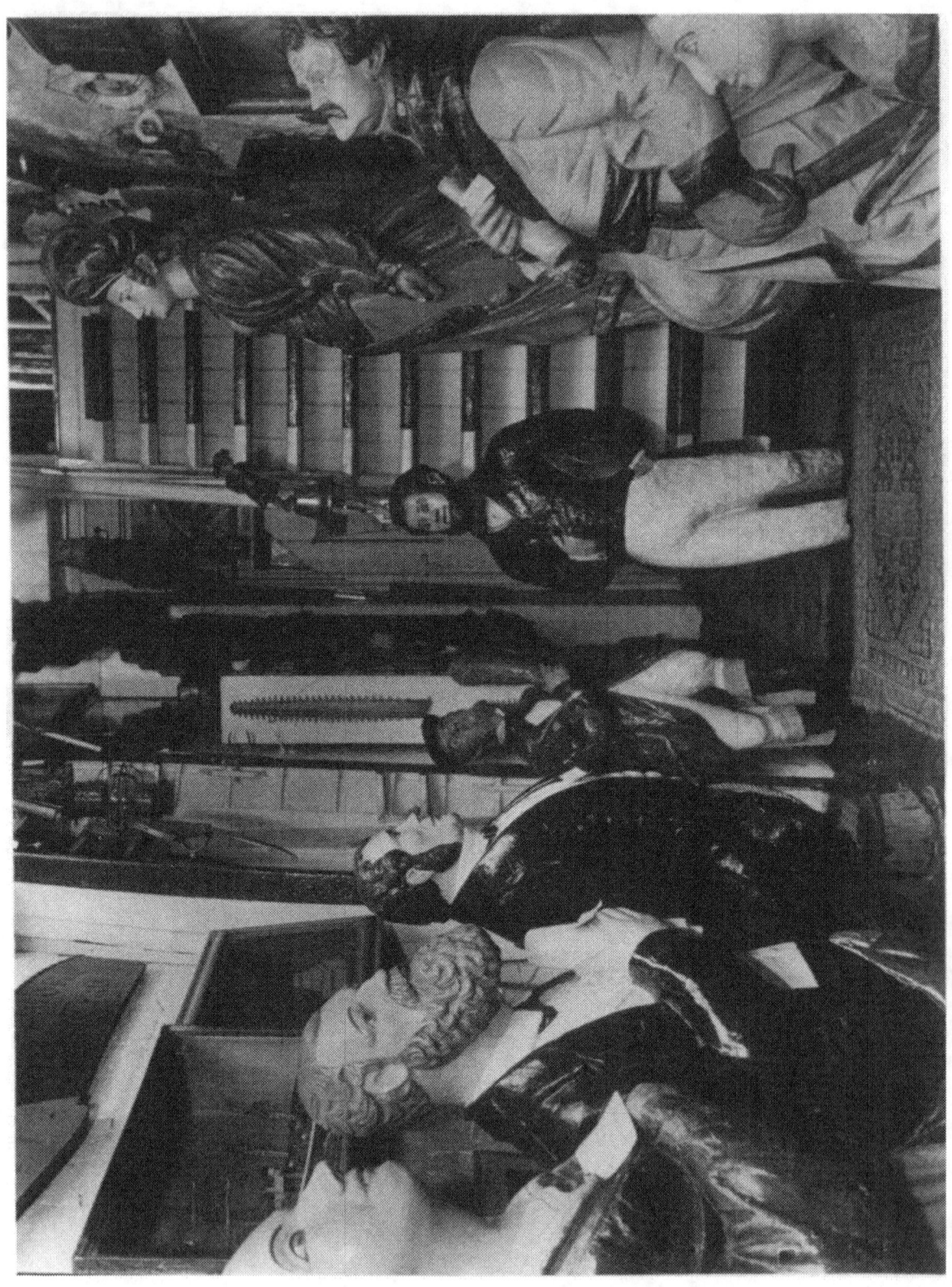

63. Captain Silver's collection of Ship's Figureheads, on his boat berthed at Gravesend.

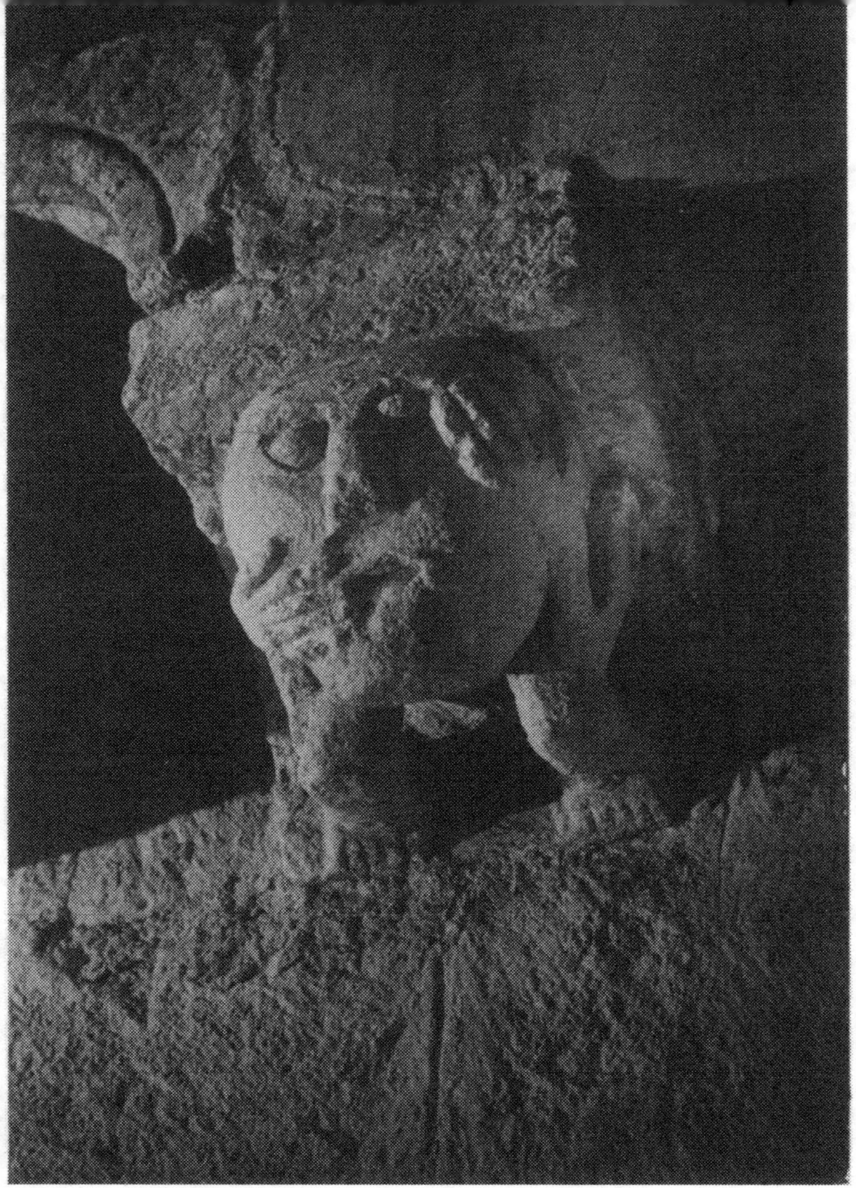

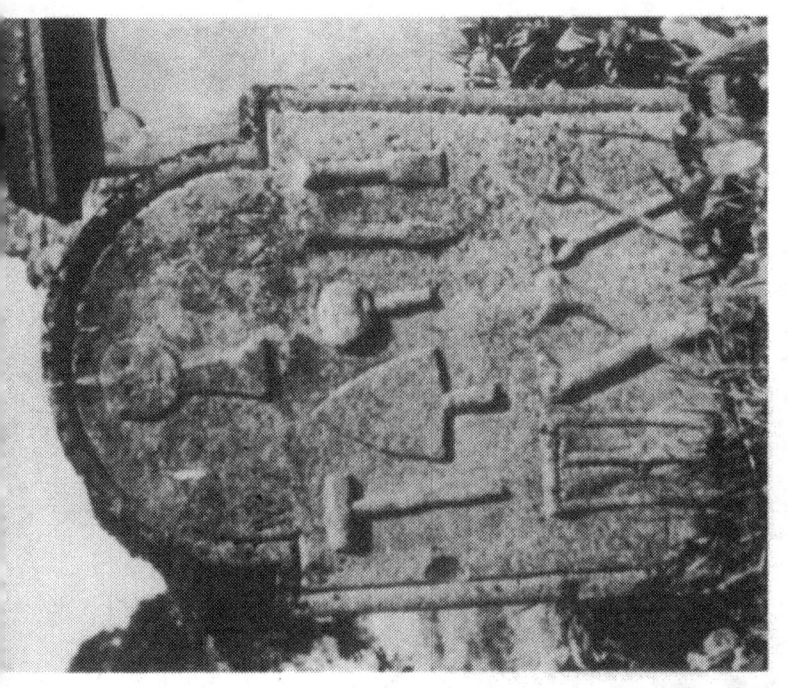

65. Tombstone of a craftsman, from a churchyard in Fife.

64. Stone carved head of a grieving figure: corbel in the library of Chichester Cathedral. *Photograph Edwin Smith.*

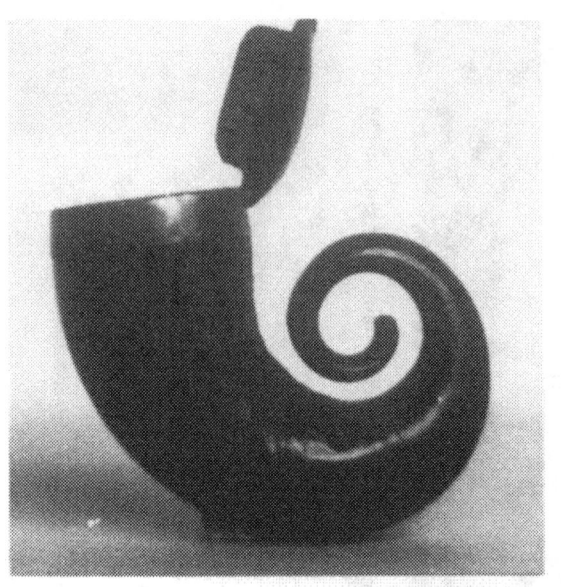

66. Snuff horn.

67. Toy made from horn.

68. Shepherd's Crook, carved in 1987 by a Roxburgh shepherd.

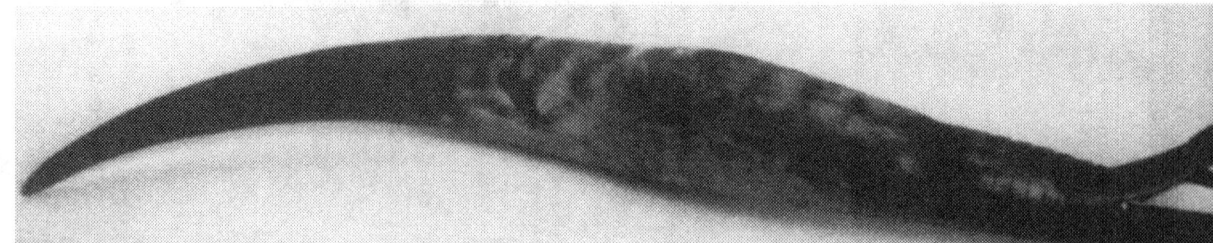

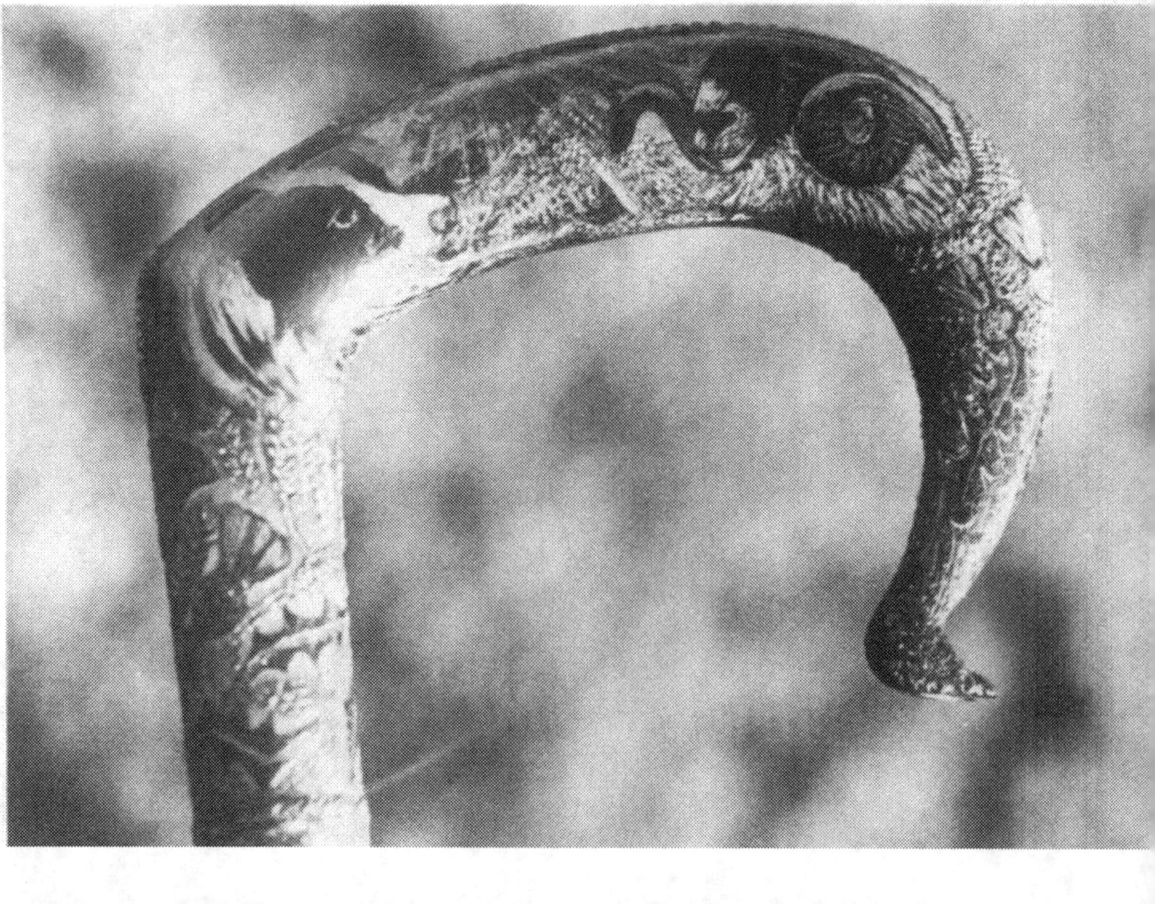

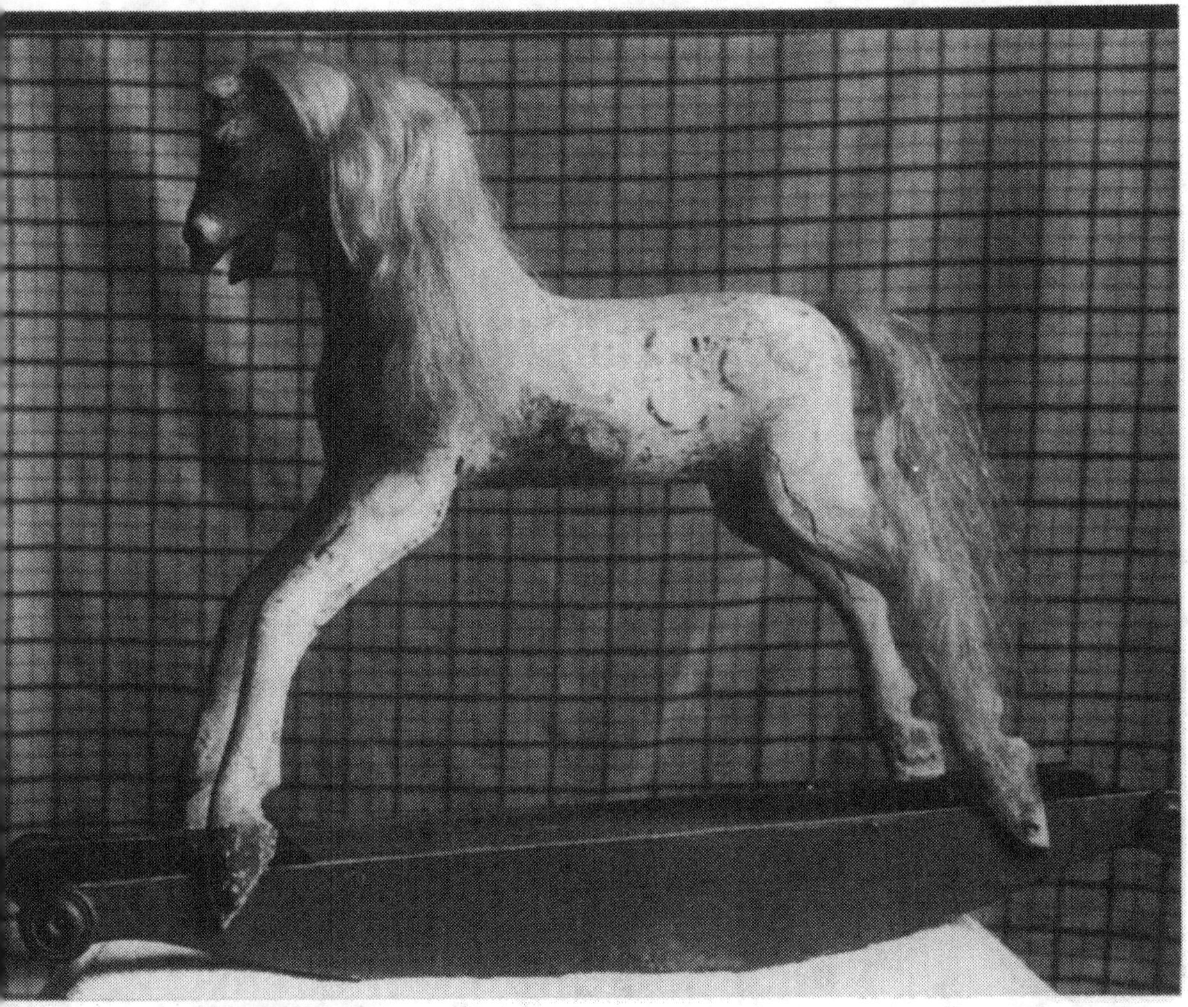

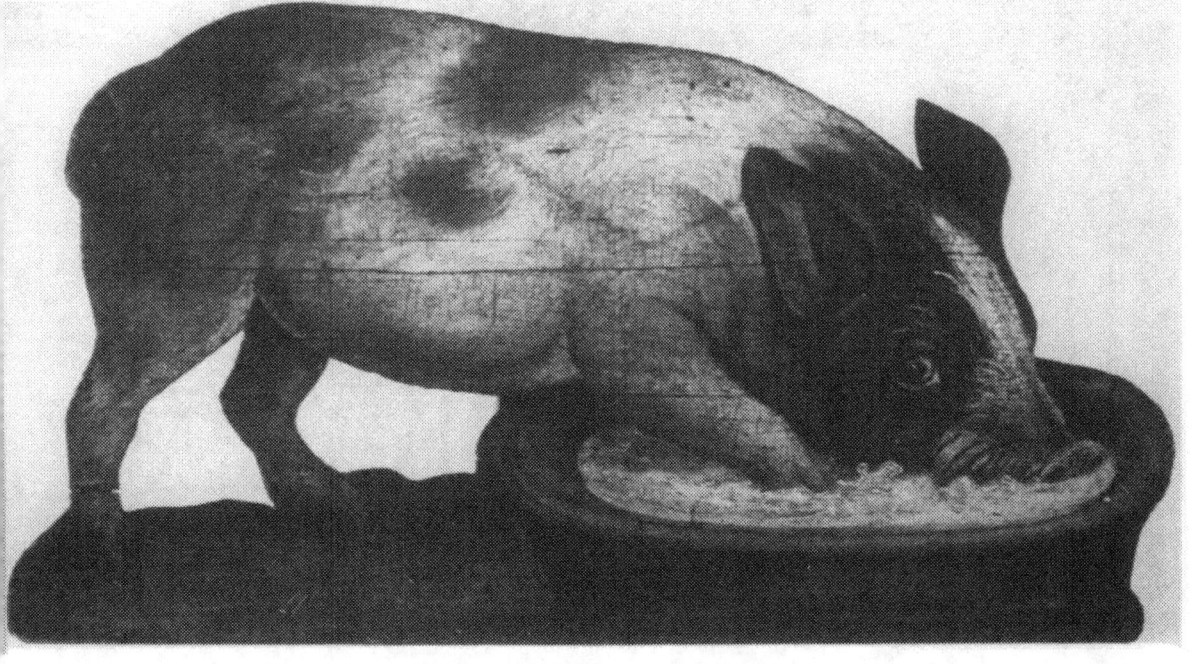

9. Eighteenth Century rocking horse.　　70. Painted dummy board pig. *Photograph V. & A. Museum.*

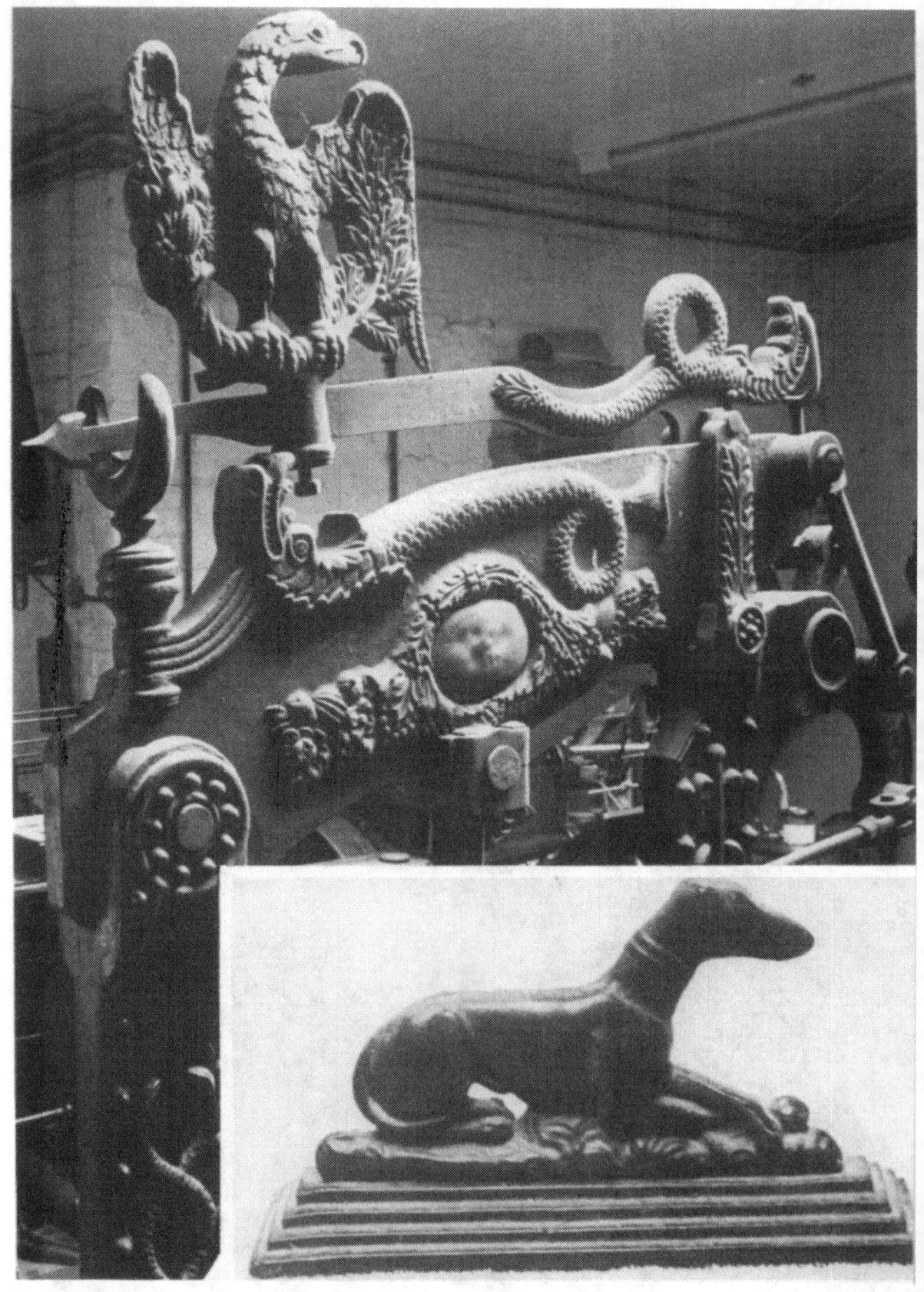

71. Ancient printing press. *Photograph Edwin Smith.*

72. Cast iron door stop.

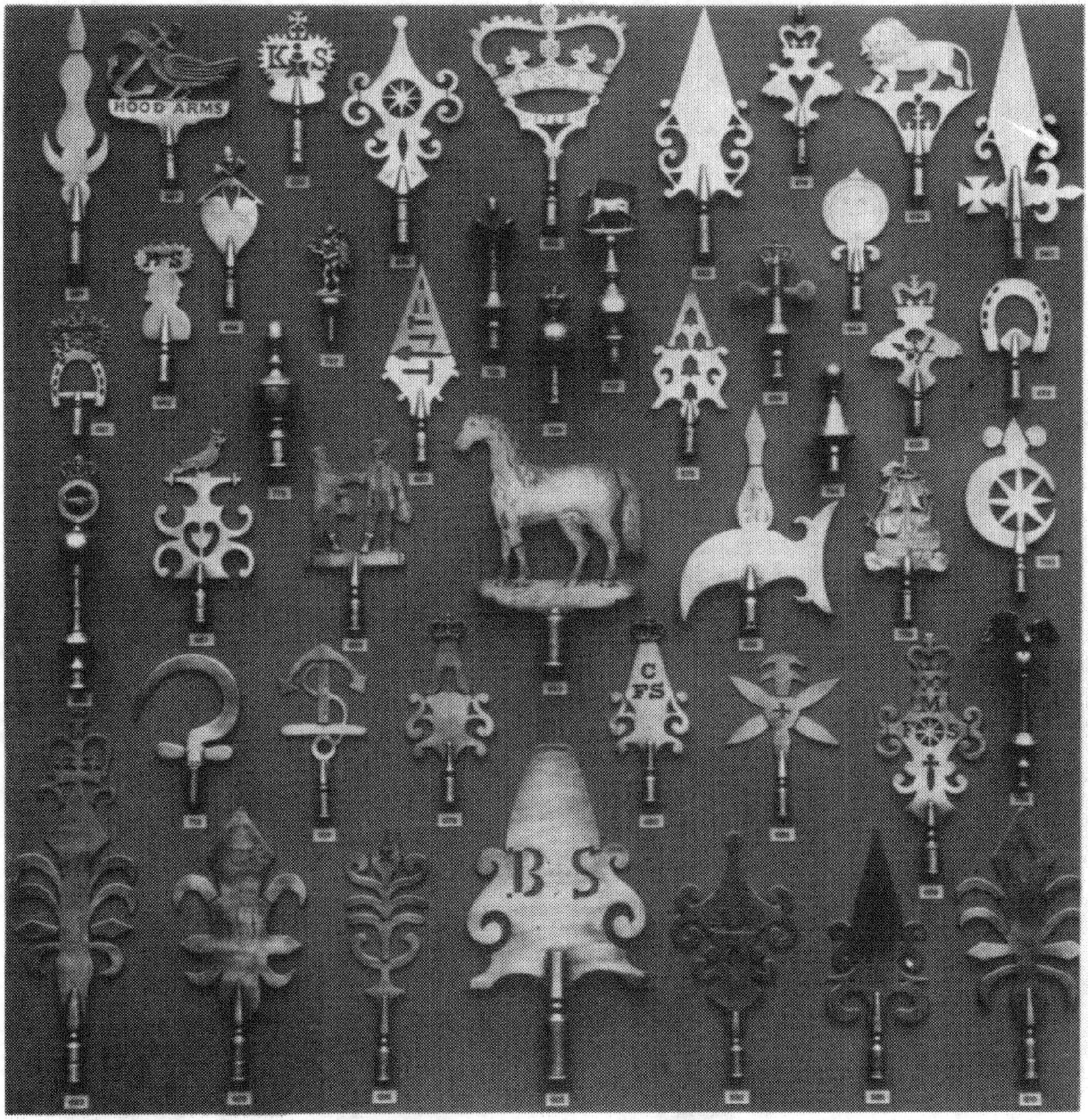

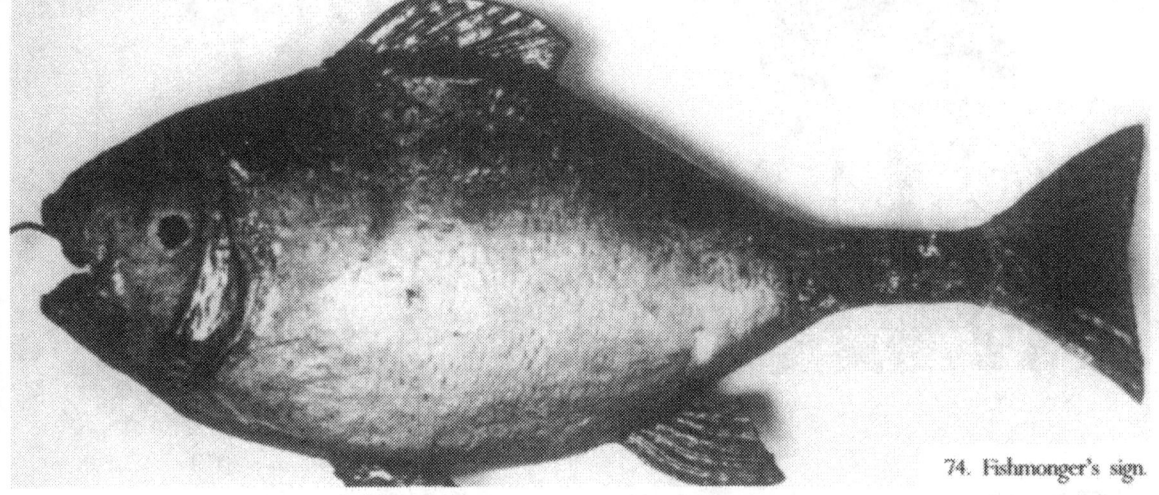

73. Friendly Society emblems.

74. Fishmonger's sign.

75. Shop sign, St Andrews.

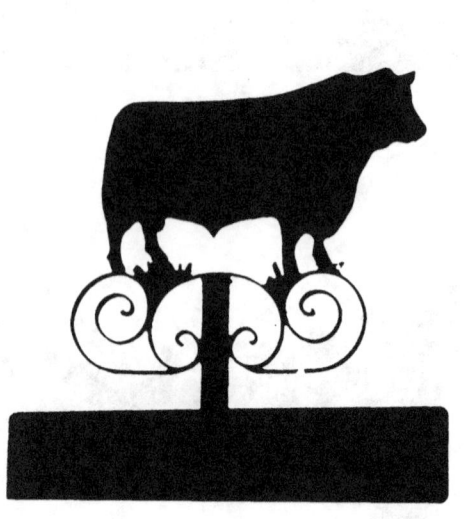

76. Farm sign, Fife.

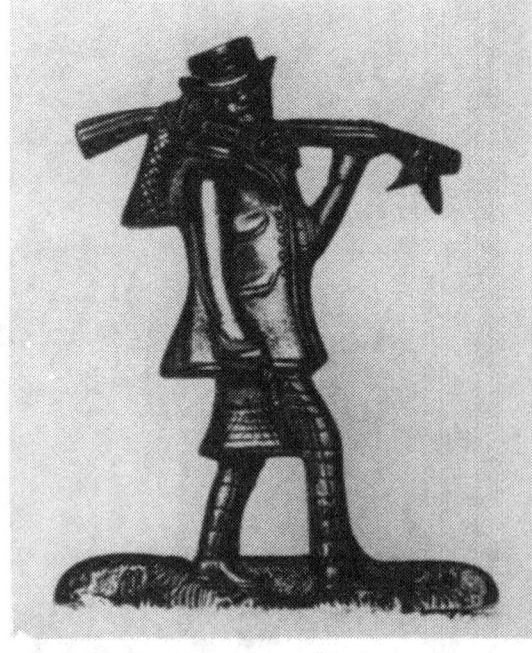

77. Chimney piece ornament, 4″ high: cast figure of a poacher in brass.

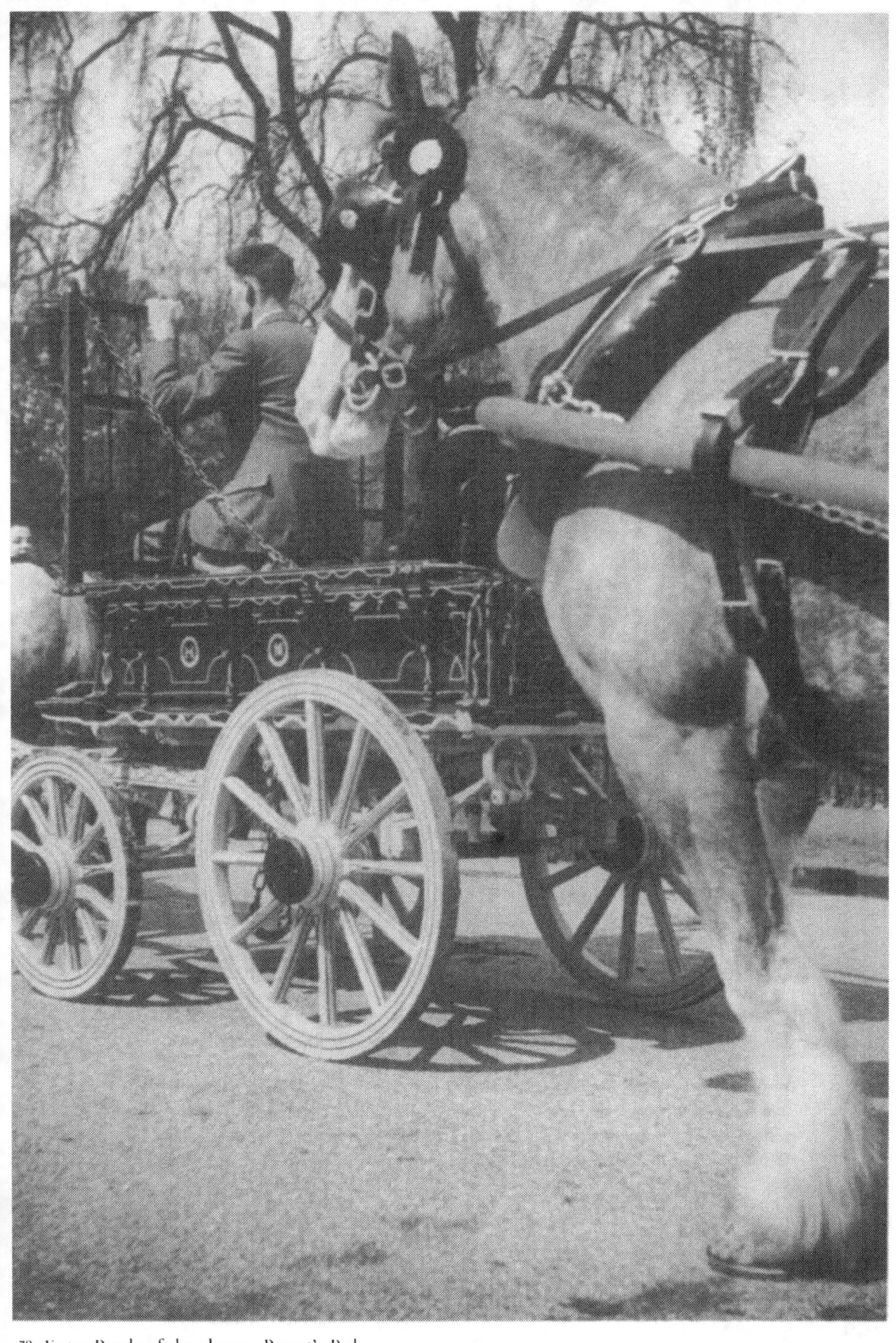

78. Easter Parade of dray horses, Regent's Park.

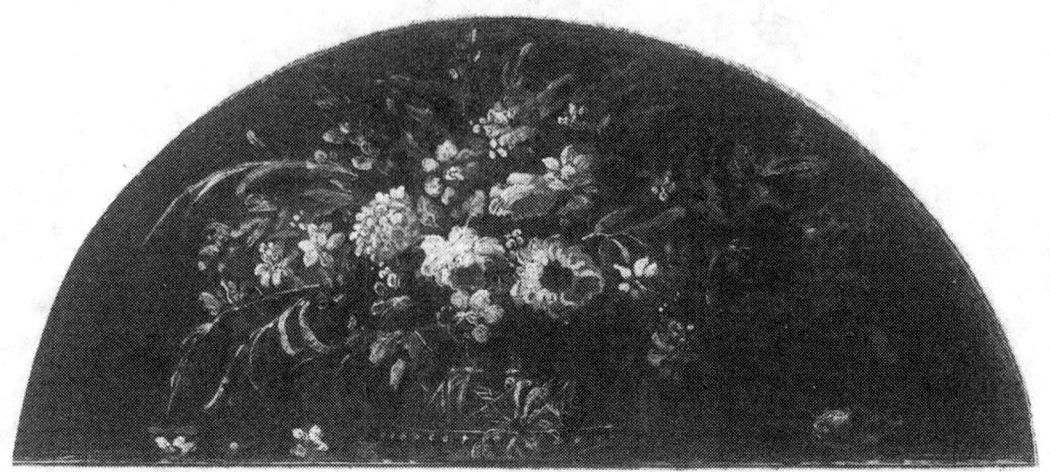

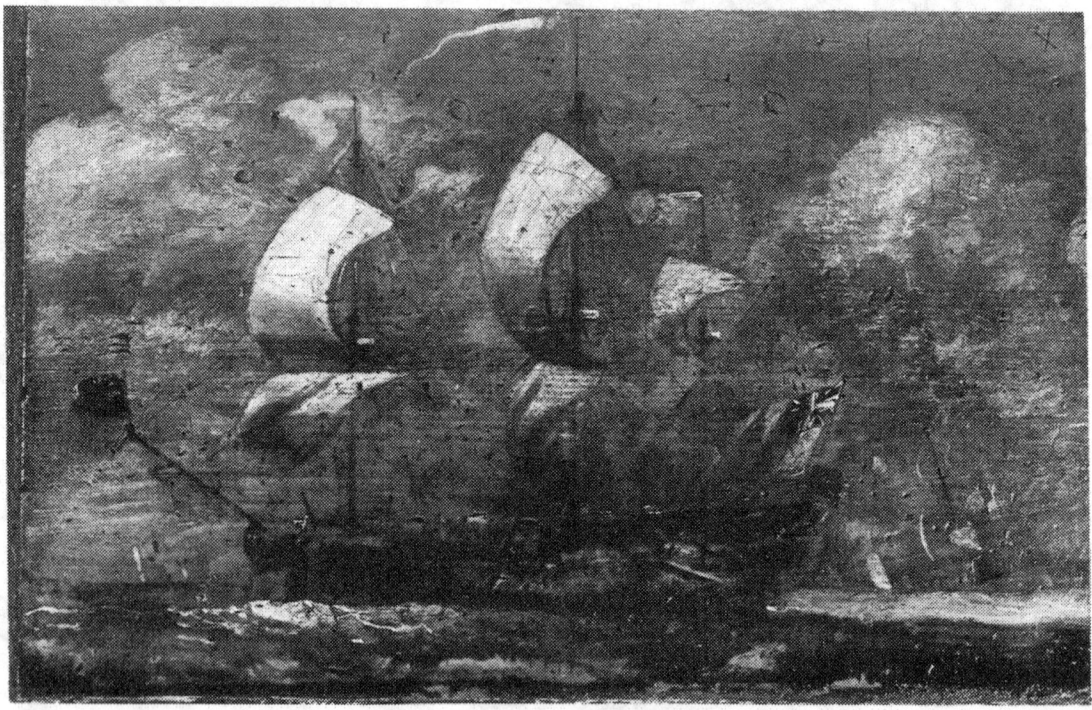

79-82. Painted panels from an old coaching inn, Bromley, Kent (now demolished).
Records show that there were originally 36 painted panels covering the walls of a
downstairs room. The panel of Edinburgh Castle (82) shows the spur demolished in
1650; it tallies with the engraving in Slezer's Theatrum Scotiae. Only the 1718 and 1814
editions show this view, size 5'4" × 2'. Many of the panels were of ships inspired by the
paintings of the Van de Velde family. The lunette of flowers was over the doorway.

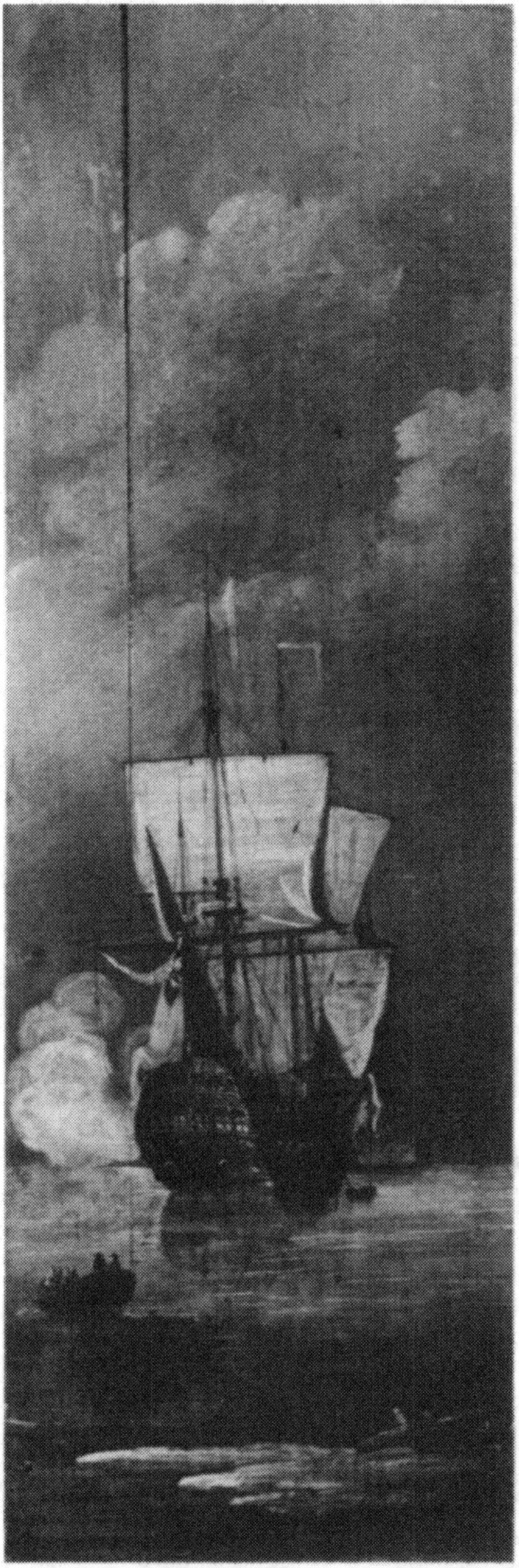

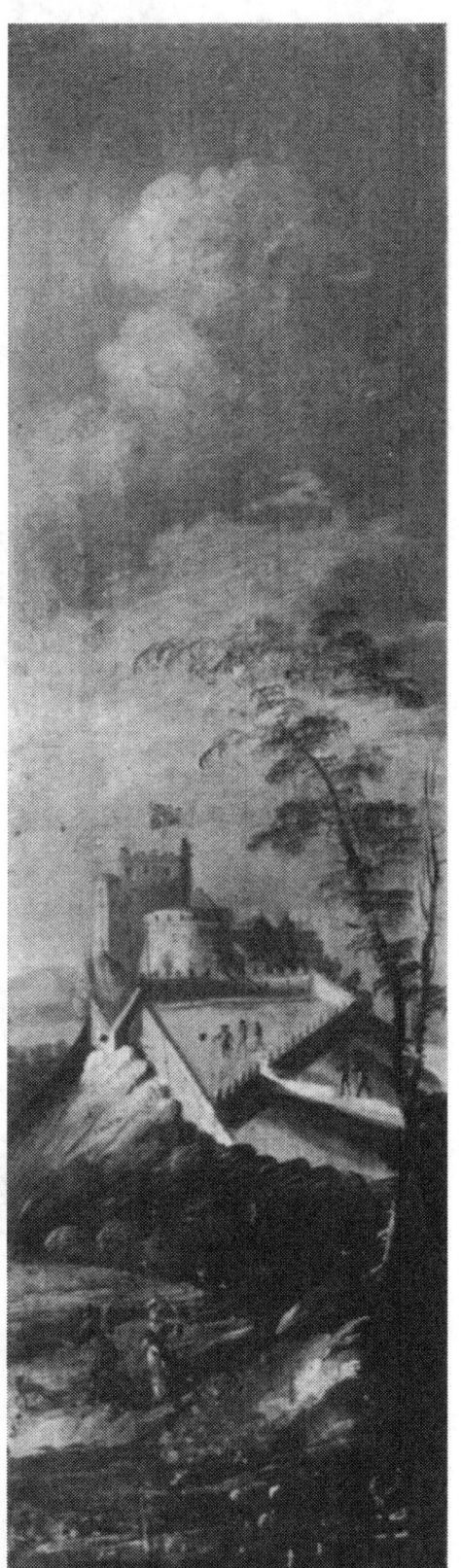

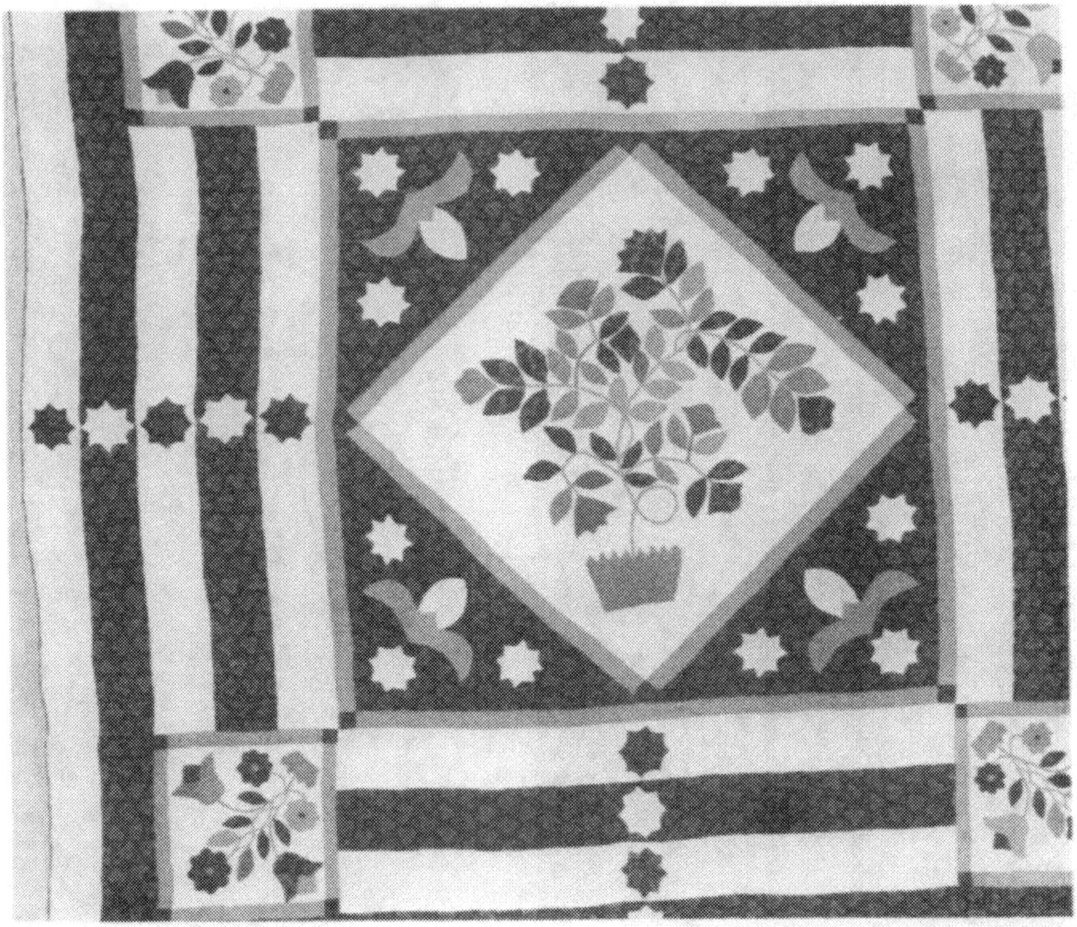

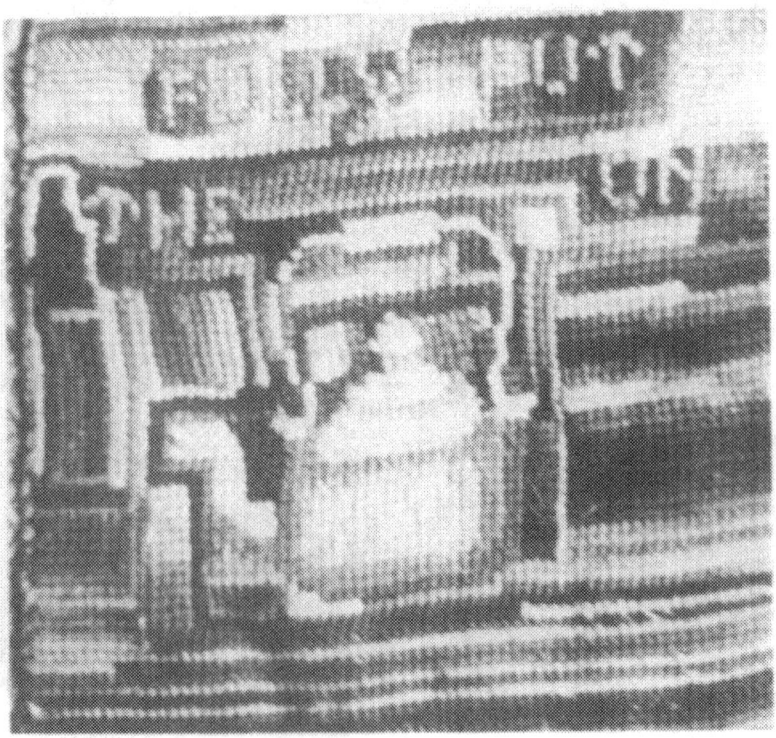

83. Beamish quilt with appliqué design.

84. Knitted kettle holder.

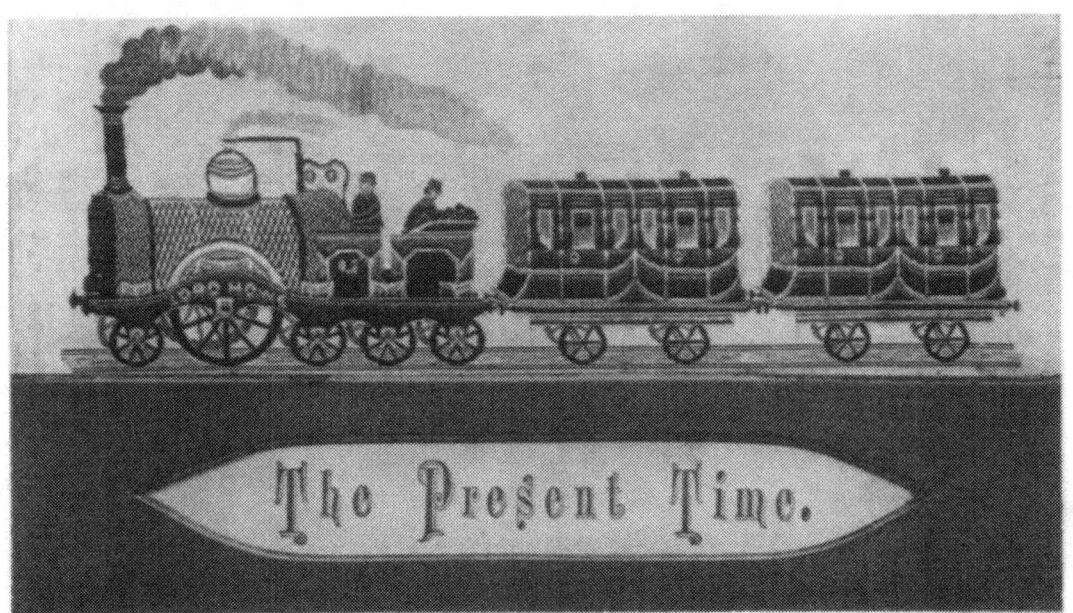

85. Coventry ribbon, The Present
    Time. The excitement of early
    rail also caused the same
    theme to be used for some
    pottery transfer designs.

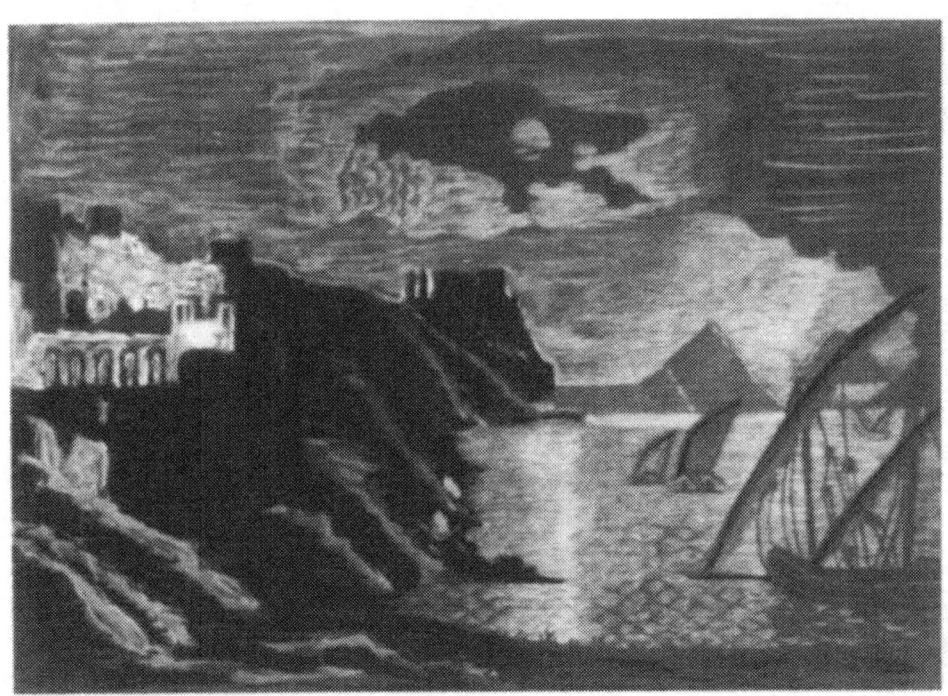

86. Sailor's embroidery of a land and seascape.

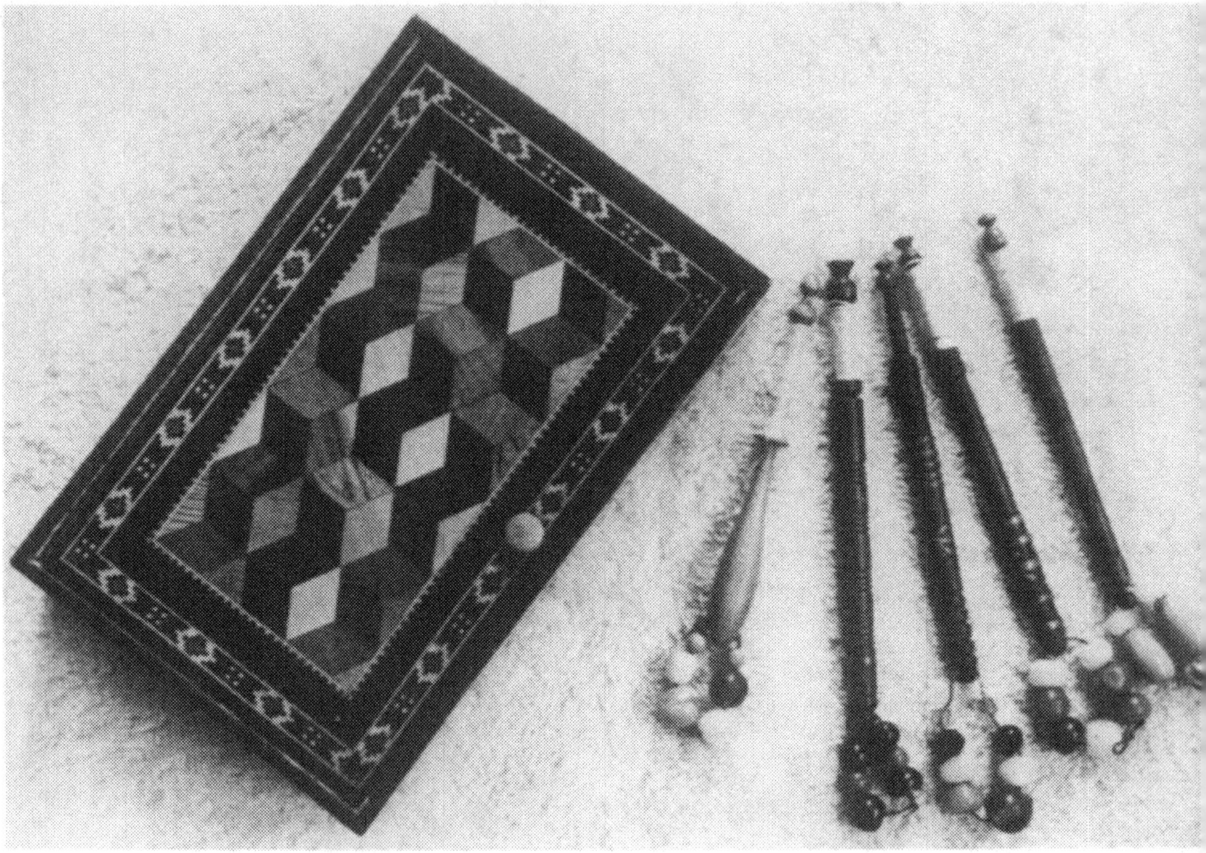

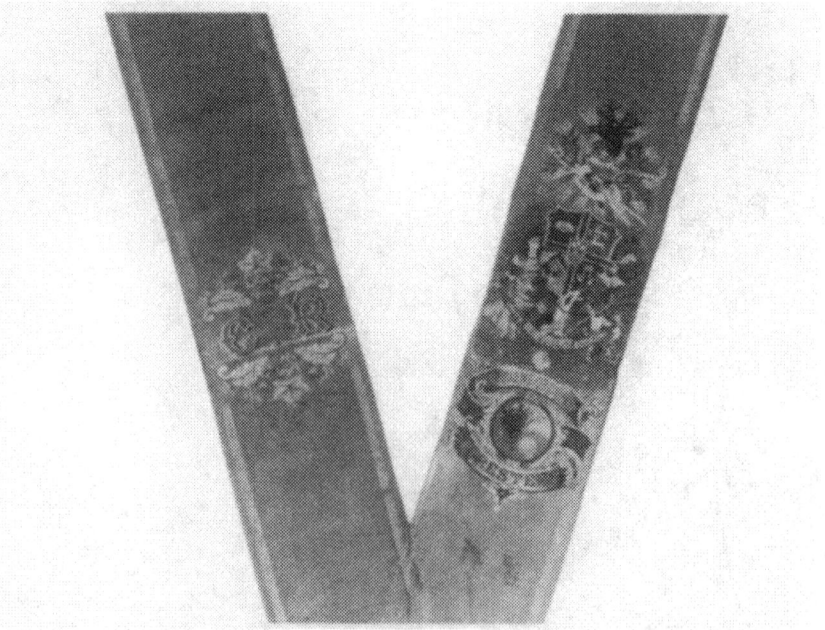

87. Tunbridge ware: bobbin box and bobbins.

88. Part of a Friendly Society ribbon of the Foresters, worn on feast and
holiday parades.

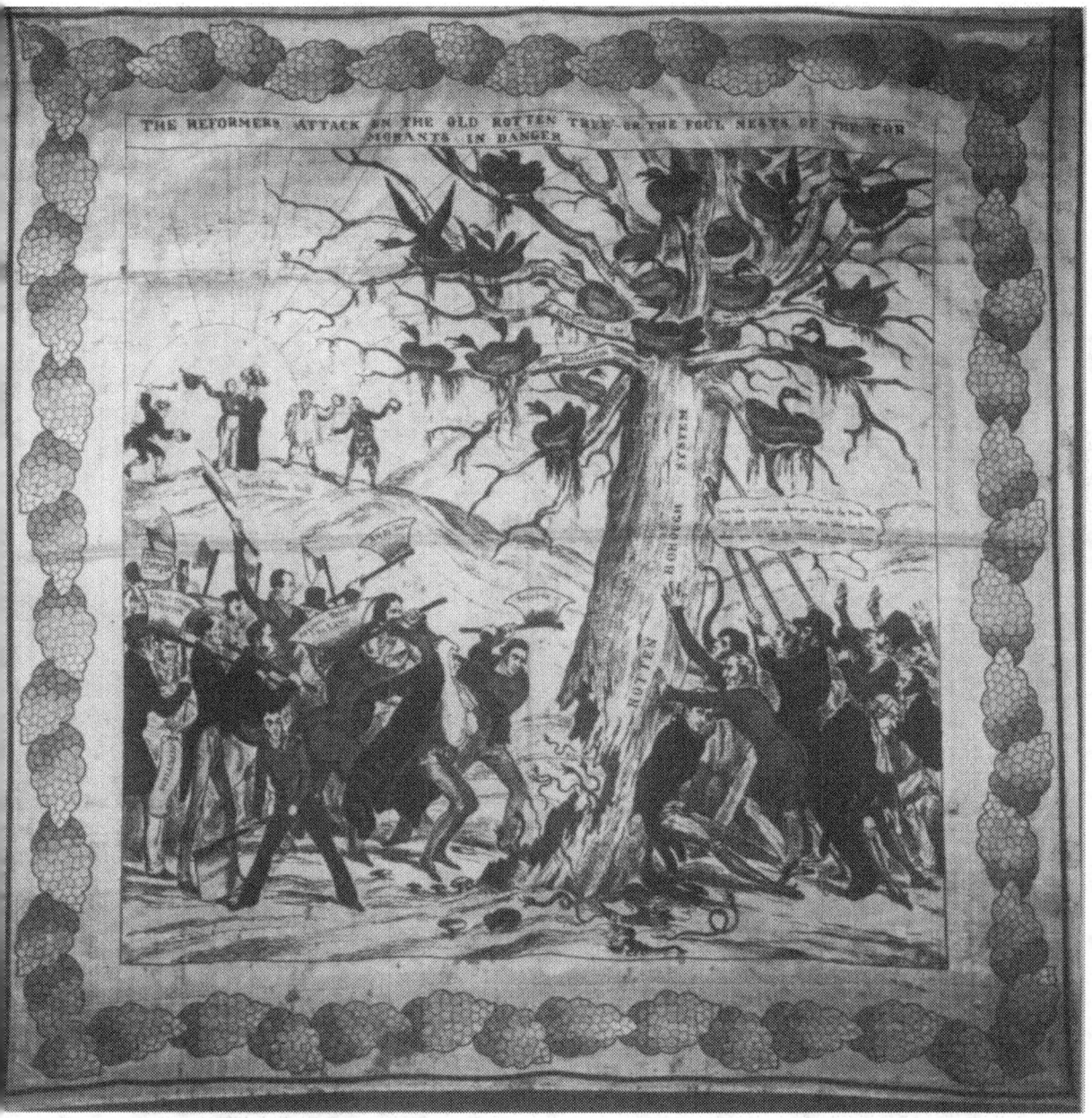

39. A printed handkerchief with the theme of the Reform Laws; such propaganda prints can be found also on transfer printed pottery.

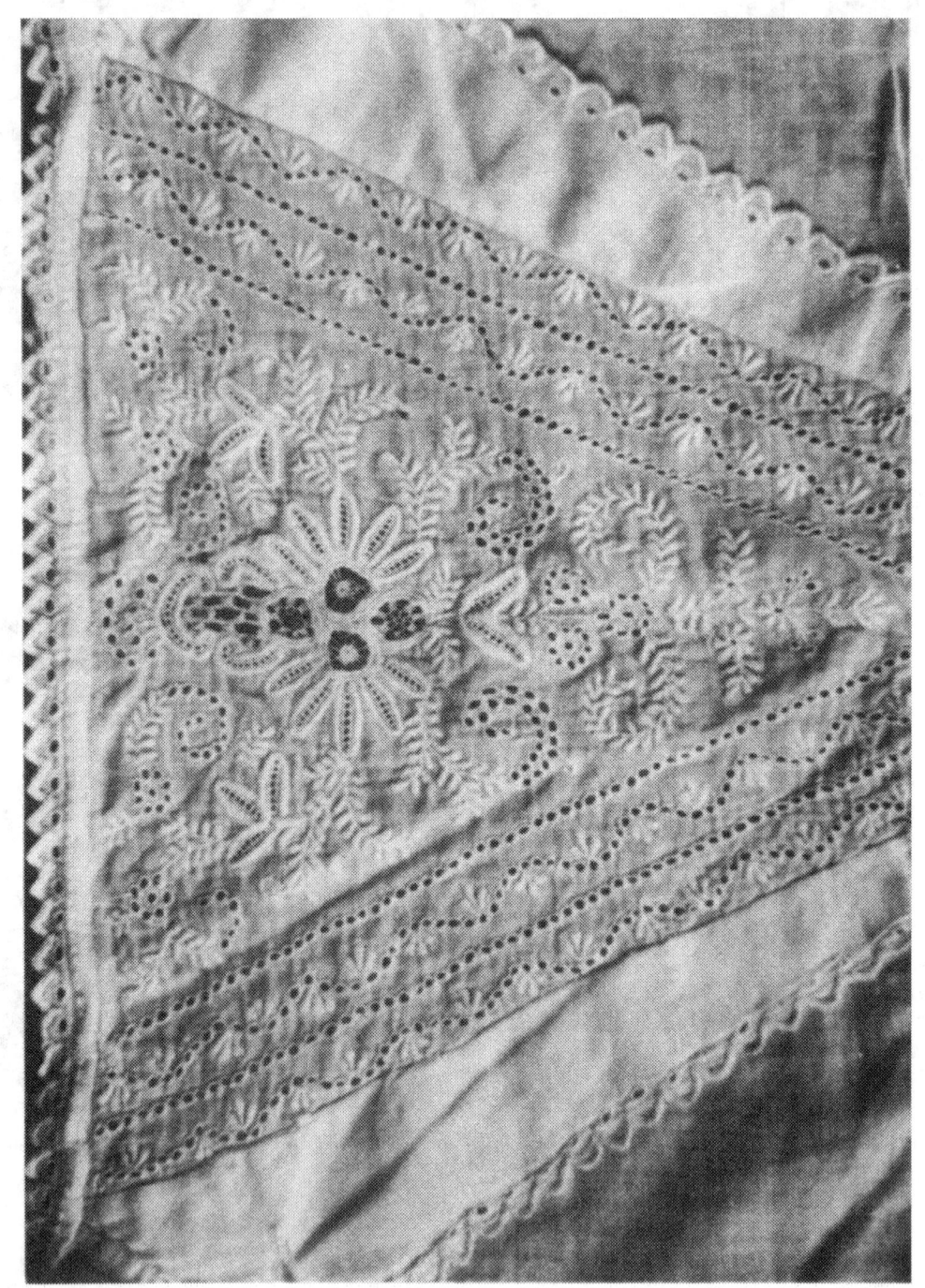

90. Nineteenth Century white work: Ayrshire embroidery on a baby's garment.

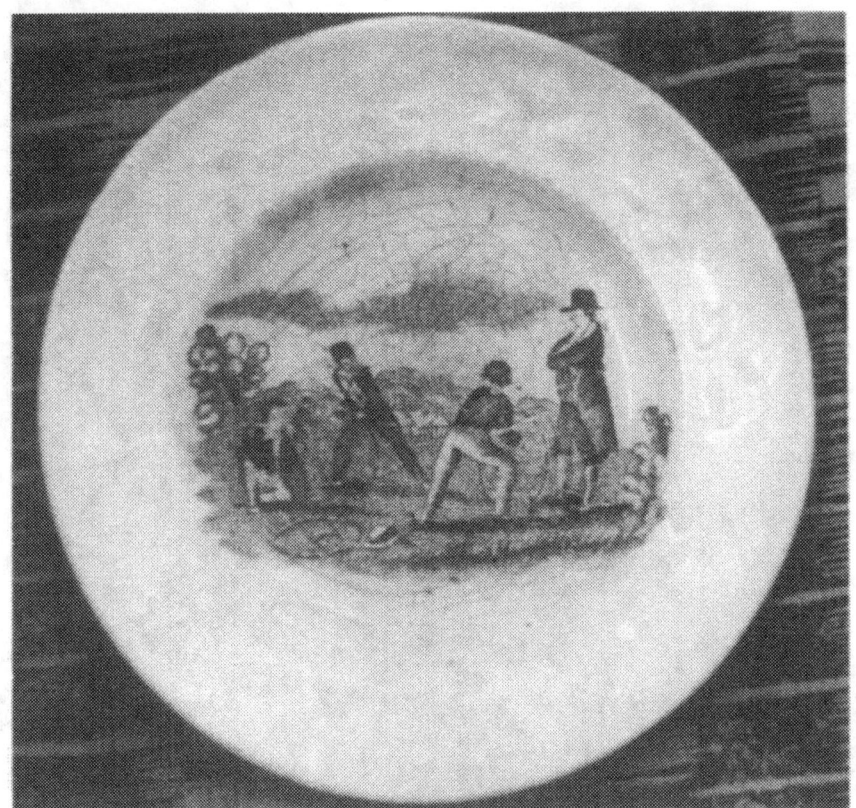

91. Two examples of transfer-printed children's plates, with embossed borders: Children at Play.

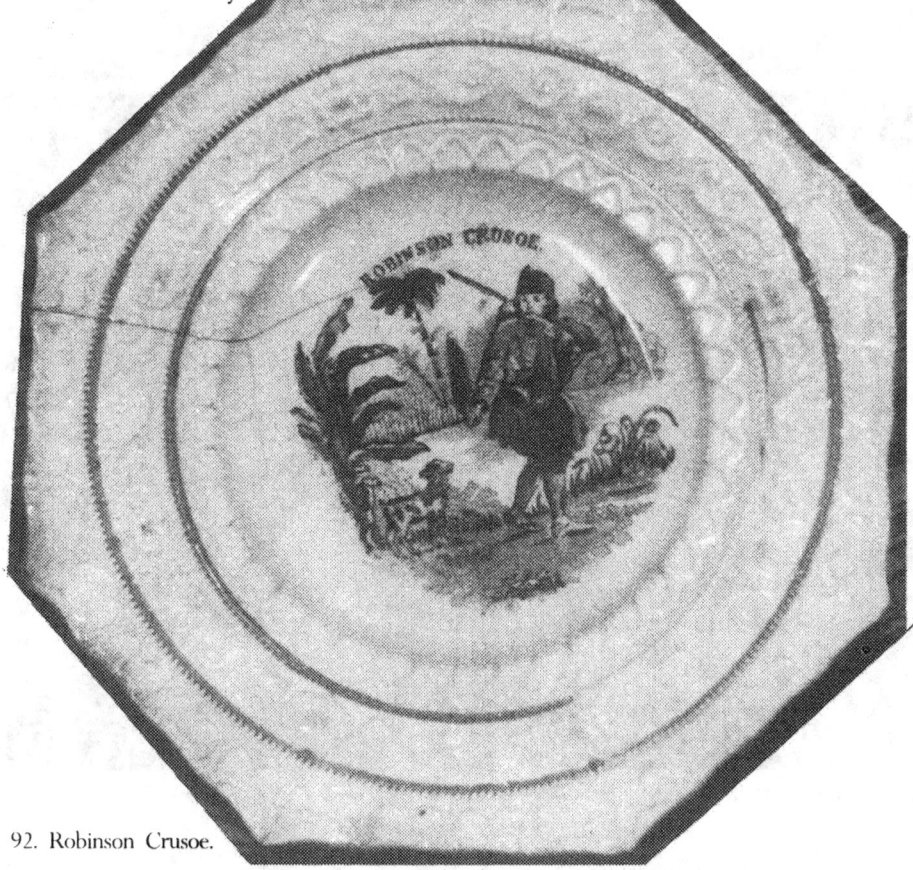

92. Robinson Crusoe.

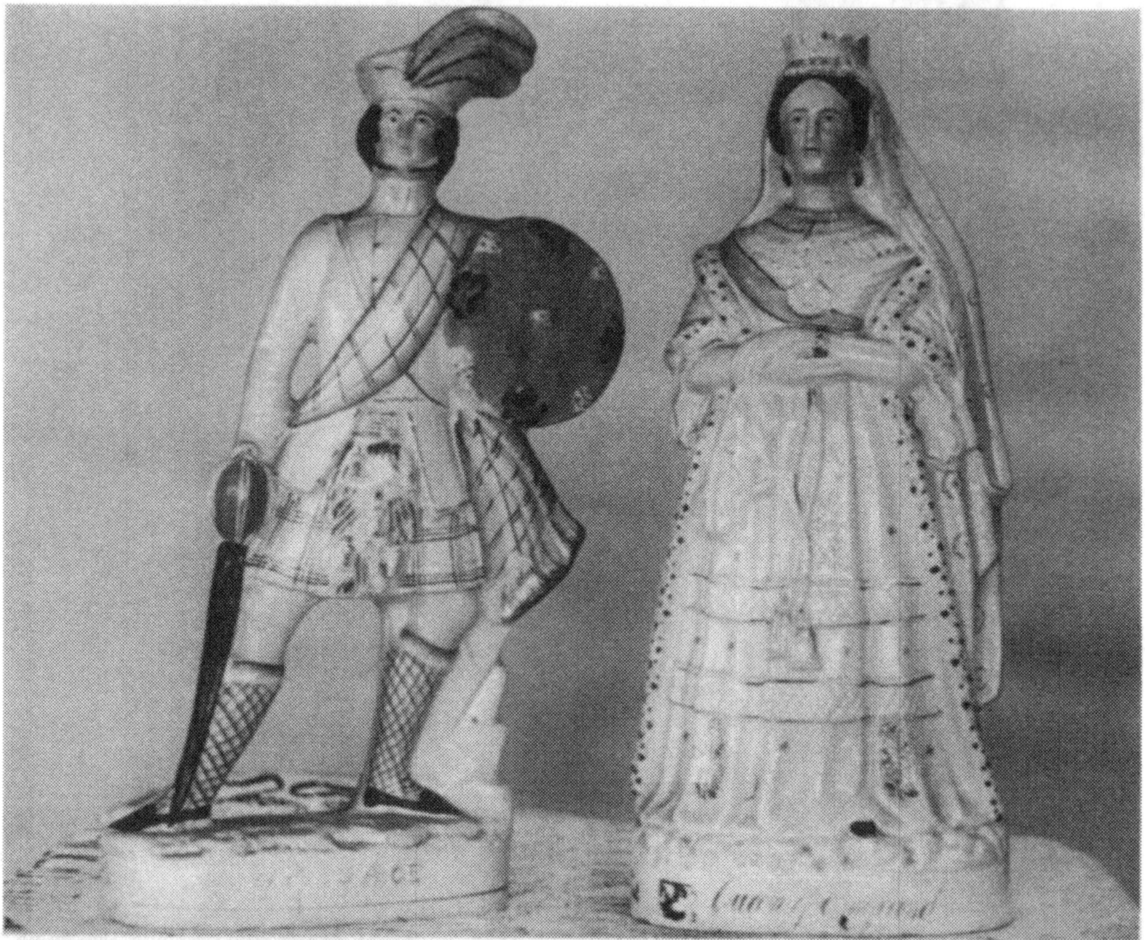

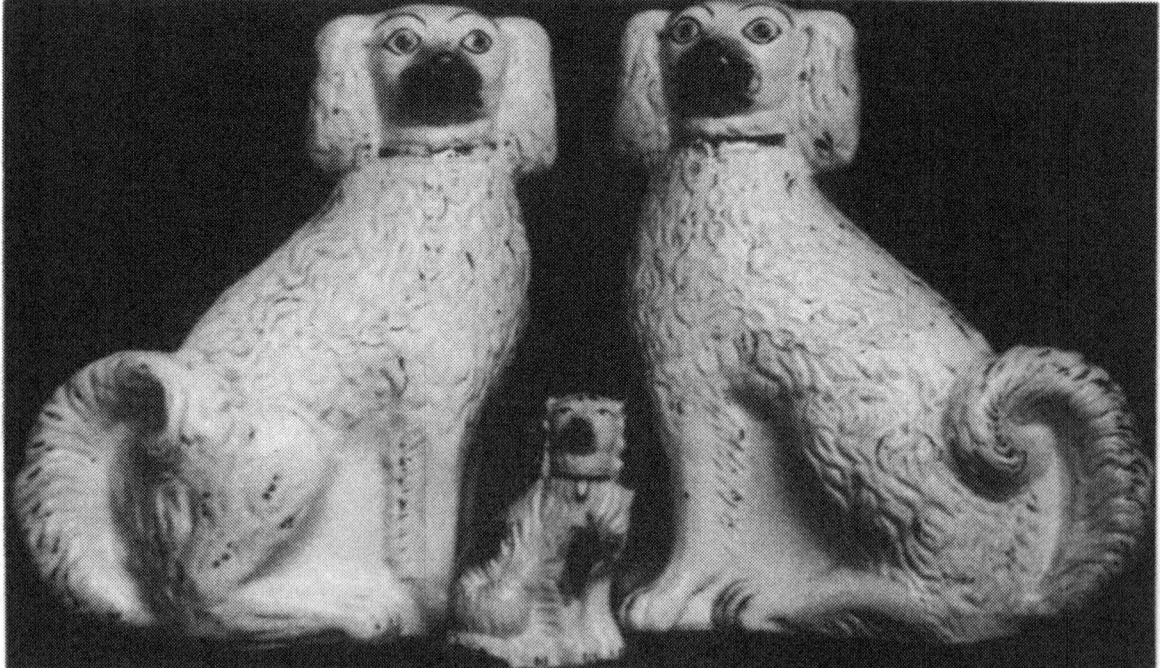

93. Staffordshire figures of Wallace and Queen Victoria.

94. "Wally" dogs.

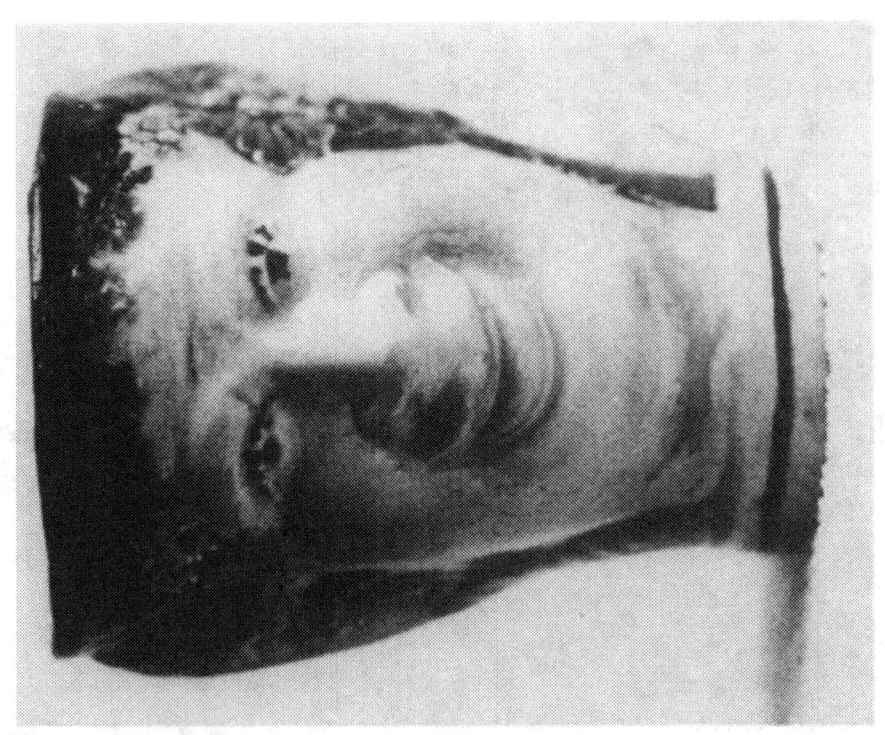

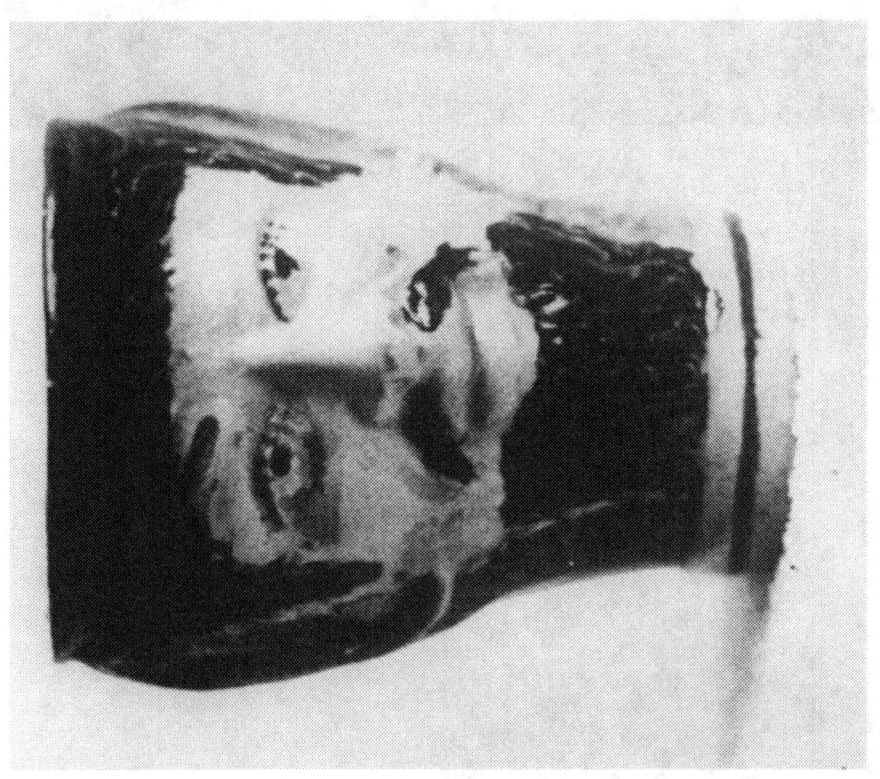

95. A stirrup cup, showing both sides of a Janus head.

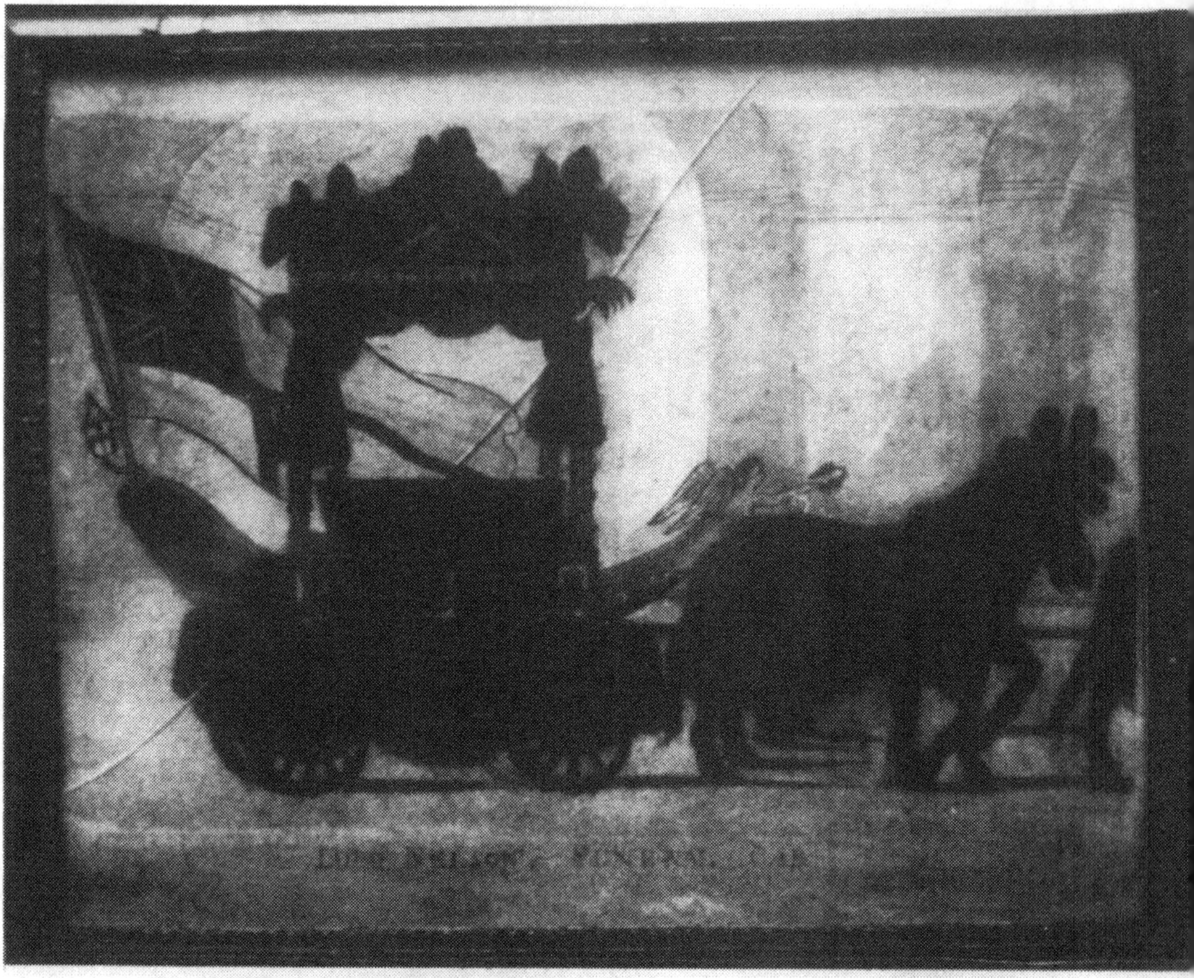

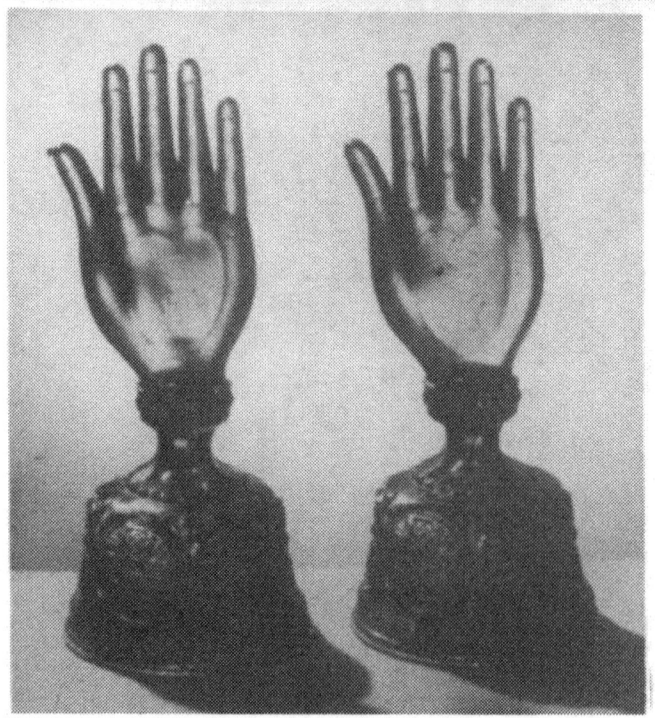

96. Nelson's Funeral: a glass painting.

97. Pressed glass hands: a Victorian conceit, possibly for use as ring stands.

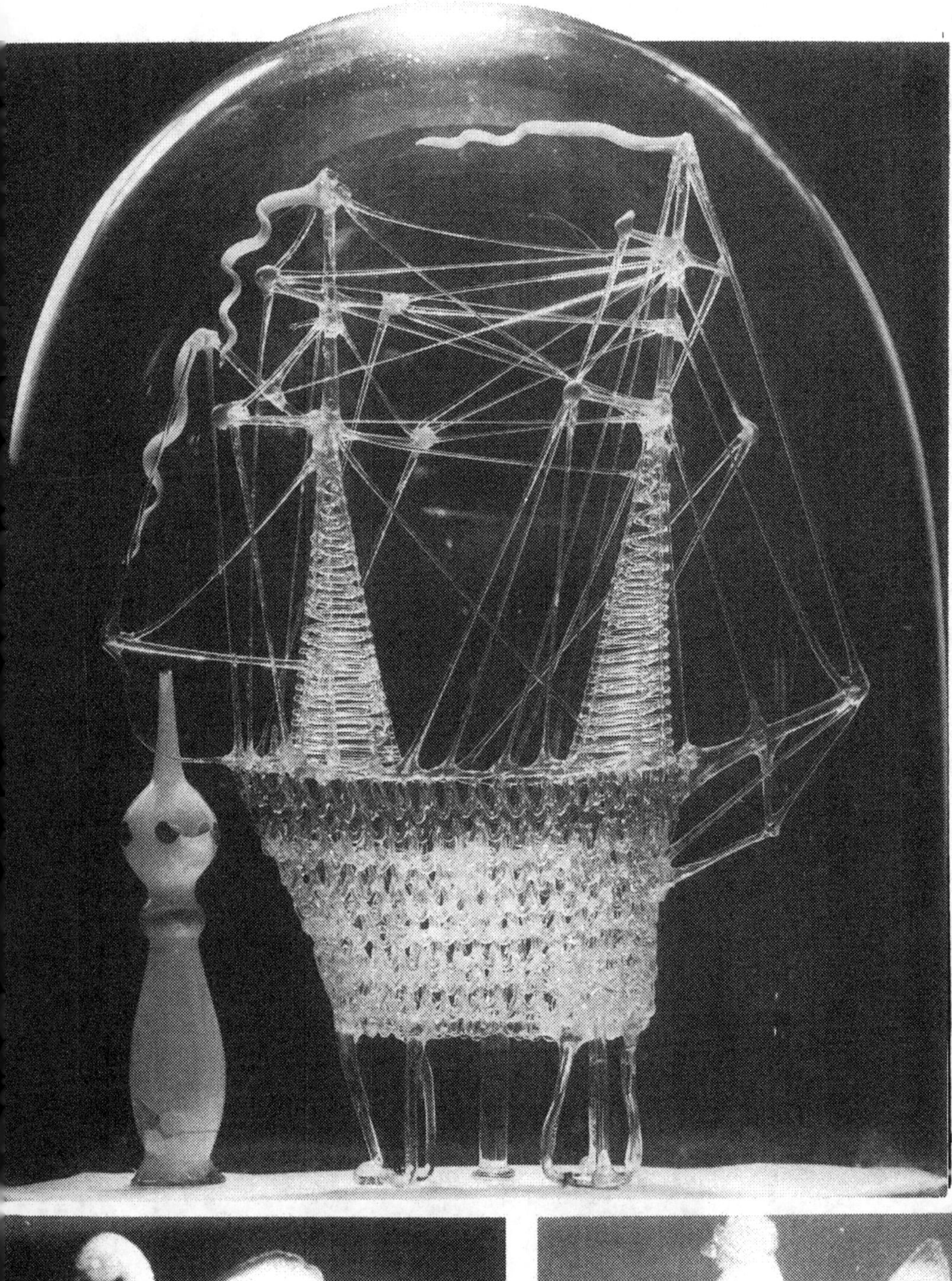

98. Spun
   glass ship.
   *Photograph
   Edwin Smith.*

99, 100.
2 tiny
pressed glass
containers,
1½″ × 2″.

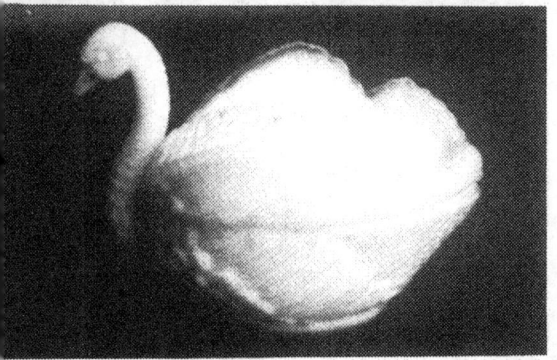

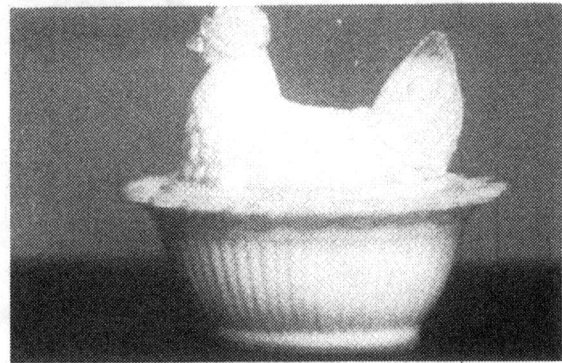

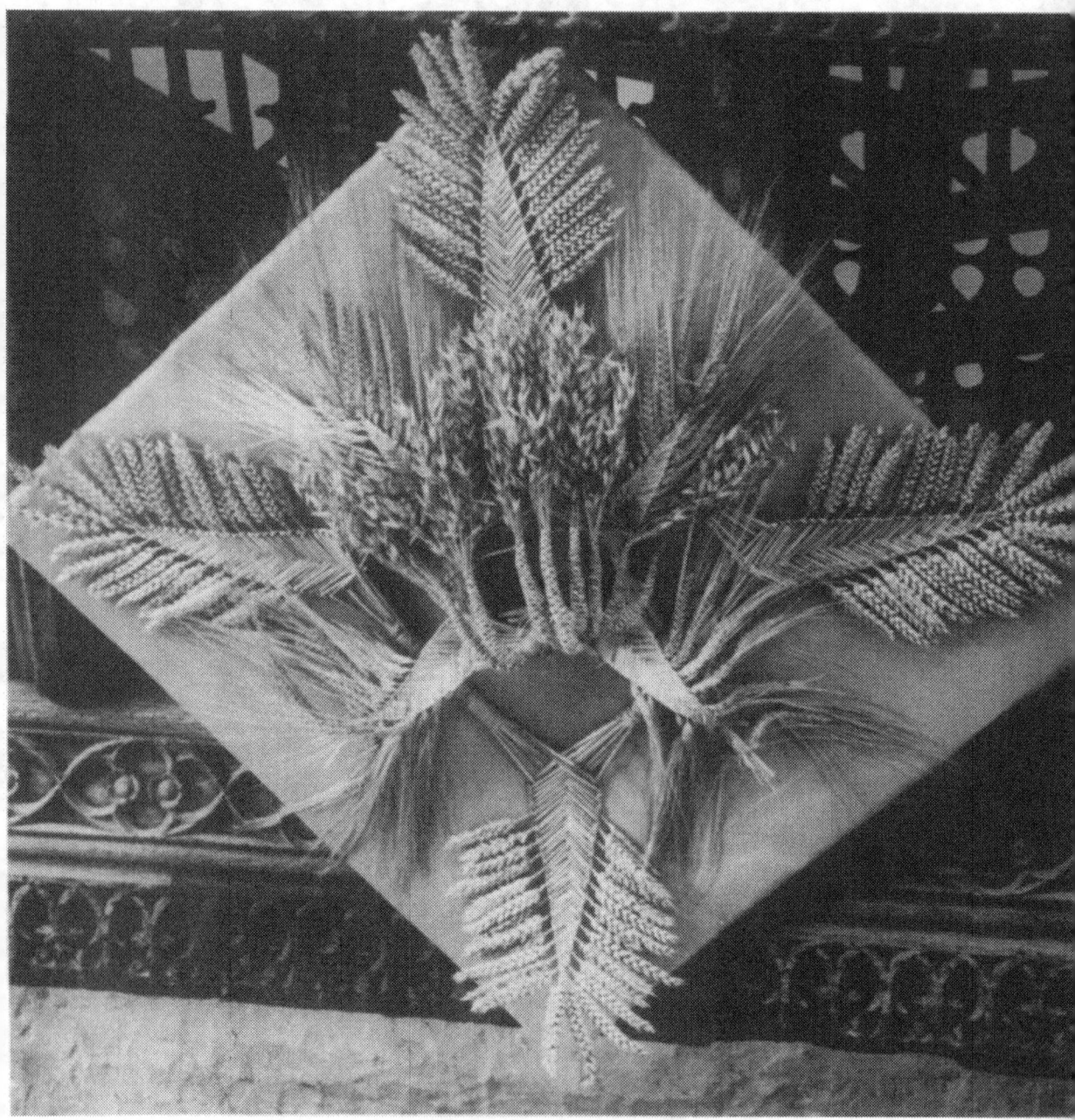

101. Corn dolly for Harvest Festival, in a Monmouthshire church. *Photograph Edwin Smith*.

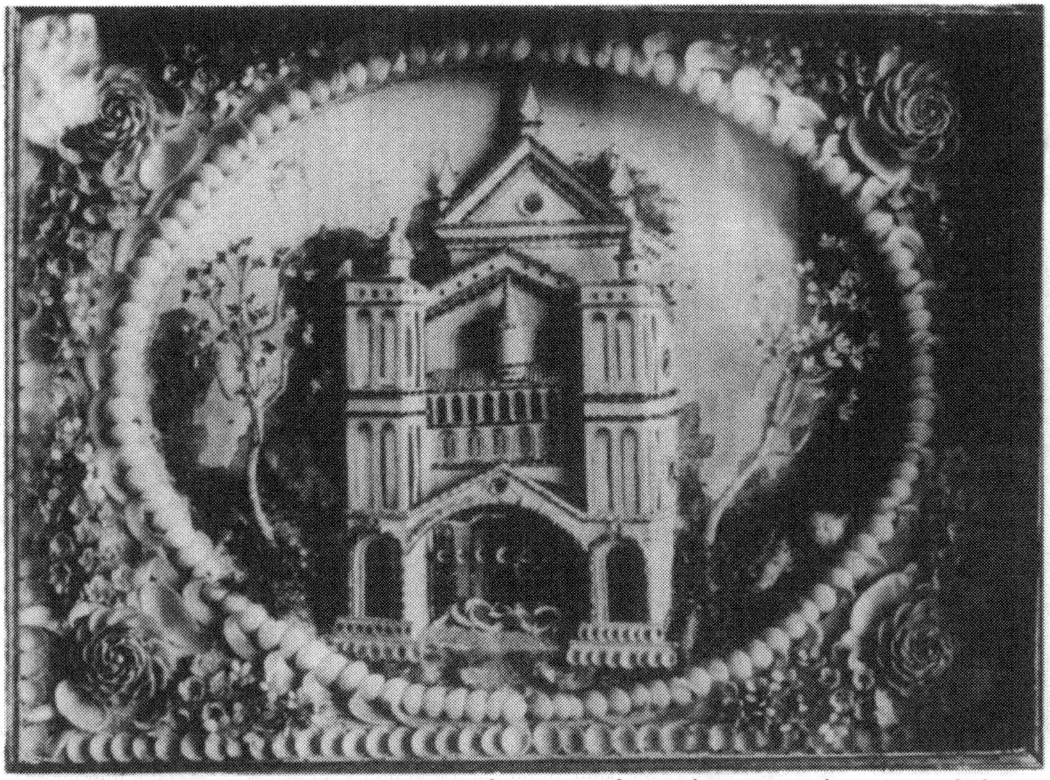

102. Shell decor masking a fireplace in summer, from La Ronde, Topsham, Devon, by courtesy of The World of Interiors.

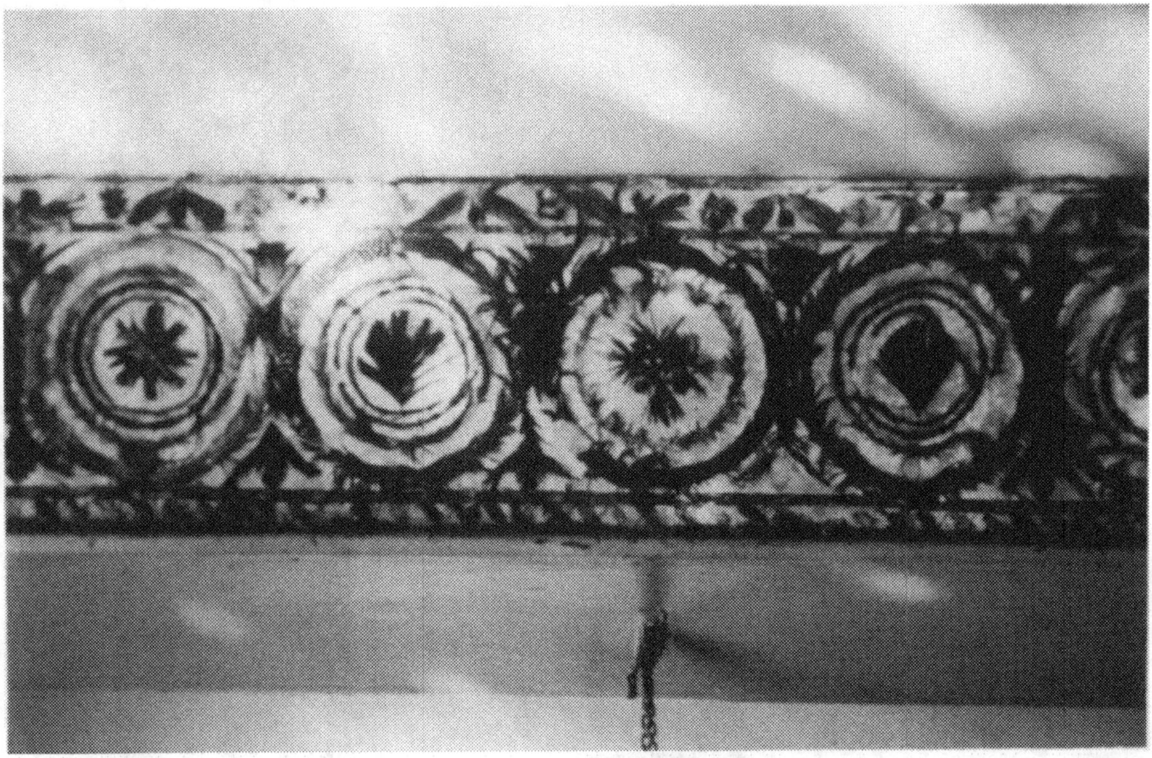

103. Part of feather work border round the Shell Gallery in La Ronde, Topsham, Devon, by courtesy of the World of Interiors.

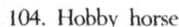
104. Hobby horse.

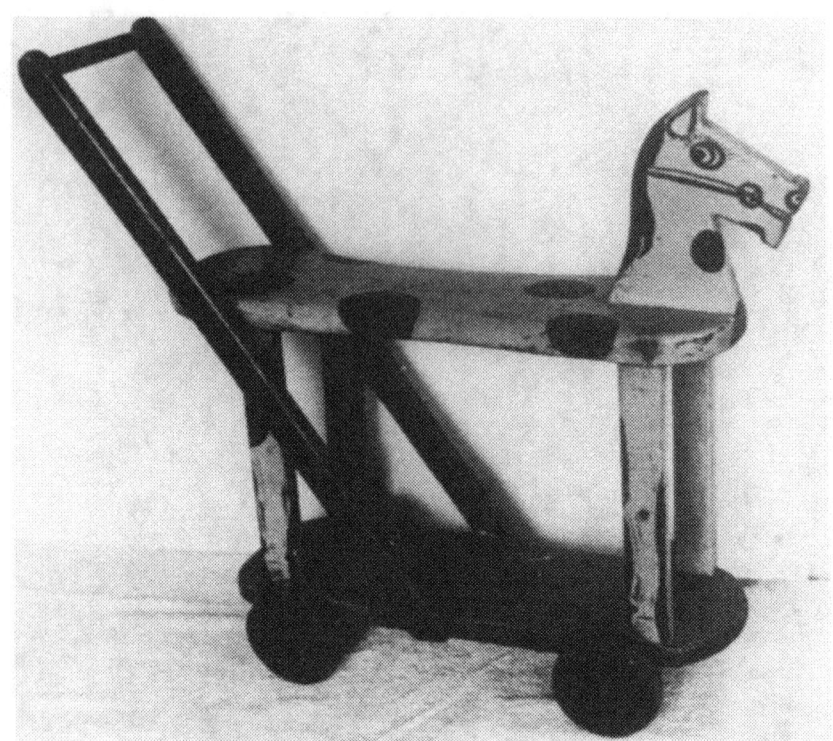

105. Dog, made from
packets of
Woodbine cigarettes.

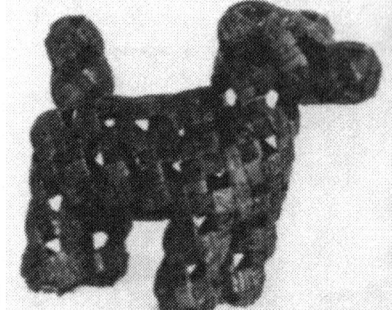

106. Horse and Cart, a gift to Mary Ramshaw by her father in 1808. 5″ long and
2½″ high.

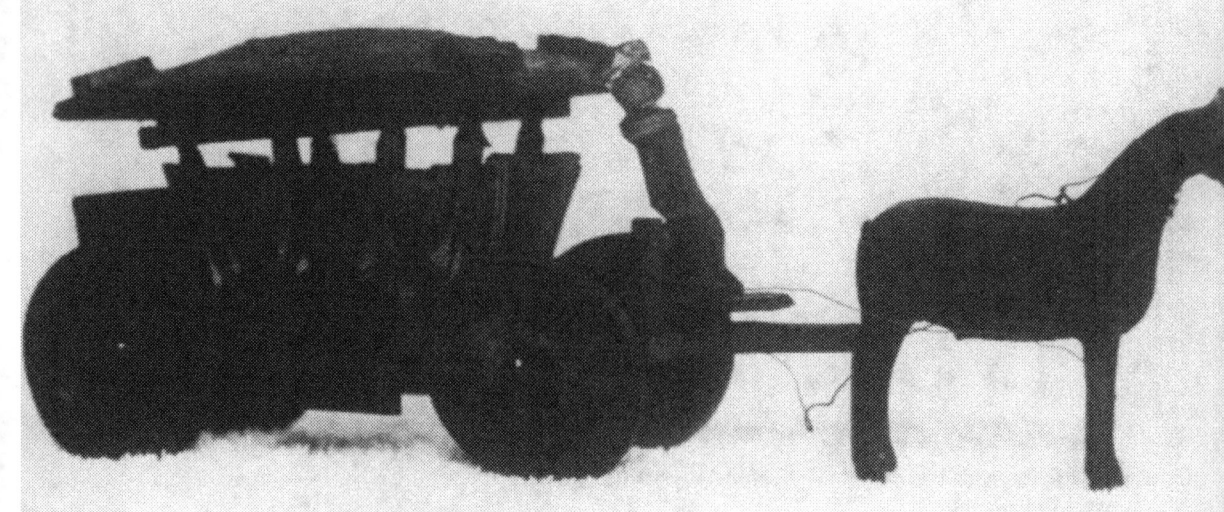

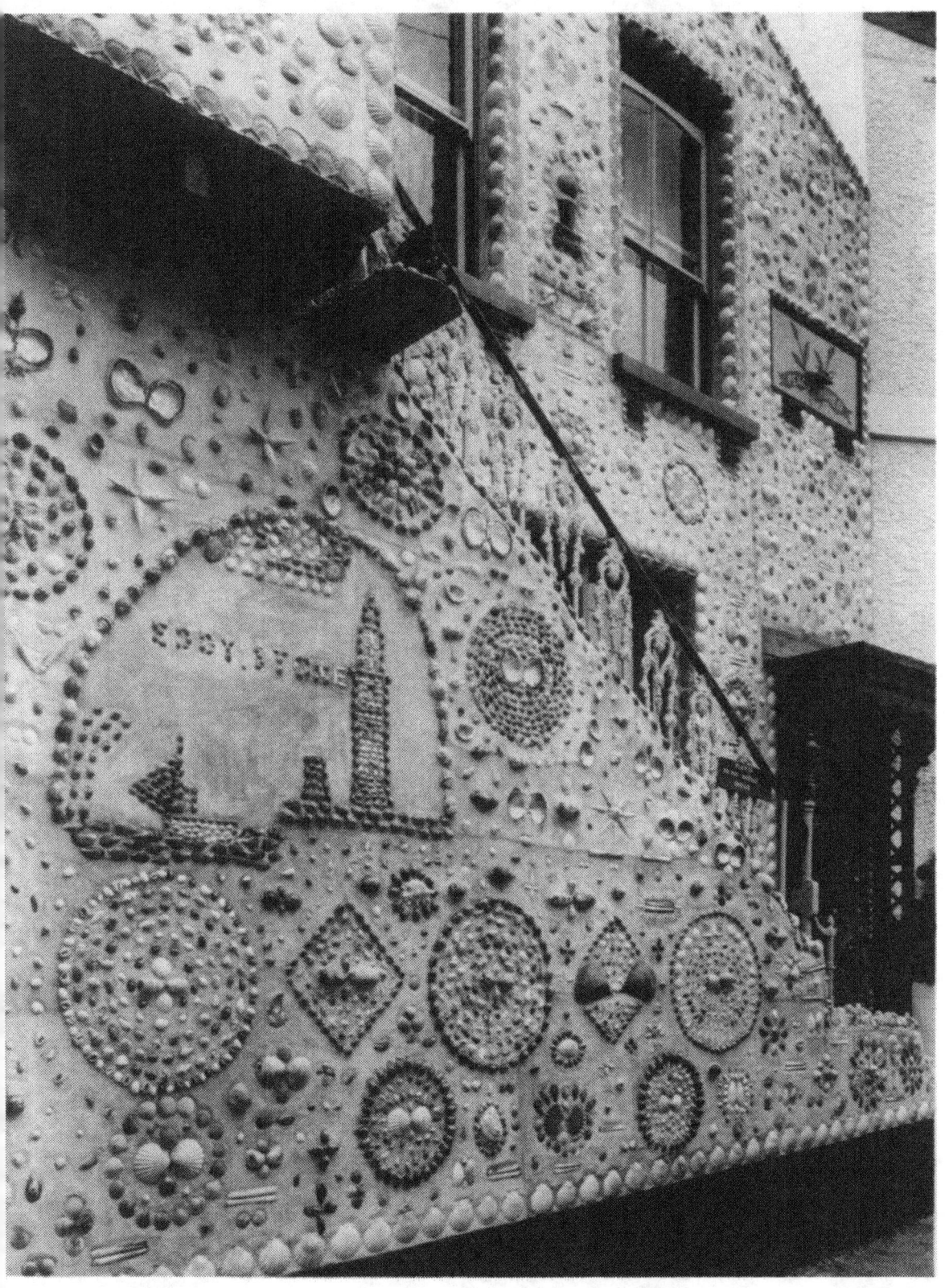

107. Pebble parge decoration, Cornwall. *Photograph Edwin Smith.*

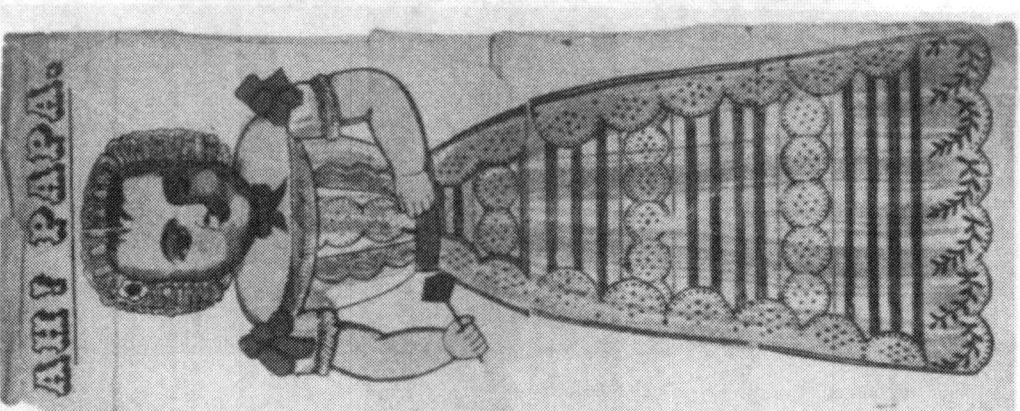

THE FINEST OLD TOM.

AH! PAPA.

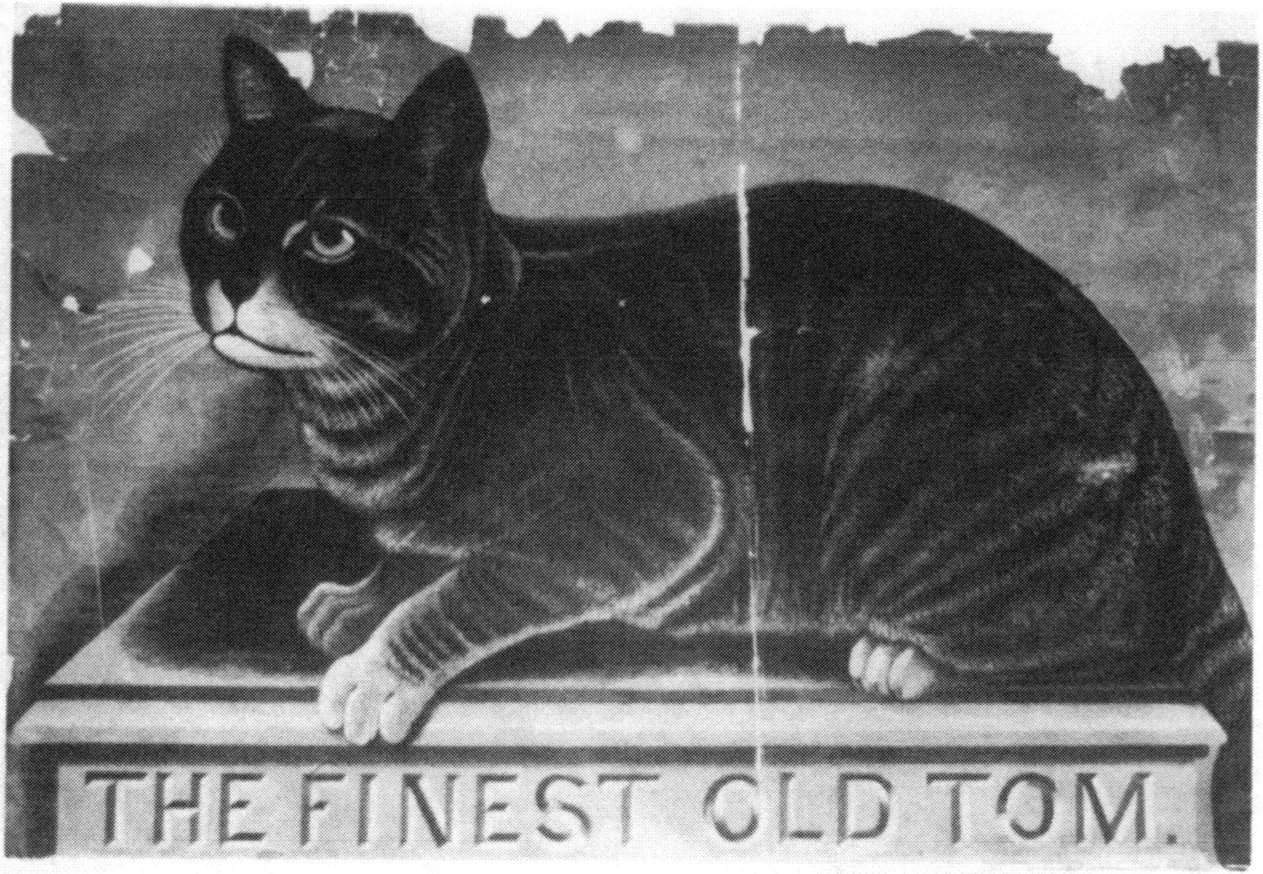

109. Old Tom: a poster advertising gin.

108. Valentine.

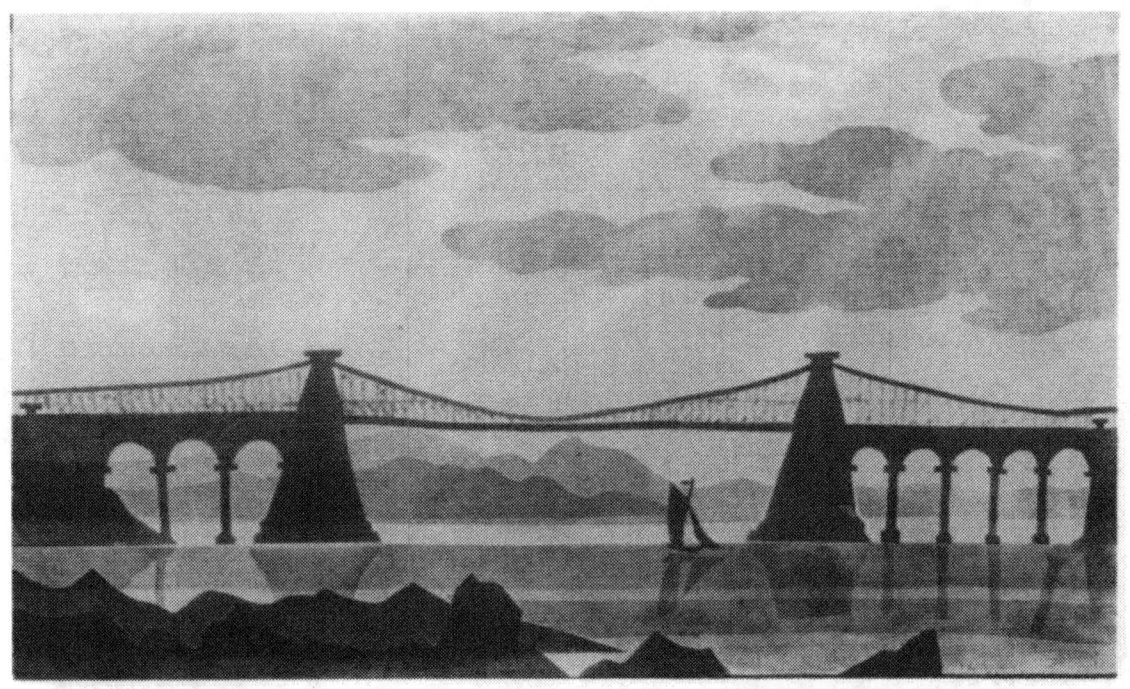

110. Collage formed from layers of different thicknesses of paper, to give the effect of chiaroscuro.

111. Tobacco label

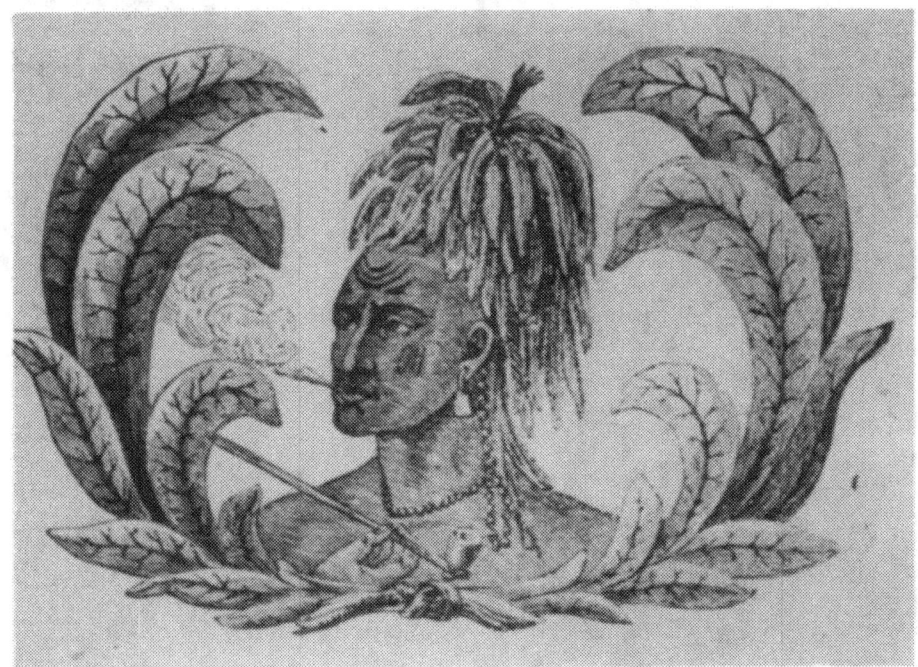

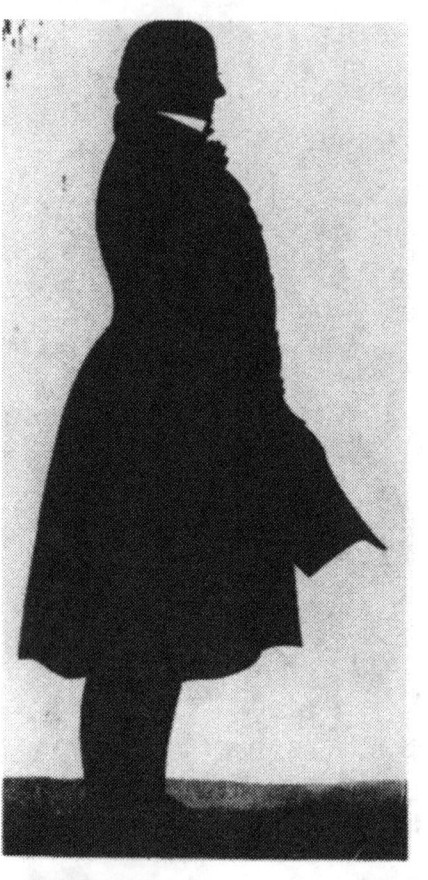

112. Silhouette of a gentleman.

113. Bill head for an open
air election meeting.

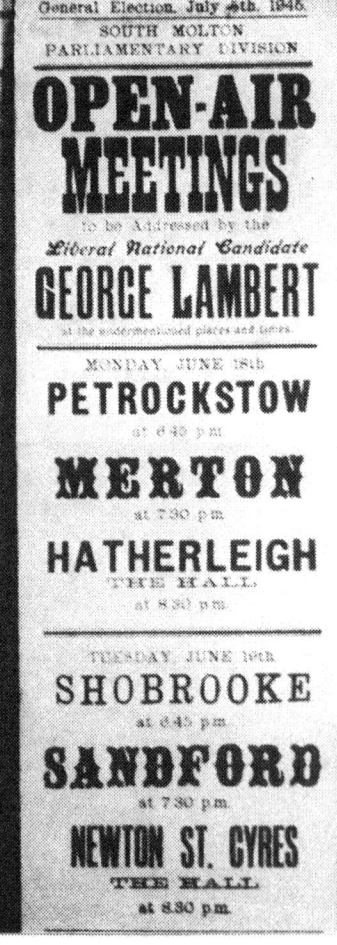

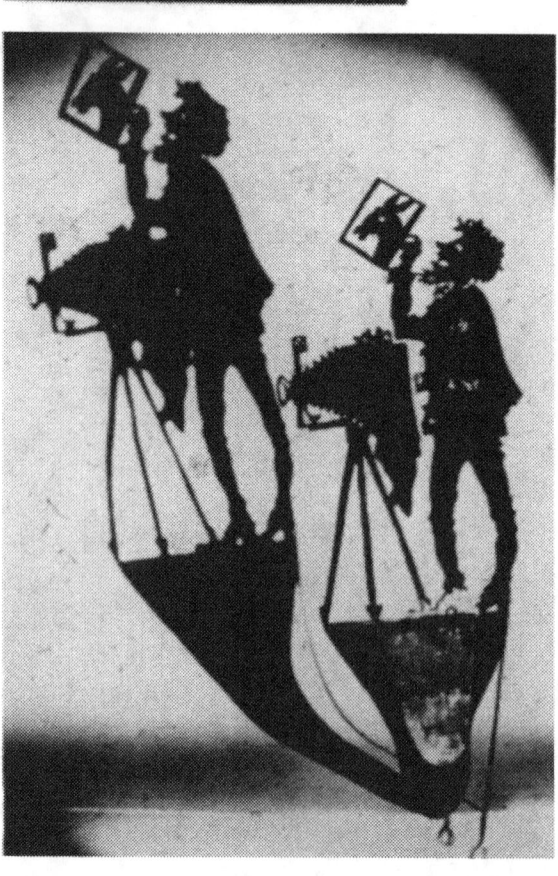

114. Figures from a galanty shadow-figure show,
described in George Speaight's 'History of the
English Puppet Theatre', pub. 1955.

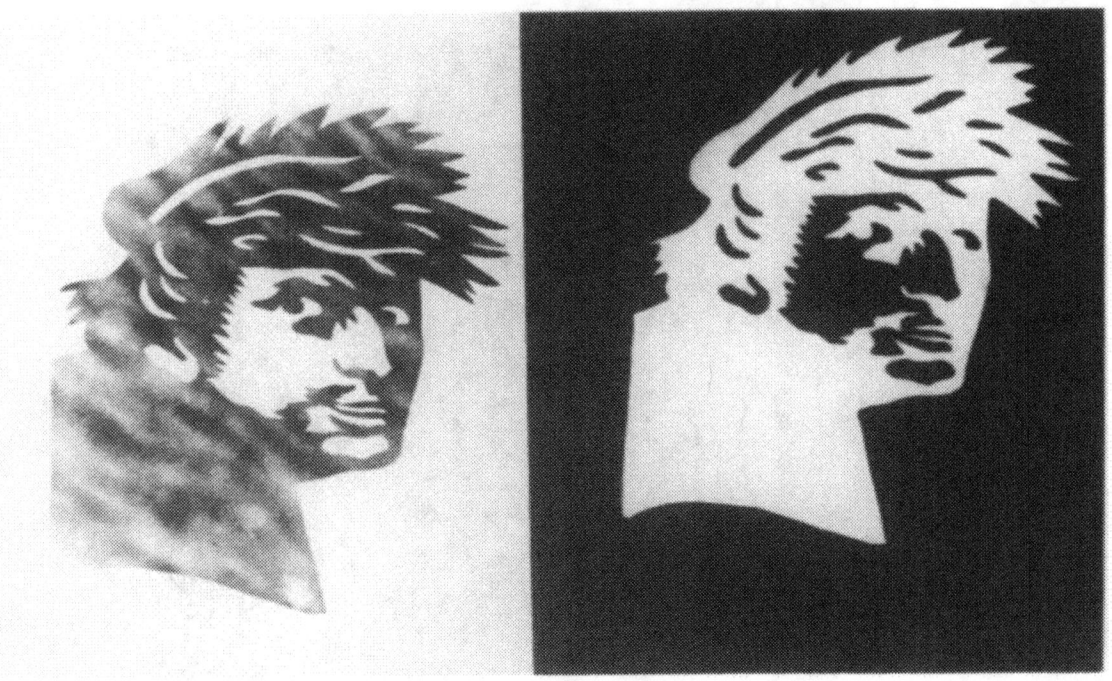

115. The shadow of a head cast by the cut-out paper on the right.

116. A fine example of a cut-out paper scene, 'The Choice of Paris'.

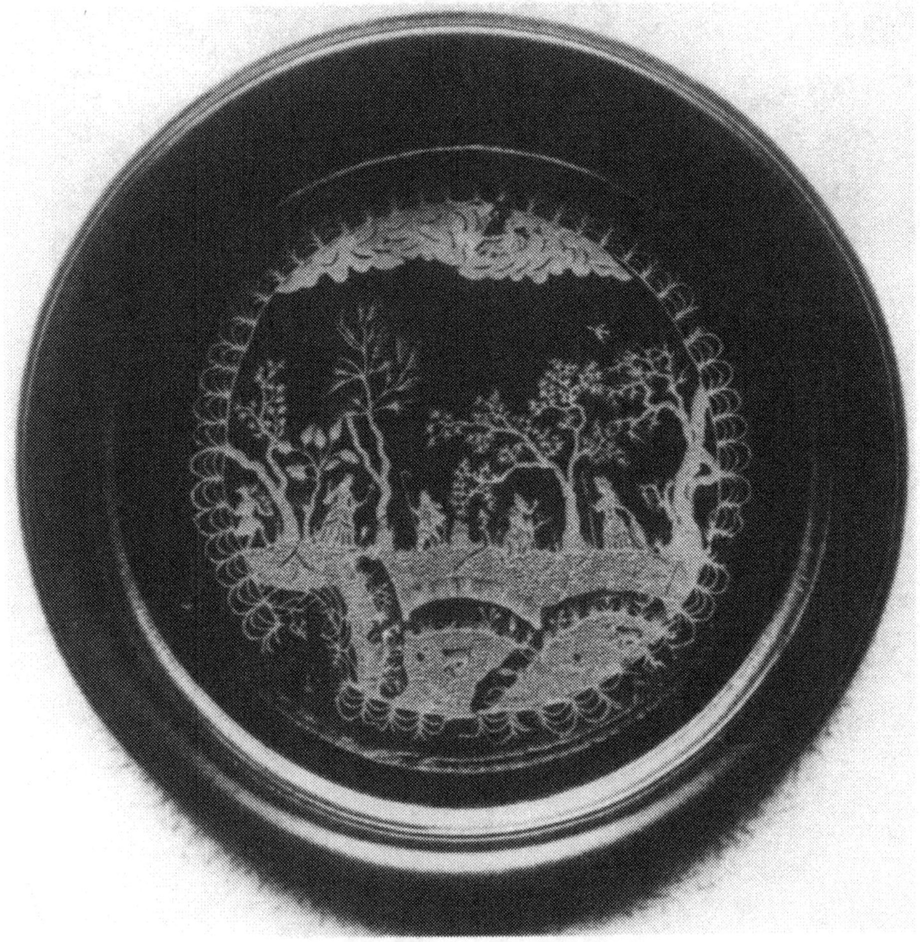

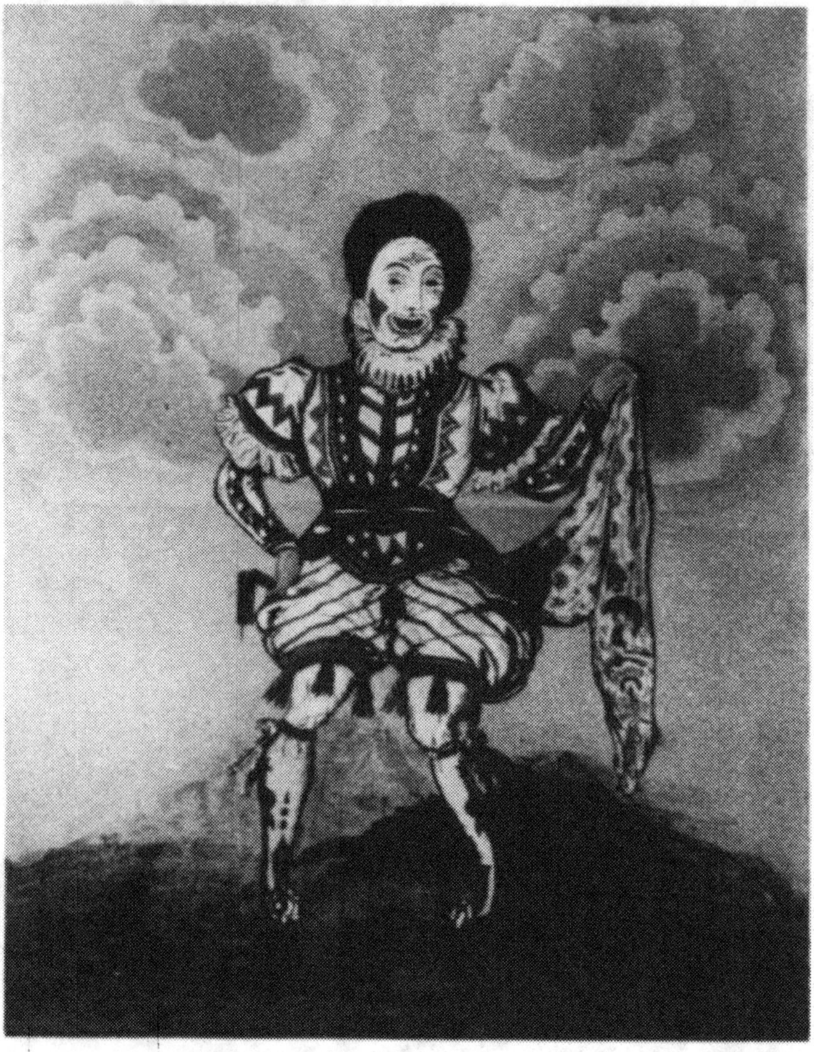

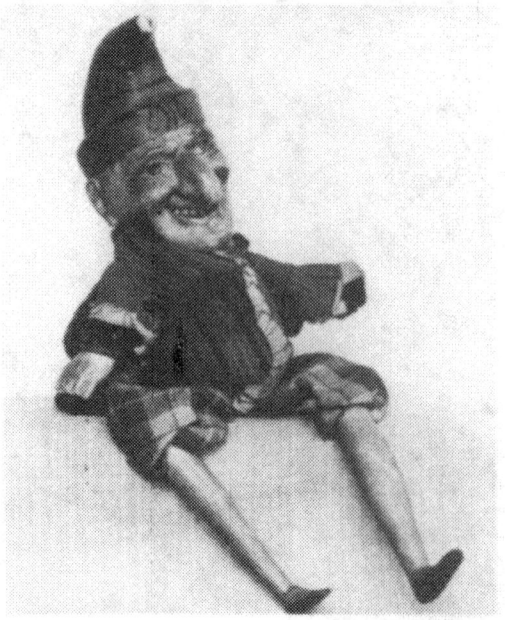

117. Grimaldi: famous
Islington clown.

118. A small carved figure
of Punch.

figures by using grease as a resist. They are a very impermanent form of decoration, for traditionally the children should roll them down a grassy slope; nonetheless much care and ingenuity go to their decoration.

Maidens' Garlands

A curious special form of church memorial decoration, once common in many parts of England, but now surviving in only a few places, is the maidens' garlands. They are hung in the church to commemorate a parishioner who has been born and baptised in the parish and of un-blemished life—usually young and unmarried and usually a girl, but we sometimes find them commemorating boys and older persons also. The forms varied somewhat from district to district. At Abbotts Ann in Hamp-shire, where the custom still persists, the earliest surviving garland dates from the eighteenth cen-tury, and the present churchwarden, Mr. Threadgill, recollects see-ing five such garlands hung up. Here they are made in the form of a crown out of bent hazel rods (first-year hazel stems without blemish are specially cut). The rods are bound in white parchment and decorated with **circular** white parchment flowers painted with black crosses; from the lowest circular hoop hang four gloves,

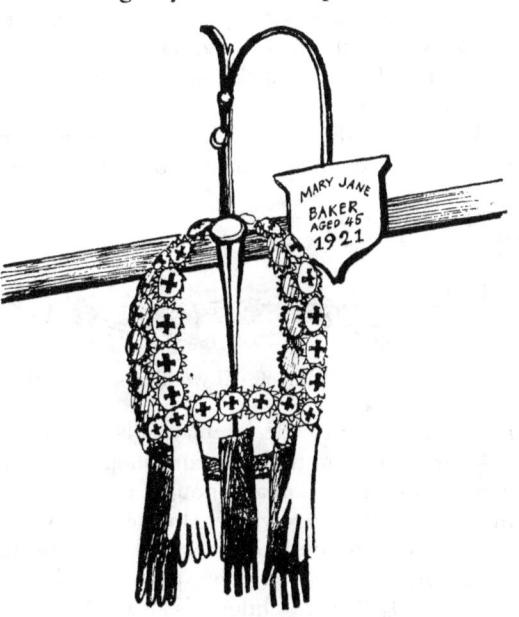

Maiden's Garland from Abbotts Ann

also cut out of white parchment and inscribed **with** sacred verses, whilst the name and dates are written on another glove hanging in the middle. The garlands are carried in the funeral procession and hung for three Sundays under the church gallery, when in theory objections can be raised to their award, though Mr. Threadgill has never known a case. They are then hung from the roof of the chancel, where they remain untouched until they fall to pieces.

Gilbert White of Selborne mentions similar customs, so does William Howett, though he says that in his mother's youth "the garlands were originally of actual flowers—lilies and roses—and the gloves of white kid." But by his time (1838) the practice was already dying out and the garlands were "imitative roses and lilies wreathed round a bough of peeled willow—

a pair of gloves cut out in white paper, and a white handkerchief, also of paper, on which was written a text."

Toys

Children's taste in toys does not change with any great rapidity. We find the same basic types recurring through the centuries; little human or animal figures, realistic or grotesque, reflecting the world in miniature, or the many action toys like balls, hoops, tops, boats to sail or kites to fly. The adaptation of spring mechanisms, though it made possible the production of an immense range of automata and mechanical toys, did not produce any great revolution in taste; the clockwork train or motor-car replaces the bullock-wagon or horse-and-cart of earlier generations. Hawkers on Hampstead Heath last year were selling little clay donkeys with spring legs, but in shape not very different from clay horses made in Greece more than two thousand years ago.

But though the basic ideas do not vary very much, trappings change with the surrounding world. Toy soldiers or dolls' clothes, houses and

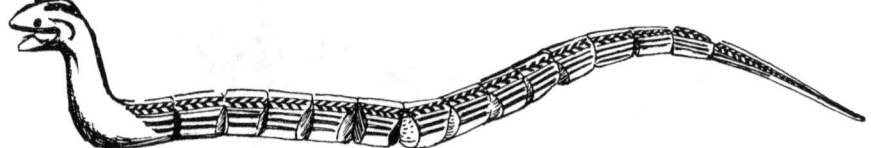

A Penny Toy: jointed wooden snake with coloured straw work

furniture often provide a remarkably faithful record of past fashions. The butchers serving in the miniature shop (54) wear their traditional blue and white costume, familiar enough to the older generation amongst us, though nowadays rarely seen. In the same way the many doll pedlars with their wares, so common during the nineteenth century, recall vanished social customs. Ideas as to what is a suitable toy for children change much more rapidly than do children's tastes. Modern parents may hesitate about giving children toy soldiers; they would be shocked by an early nineteenth century cheap toy, carved in wood, which represents a poacher caught in a man trap; by pulling a string he can be made to kick his leg, open his mouth and groan.

Amongst the cheap toys that might be sold in the streets for a penny or two, but none the less were often beautifully made, we find many examples of popular art. Little jointed wooden dolls, usually called "Dutch" (*VII*), have been made in England since the eighteenth century, and can still sometimes be bought for a few pence. They were dressed by their owners in different characters to suit individual fancy, often with much charm and taste.

By the nineteenth century the making of inexpensive toys, mainly for sale in the streets, had become a full-time family occupation, though in England it never reached the degree of specialisation attained on the

Continent, where whole villages might make one particular toy, or even a part to be assembled elsewhere. Many of these English penny toys, such as lambs, horses-and-carts, bird-cages, money-boxes, Jack-in-the-boxes, Noah's arks, were made of wood, and some were made of clay or even paper. They were mostly gaily coloured; the jointed wooden snakes, at a penny each, had coloured split straw work to represent scales. The penny-toy makers, especially in the big cities, often lived in slum conditions, such as Mayhew describes in *Life and Labour of the London Poor*, and worked with the simplest tools and cheapest materials. But for all this, the penny toys are often delightful examples of popular art, lively and endlessly ingenious.

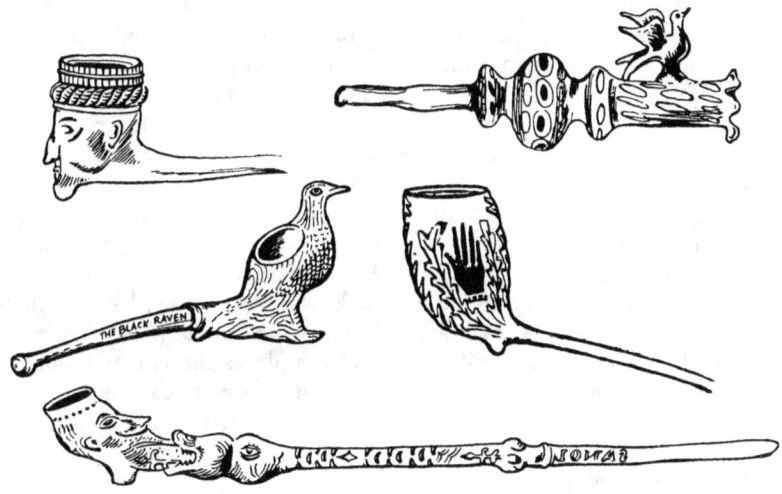

Clay Pipes. *Top right*: Nailsea Glass Cigar-holder

Pipes and Smoking

Smokers have been well served by popular art; we find their equipment—pipes, stoppers, snuff-boxes—decorated in all sorts of ways, some patriotic, some humorous. For all so many pipe smokers prefer wood, carved pipes are rare in England; the pipe *par excellence* for carved decoration is the meerschaum, and these are mostly carved by the Viennese, who have a long tradition in this kind of work. The most common English decorated pipe is the ordinary clay, as it was also the first to be in general use. The earliest clay pipes had short stems and small bowls (tobacco was very dear) ending in a heel instead of a spur. The long clay pipes are reputed to have come in with King William from the Netherlands. Clay pipes are moulded, so they can easily be decorated, and they have been since the seventeenth century. One such, now in the Folk Museum at Balize Castle near Bristol, has Jonah's head on the bowl, whilst the stem is the whale swallowing him; it has the date 1683 and "Jonah" in reverse lettered on it. Public-houses often provided patrons with clay pipes lettered with the name of the inn and also sometimes decorated with it, like "The Raven," which formed the bowl. They also provided large communal snuff-boxes with their device, often handsomely engraved in brass. We can still buy for a few pence clay pipes made in the old moulds, with grotesque heads or charming designs in relief—acorns and oakleaves, or a dancing Scotsman surrounded by a leafy swag.

The Staffordshire potters also turned their hands to fancy pipes in glazed earthenware, snake pipes with elaborately interlaced stems, or portraits of Napoleon, or a hand holding a pipe in its fingers. A favourite model was the figure of a man, or even a woman or a monkey, with the pipe stem running through their mouths to look as though they were smoking it; the figures are some standing, some sitting. But these complicated types, like the Nailsea glass ones, seem more ornamental than practical.

Tobacco stoppers have been carved in wood or bone or cast in metal with an immense variety of devices, some abstract, some pictorial, like a hand or a leg or little figures—even St. George has been made into a tobacco stopper (**15**). Metal ones were sometimes made as rings. Tobacco jars too give plenty of opportunity for invention; we find them in wood, metal, earthenware, stoneware—the roughening for striking matches is naturally a late development. Snuff-boxes lend themselves to particularly delicate decoration; they may be in wood, horn or pewter, like the little shoe snuff-boxes (p. 23), in brass or even in *papier mâché* or Tunbridge ware; a whole class are souvenir presents from places. Early match holders too are often charmingly decorated, though the cigarette case and ash-tray come rather too late to be assimilated to popular art. Even the blacksmith played a part; he provided miniature tongs for picking up hot coals to light a pipe, whilst the printers supplied some delightful designs for early tobacco labels, wrappings and advertisements.

Chapter Seven

PRINTING

Ballads and Broadsides

"I love a ballad in print, for then we know it is true," says one of Autolycus' customers in *A Winter's Tale*. Printing, which is essentially a method of cheap mass production, once introduced in England, was rapidly adapted to the needs of popular art, notably as "street literature." In the early days this cheapest form of reading matter consisted of printed ballads and broadsides, which continued from Tudor times right down to the middle of the nineteenth century. Before the introduction of printing, the itinerant ballad singer had travelled the countryside, often combining this with miscellaneous peddling. Printing made it possible for him to sell copies of his ballads as well as singing them, and he carried them all over England in his pack.

The public for whom these wares were mainly intended was not very literate, so the ballads would normally take the form of new verses set to an old familiar tune. In addition, they would be illustrated by a large woodcut, set at the head of a long strip of paper, the length varying according to the amount of matter to be printed. They were very crude productions, both in style and execution, roughly printed in heavy black letter, and the woodcut often coarsely done. Nevertheless, these broadside woodcuts, for all their lack of skill, have at their best great charm, with a force, directness and freedom reminiscent of primitive paintings. They follow the same spirit as the humours and grotesqueries of Gothic carving, in pew ends, gargoyles, misereres and the like, and are full of exuberant fantasy.

This natural fantasy was enhanced by the demands of their public for sensation, broad humour and drama. The marvellous had a special appeal, like the ballad Autolycus carried "of a fish that appeared upon the coast, on Wednesday the fourscore of April, forty thousand fathoms above water, and sung this ballad against the hard heart of maids." The portrayal of such wonders often entailed a glorious juxtaposition of incongruous objects, more startling to our modern eyes perhaps than to that of the contemporary public, steeped in a tradition of symbolic representation and accustomed to the Emblem Books, with their combinations of literal realism and hidden meanings.

These printed ballads and broadsides survived in much of their traditional form until, in the mid-nineteenth century, they succumbed before what Peacock satirised as "the March of Mind" and the "Steam Intellect Society," namely the spread of popular education and the provision of other sources of cheap literature. But in their heyday, such was the demand for them that not only their production but also their sale became a specialised occupation in the towns. They were distributed by "Flying Stationers" or "Running Patterers," who would run through the streets blowing a horn and crying extracts from their wares, the latest "bloody battle" or "horrid murder," creating so much uproar that, in 1839, these activities were restricted by Act of Parliament. Our English weather being what it is, the street ballad sellers would often carry their wares fastened to the inside of an umbrella, and open it to display them. Silas Wegg in *Our Mutual Friend* is a typical example of the Flying Stationer as he had developed by the nineteenth century; he dealt exclusively in "street literature," although in the country districts it still formed part of the general pedlar's pack.

Before their final demise, the ballads and broadsides inevitably declined

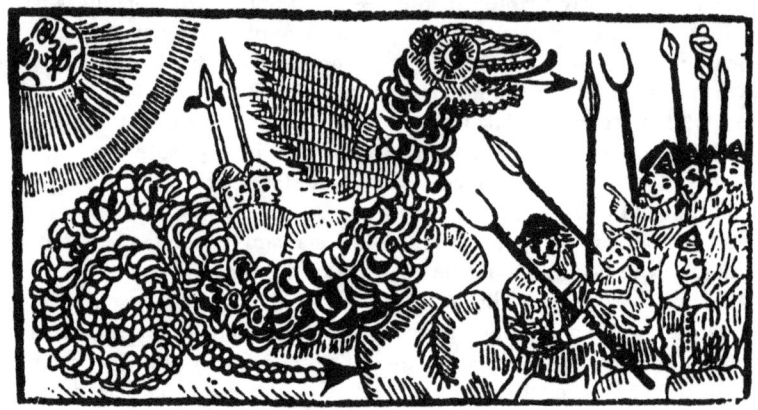

The Flying Serpent: Broadside Woodcut dated 1669

in the social scale, circulating mainly amongst the rougher and more brutal elements of society, especially in the towns. Sensation-mongering became their chief appeal, with, of course, murder heading the list. When sensations ran short, an old one would be rehashed and palmed off as new to the unsuspecting buyer; hence the title "catchpenny." Till public executions were stopped in 1868, these occasions provided a ready sale for the "gallows literature" type of broadside, such as the "Copy of Affectionate (*sic*? affecting) Verses" and "Last Confessions," done into doggerel rhymes, highly moral in sentiment, and written, the Patterer would assure his public, "from the depths of the condemned cell, with the condemned pen, ink and paper." These verses would be decorated with a rough woodcut portrait of the murderer or perhaps merely a gallows. Minor sensations, suicides and the rest, were given stock pictures, the old blocks doing service again and again, and from time to time being recut from earlier originals. As portraits they were as bogus as the "Last Confessions," which also passed muster for many a murderer. But the broadside public never seems to have cared about factual acuracy; indeed it would probably have only impeded a semi-literate society accustomed to recognising stock

figures in the human scene, much as it applauded or hissed the various set
characters in melodrama and pantomime.

Major sensations might be given a new and exclusive *mise en scène*, with
pictures not only of the murderer and his victim, but a vivid reconstruc-
tion of the crime, and views of its scene; though these were still not in
terms of factual accuracy. One such *cause célèbre* was the murder of Maria
Marten in the Red Barn, which was also put on the stage and represented
in Staffordshire figures—indeed it seems likely that these figures were
taken from the broadsides. Or the Pegsworth and Greenacre murders,
both in 1837, which called forth an immense pictorial literature, some

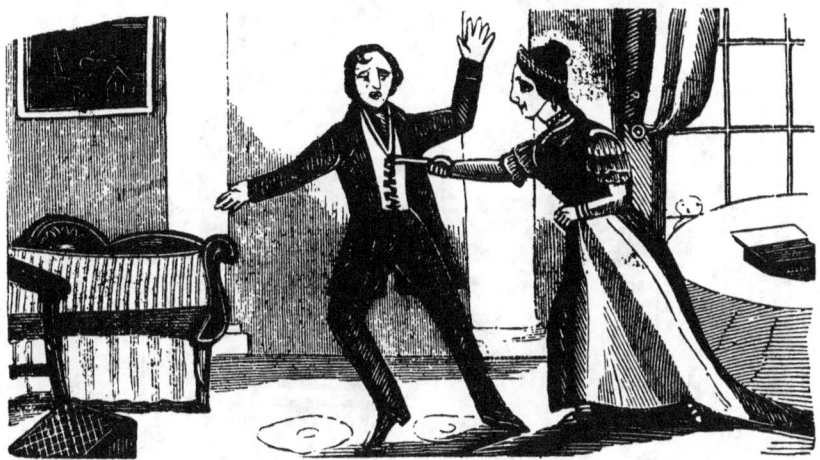

Murder of Captain Lawson.

A Catnach Broadside

even in colour, flat washes applied by hand. One printer, Orlando Hodgson, better known for his toy-theatre sheets and Books of Fate, produced a
version of the Greenacre murder which, with its brilliant colour combinations, stands out as a superb piece of theatrical artificiality, submerging the
gruesomeness of individual details in the magnificence of the whole.

The two printers and publishers most concerned with ballad and broadside production in its final phase, at least in London, were Jemmy Catnach
and Johnny Pitts, both of the Seven Dials neighbourhood, so much so that
"Seven Dials" became a common term for this sort of literature. Through
the interest of the nineteenth century antiquarian, Charles Hindley, who
compiled various books on street literature and the Catnach Press in particular,[1] illustrating them with prints from the old blocks, we have a comparatively full record of how these printers worked, their various stratagems

[1] Charles Hindley: *The Life and Times of James Catnach* (1878), *The History of the
Catnach Press* (1886), *Curiosities of Street Literature* (1871) are a few of the titles.

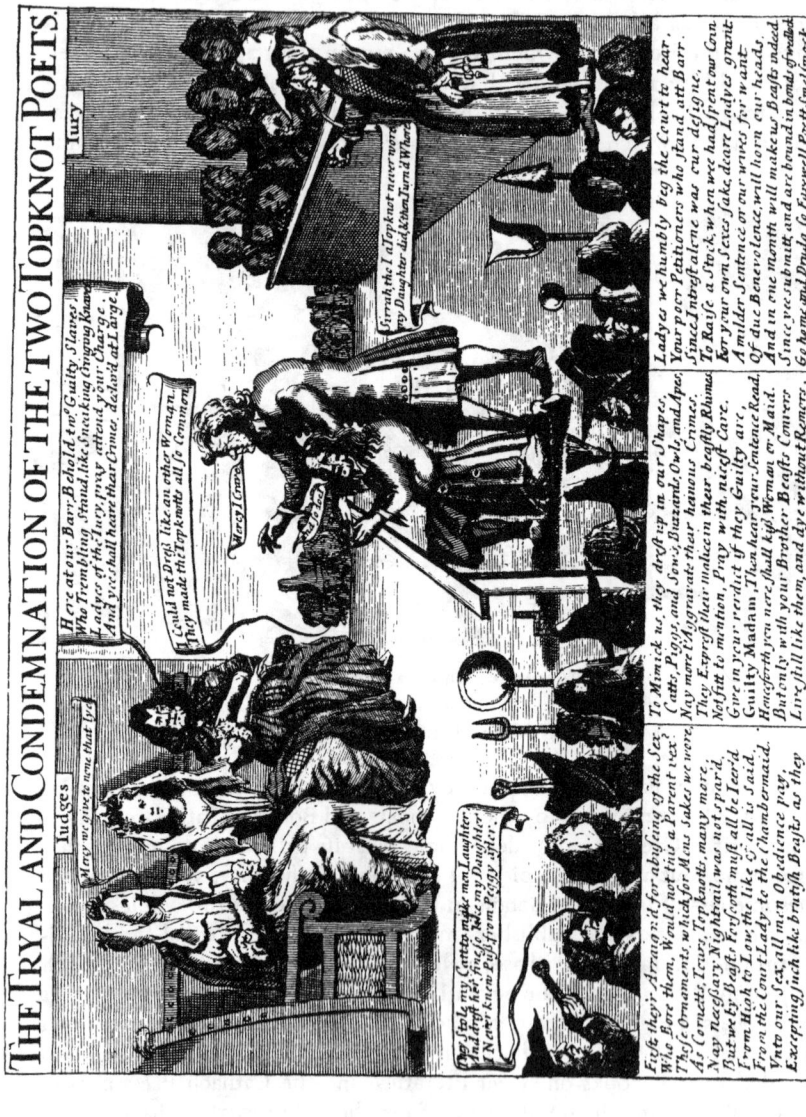

An eighteenth century Satirical Broadside

for cooking up old productions to look like new ones, evading prosecutions for libel, the spreading of false news and so on, as well as what their wares actually looked like. According to Hindley, Catnach frequently bought up not only old stocks of type but also blocks from other firms, converting them to his own purposes. He also worked out a sort of "Stop Press" technique as the speed-up of communications throughout the country brought an increasing demand for hot news. If some illustrious personage looked like dying, he would start on a broadside portraying the funeral, using stock figures and adding more and more details of the procession, trappings and so forth, until he was ready to market his version almost before the event happened.

Though sensationalism and scandal bulked large, broadside publishing, even towards the end, was by no means confined to it. Dialogues of all kinds, humorous, elevating, satirical; political squibs; moral tracts; songs "three yards a penny," comic, romantic, religious; drinking songs, love songs, patriotic ballads, were produced in abundance, all embellished with cuts, some most inappropriate to the subject. The broadsides catered for all tastes and views. One of the last great events to be recorded in their chronicles was Queen Victoria's marriage to Prince Albert in 1840; the same publishers put out versions portraying Albert as Prince Charming and others ridiculing him as a German sausage-maker. They also shamelessly pirated other people's popular successes. Pierce Egan, author of *Tom and Jerry, or Life in London*, which appeared in instalments in 1821 and took the town by storm, complained of no less than sixty-five publications lifted from his work, and that, less than twelve hours after his own publication, Catnach had a pirated version, price twopence, on the streets. It was a "whole sheet," with twelve cuts, roughly copied from the original Cruikshank illustrations, but in reverse and with a little verse underneath each.

In wartime, especially during the Napoleonic Wars, the broadside and ballad writers were in their element. As Douglas Jerrold wrote in 1841, "With the fall of Napoleon, declined the English Ballad Singer. During the war, it was his peculiar province to vend halfpenny historical abridgements to his country's glory, recommending the short poetic chronicle by some familiar household air, that fixed it in the memory of the purchaser' who thus easily got hatred of the French by heart with a new assurance of his own invulnerability. No battle was fought, no vessel taken or sunken, that the triumph was not published, proclaimed in the national gazette of our Ballad Singer. . . . It was his narrow strips of history that adorned the garrets of the poor; it was he who made them yearn towards their country; albeit to them so rough and niggard a mother."

News purveyor, sensationalist, scandalmonger, humorist, patriot, he was also, oddly enough, a great moralist. All through their career we come across ballads and broadsides dwelling on the vanities of this world and the imminence of death. So popular was this theme that earlier verses might be revived and given a new contemporary illustration, as in the various "Messenger of Mortality" broadsides in the Douce collection.

For all their crudity, the simplicity and directness of the broadside woodcuts made them extremely effective propaganda. George Cruikshank, for instance, adopted this technique in his campaign to abolish the death penalty for forgery, and the same type of pictures adds point to the political tracts of William Hone and other pamphleteers.

Chapbooks and Children's Books

Closely akin to the broadsides and ballads are the chapbooks. Though they were invented somewhat later, they were often produced by the same printers and covered many of the same topics. Slim, small volumes, they fitted easily into the pedlar's pack, to be carried all over the country; it is from the pedlar or "chapman" that they take their name. Chapbooks flourished exceedingly from the mid-seventeenth century onwards; the pamphleteering habits associated with the Civil Wars, far from driving them out, gave them an extra fillip. By the beginning of the eighteenth century they were being printed in many county and even market towns.

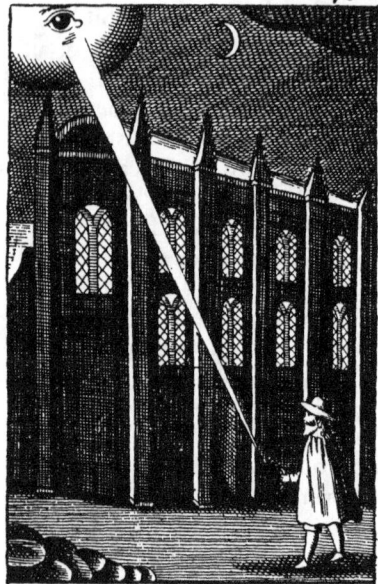

The wicked is snared in ye work of his own hands. Psalm.9.16. Thou hast seen it, for thou beholdest mischeif & spite, to require it with thy hand. Psal:10 14.

Copper-engraved Illustration from the Book of Common Prayer, printed in 1710

The earliest chapbooks had leather covers, later abandoned for paper. Paper cover and frontispiece are usually decorated with small woodcuts or type ornaments, and cuts are often interspersed in the text, as pictures or swags. These little woodcuts are indeed the great attraction of the chapbooks; they have the *naïveté*, directness and fantasy of the ballad and broadside decorations, but being on a smaller scale, are more delicate. In both chapbooks and broadsides the pictures harmonise well with the rough handmade paper and weight of type, at first very heavy but growing lighter as the elegancies of the eighteenth century approach. The paper covers of the chapbooks deserve special attention; they were often gaily coloured (yellow was a favourite ground) with, sometimes, little stuck-on labels for the titles, surrounded by decorations of type ornaments and perhaps a woodcut, hand coloured. Such coloured illustrations came in towards the end of the eighteenth century, and could at first only be done by hand with water colour, applied in flat washes for speed. When chapbooks began to be made specially for children, Dutch embossed and decorated papers were also used with great effect, as also patterned and marbled papers. But some of the cheapest chapbooks had no covers, being merely folded sheets, which the purchaser could stitch to please himself, in coloured threads perhaps. Prices of chapbooks would range from a penny or less to sixpence.

In contents the chapbooks covered, like the broadsides, an immense range. A rough classification of topics, made by John Ashton, the nineteenth-century antiquarian and collector, reads: "Religious, Diabolical, Supernatural, Superstitious, Romantic, Humorous, Legendary, Historical, Biographical and Criminal." The texts can rarely lay claim to any literary merit, and when, as they often were, they have been adapted from earlier versions, they may have been so hacked about and badly compressed as to be almost unintelligible. The stories are sometimes based on real events, sometimes on the old mediaeval romances, like Sir Bevis or Sir Guy of Warwick or Robin Hood, others again are crude pirated versions of popular books, like *Gulliver's Travels* or even *Moll Flanders*, but are generally told so flatly as to lose all sense of drama. Nevertheless the chapbooks pleased their public, grown-up children and real children, who bought them in vast numbers.

Their miniature size makes chapbooks specially attractive to children, yet chapbooks specially written for them were a late development, as were all children's books not primarily intended as an adjunct to instruction or for moral improvement. Till then, children bought and delighted in the chapbooks primarily intended for grown-ups, especially the fables and romances, as we knew from Uncle Toby, who says: "When Guy, Earl of Warwick, and Parismus and Parismenus, and Valentine and Orson, and the Seven Champions of England (*sic*) were handed around the school— were not they all purchased with my own pocket money?" Steele, writing in *The Tatler* in 1709, describes his little godson as an authority on Aesop's Fables, the lives and adventures of Don Bellianis of Greece, Guy of Warwick, the Seven Champions, John Hickathrift and other chapbook heroes, which, according to Mr. Harvey Darton,[1] the great authority on English children's books, were not then accessible to children in any other form.

When at last a real publisher of books for children appeared—John Newberry, publisher and friend of Johnson, Goldsmith and Smollet—he naturally followed the chapbook practice of small pictures and miniature size, giving them gay Dutch paper covers; indeed, the small woodcuts in his *Little Books for Little Masters and Misses* are pure chapbook; only the text has been specially written for children. Even the great Bewick follows the old chapbook styles in his wood engravings for the children's books published by Saint, of Newcastle, some few years after Newberry; for instance in the delightful *New Lottery Book of Birds and Beasts* (1771).

This idea of a special literature for children was quickly seized upon by the chapbook and broadside printers themselves. Real children's chapbooks were now produced, together with a great number of rhyme sheets,

1 W. J. Harvey Darton: *Children's Books in England* (Cambridge, 1932).

FROM
LUMSDEN & SON'S
𝔍𝔲𝔟𝔢𝔫𝔦𝔩𝔢 𝔏𝔦𝔟𝔯𝔞𝔯𝔶,

60, *Queen-Street*,
GLASGOW,
Price Twopence.

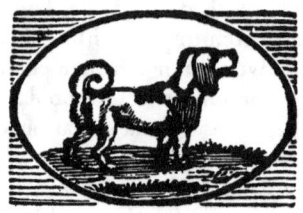

Bow, wow, wow.

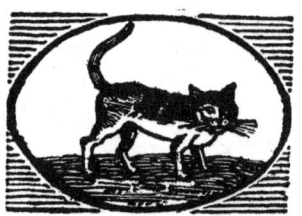

Mew, Mew, Mew

THE

WORLD
TURNED UPSIDE DOWN;
OR,
No News, and Strange News.

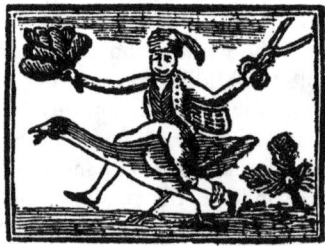

TAILOR RIDING A GOOSE.

𝔜𝔬𝔯𝔨 :
Printed and Sold by J. KENDREW, Colliergate.

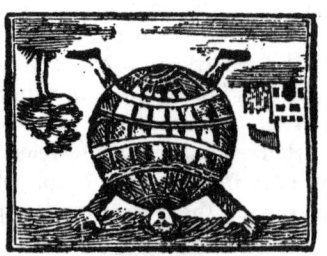

Here you may see what's very rare,
The world turn'd upside down ;
A tree and castle in the air,
A man walk on his crown.

Covers and Woodcut Illustrations from Children's Chapbooks.   (Actual size.)

songs, games and the like, some purely for entertainment, others, like the many ABC's, instructional also. Catnach himself was very active in this field. His advertisement runs:

> Little Boys and Girls will find
> At Catnach's something to their mind.
> From great variety may choose
> What will instruct them and amuse;
> The prettiest plates that you can find,
> To please at once the eye and mind,
> In all his little books appear,
> In natural beauty shining clear.
> Instruction unto youth when given,
> Points the path from earth to heaven.
>
> He sells by Wholesale and Retail,
> To suit all moral tastes cant fail.

Compared with the delicacy and charm of the better-class children's books of the early nineteenth century, these street literature versions appear rough and crude. But they have a force and simplicity particularly attractive to children, while the morality of the text is impeccable. Nevertheless, at no stage of their career were chapbooks approved by moralists and educationalists; they were constantly denounced for putting fanciful ideas into children's heads. As Mr. Harvey Darton has pointed out, the battle of the Puritans between Penny Merriments and Penny Godlinesses raged as fiercely in the world of chapbooks as elsewhere. We must be thankful that godliness was not everywhere triumphant for, apart from their intrinsic charm, the chapbooks have made two immortal contributions to our nursery archives, by preserving in print the fairy-tale and the nursery-rhyme, which would else have disappeared with the aural traditions which first put them into circulation.

Bills, Trade Cards and Advertisements

Broadsides and chapbooks are but two manifestations in the immense field of what M. P. L. Duchartre, the great French authority, has so aptly termed "popular imagery." Such pictures, at first simple woodcuts and later copper engravings, were used for a great many purposes. We find them on advertisements and handbills, especially in connection with fairs and circuses, where they served to whet the public appetite for the marvels on show. Many other public announcements were decorated with pictures; sailing and steamship and early railway bills, for instance, or coach guides.

A special group are the Trade Cards, at their zenith in the mid-eighteenth century. They are not really cards at all, but a form of decorated handbill printed on a piece of paper, varying in size from small octavo to large quarto or even folio. As they were intended as advertisement, they carry the name and address of the shop with the type of goods sold, and very often the shop sign or device as well. This picture is not, of course,

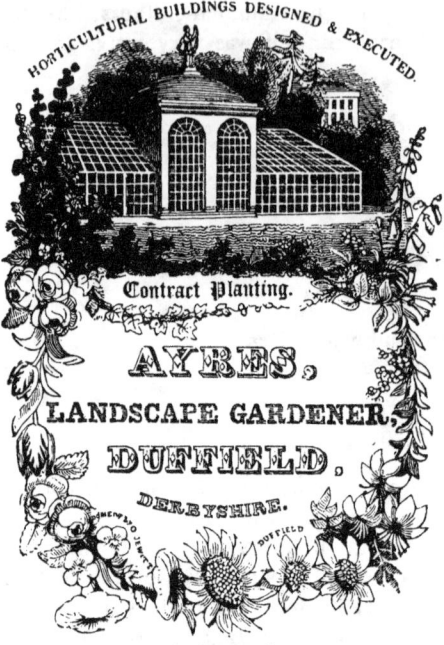

Trade Card

an exact reproduction of the painted signboard, but is a decorative rendering of it, translated to suit the medium of a copper engraving and often enclosed in a cartouche, whilst the whole card may have an ornamental border, curved and scrolled as befits eighteenth century elegance. Many of these trade cards are very delicate engravings. Less elaborately decorative is the billhead, set at the top of the sheet on which the customer's accounts were written. Here space and convenience dictated a simpler design; the owner's name and address and trade, with, perhaps, the sign.[1]

A special form of trade card are the little round watch papers which used to be set inside watch cases and gave the maker's name and address. Here the lettering is designed to fit into a circle, and the results are often delightful.

The trade cards rely for much of their appeal on decorative lettering with elegant flourishes and curls. In this they reflect the influence of the writing masters and the vogue for ornamental penmanship which was to

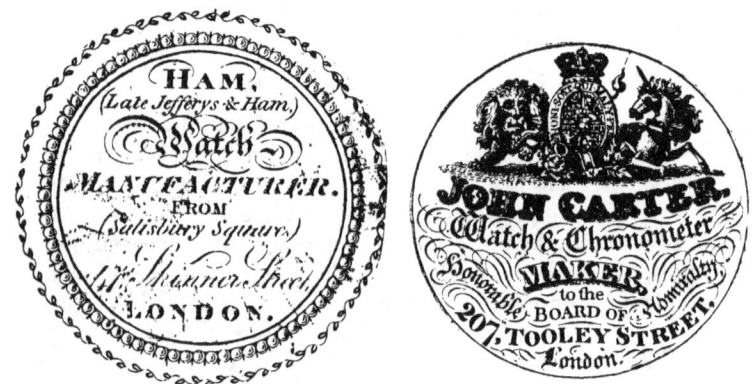

Eighteenth-century Watch Papers

[1] Sir Ambrose Heal has illustrated many tradecards and billheads from his own fascinating collection in *London Tradesmen's Cards of the XVIII Century* and *The Signboards of Old London Shops*.

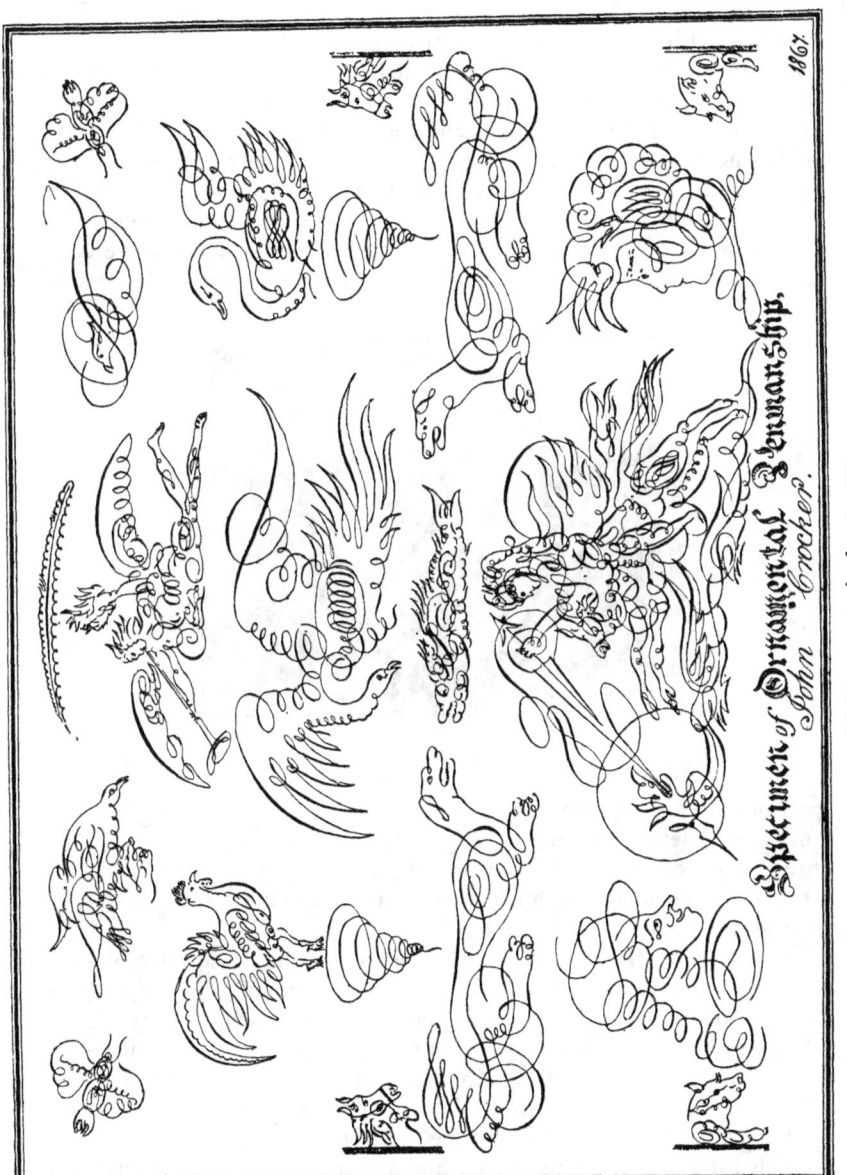

Writing-master's sheet, 1867

persist right down to the mid-nineteenth century (p. 103). Sir Ambrose Heal in *The English Writing Masters* gives many specimens of this work. Nowadays, with the advent of the typewriter and other mechanical aids, it is hard to realise the important part which handwriting once played in everyday English life and how decorative penmanship can be.

The exuberant love of ornament which burst out in the nineteenth century, after the sober elegance of an earlier age, affected printing like everything else. Type-faces, especially for display printing, work mostly done by the humble jobbing printers, became extremely ornate, at times verging on the grotesque. Letters took on strange, fantastic shapes; they might be decorated with flowers, set in little scenes, or be composed of leafy boughs or other romantic objects, much after the style of the cast-iron rustic garden furniture then so much admired. Sizes and styles of

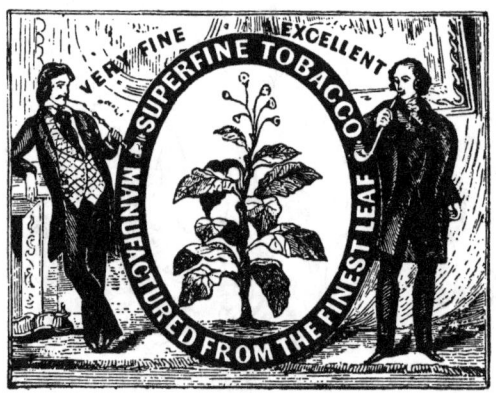

Tobacco Label

type would be happily jumbled together, with little regard for legibility or printing proprieties, but making a splendid show of magnificence. As the century wore on, some of these extravagances began to degenerate into merely weak eccentricities, but at their best we cannot but respond to their tremendous vitality.

A wholly delightful feature of this humble printing is the use of little type ornaments to decorate the text—head and tailpieces composed of printers' flowers or little scenes, a balloon, a stage coach, railway engine, paddle-steamer or sailing-ship. Looking through an old catalogue of printers' ornaments we find hundreds of different motives, pleasantly recalling the little woodcuts from which they were doubtless derived and providing a miniature panorama of the life of the times.

Labels for goods were also given pictures, more or less appropriate to the goods they advertised—early tobacco labels, ranging from nigger boys to Red Indians, are a particularly interesting and attractive class, to select but one example from a vast field.

VOCAL CONCERT,

AT THE

MARINE LIBRARY,

RAMSGATE.

THE CELEBRATED

MINSTREL FAMILY

MR. FROST, HIS SON AND THREE DAUGHTERS,

Who are making a tour of Kent, and whose Performances have been received with rapturous applause in various parts of the Kingdom, and have been Patronized by many of the Principal Families, most respectfully announce that they intend to give a

MISCELLANEOUS VOCAL

CONCERT

FRIDAY Evening, NOV. 3rd, 1837.

Mr. FROST, Jun. will preside at the GRAND PIANOFORTE and ROYAL SERAPHINE, or Miniature Organ, which Instruments, to give effect to the Concerts, are removed from place to place with the Family.

PROGRAMME:—

PART I.

GLEE—" We Fairies Gay."..................BISHOP
SONG—" There's a Holy Chorus in Night."..............ROSSINI
DUET—" Love's sweet art Flower."..................HORN
The celebrated Tramp Chorus in " Rob Roy,"..............BISHOP

SOLO—ROYAL SERAPHINE.

TRIO—" Silently, Silently over the Sea."..................LANZA
FINALE in CINDERELLA" Now with Grief."..........ROSSINI
DUET—" Sweet Sister, Fay."..................BARNETT
TRIO—" Full of Doubt ; or the Deaf Old Woman."........BISHOP

PART II.

GLEE—" Blow, Gentle Gales." (Five Voices) ....BISHOP
DUET—" The Master and Scholar."....................HORN
SONG—" The May Dew."..................LOVER
" Market Chorus in " Massaniello."..................AUBER

SOLO—ROYAL SERAPHINE.

MADRIGAL—" Merrily wake Music's Measure." (Five Voices)..BABE.
DUETT—" The New Sol Fa."..................BARNETT
GLEE—" The Breath of the Briar."................WHITAKER
FINALE—" God save Victoria, our Gracious Queen."..............

Tickets 3s. each, to be had of Mr. Frost, No. 2, Cliff Street, and at the Marine Library.

DOORS WILL BE OPEN AT HALF-PAST SEVEN, AND THE PERFORMANCE COMMENCE AT EIGHT PRECISELY.

CARRIAGES TO BE ORDERED AT TEN O'CLOCK.

✱✱ Families and Private Parties Attended.— Lithographic Prints of the Minstrel Family price 6d. each.

MARGATE: PRINTED BY T. M. KEBLE, 12, HIGH STREET.

Early nineteenth century Concert Bill

Pictures and Paper Games

Then there are the souvenir pictures sold to record some great event—the various frost fairs held on the frozen Thames would not have been complete without some cheap picture on sale and, at least in part, actually printed on the ice. Lithography, which came into general use at the beginning of the nineteenth century, must have been the last process used to record a Thames Frost Fair actually on the river. A later development of these souvenir pictures are the panoramas, long rolls of narrow paper illustrating some specially magnificent procession, perhaps, like George IV's coronation. Later still came peepshows made in cardboard and paper, folding flat like a concertina. They had two eyeholes in front and gave a view in depth of, perhaps, the new Thames Tunnel, where they were often sold off barrows. Specially fine ones show two levels, with boats sailing on the river above and people walking along the tunnel underneath. They are all gaily coloured.

Many cheap prints, in wood or copper engraving, were sold for framing and hanging on the walls (38, 39). In Protestant England, biblical scenes were very common, whereas in the Catholic countries of the Continent we find various patron saints and martyrs, much of this religious literature being intended for sale to pilgrims. Sporting subjects are very common both here and abroad; so are naval ones in England, whereas abroad the emphasis is more often military. There are scenes from everyday life, such as the Cries of London, echoed in France by the Cries of Paris, or Town and Country Life contrasted, or domestic events such as love and courtship, ending in marriage or parting, according as the mood is happy or sad. A strong vein of cynicism appears in some English treatments of these topics. It is interesting to compare a set of four English prints on marriage, entitled "First Meeting," "Courtship," "Marriage" and "A Year After," with the parallel French series. The concluding English scene shows the young wife sitting disconsolately alone, minding the baby. The French version is more romantic, as the titles "La Demande en Mariage," "Le Couché de la Mariée" and "Le Levée de la Mariée" indicate. Dramatic scenes, of shipwreck and rescue, for instance, reflect the impact of the Romantic movement. Political prints are specially plentiful in times of stress, nor must we overlook the many political and other caricatures, of which Gilray, Rowlandson and Dighton are the highlights, although large numbers of others were produced by less skilful hands.

These popular pictures began to be coloured towards the end of the eighteenth century, in brilliant water colours, applied by hand, at first in detail and later in broad, sweeping stencils. As the nineteenth century progresses, the colours become stronger and more violent. We find these hand-coloured prints illustrating cheap booklets also, like Books of Fate or Books of Dreams, where the frontispieces often contain a most dramatic jumble of queer symbols. Coloured sheets were also produced for the many games for children, some quasi-educational, others simply for amusement.

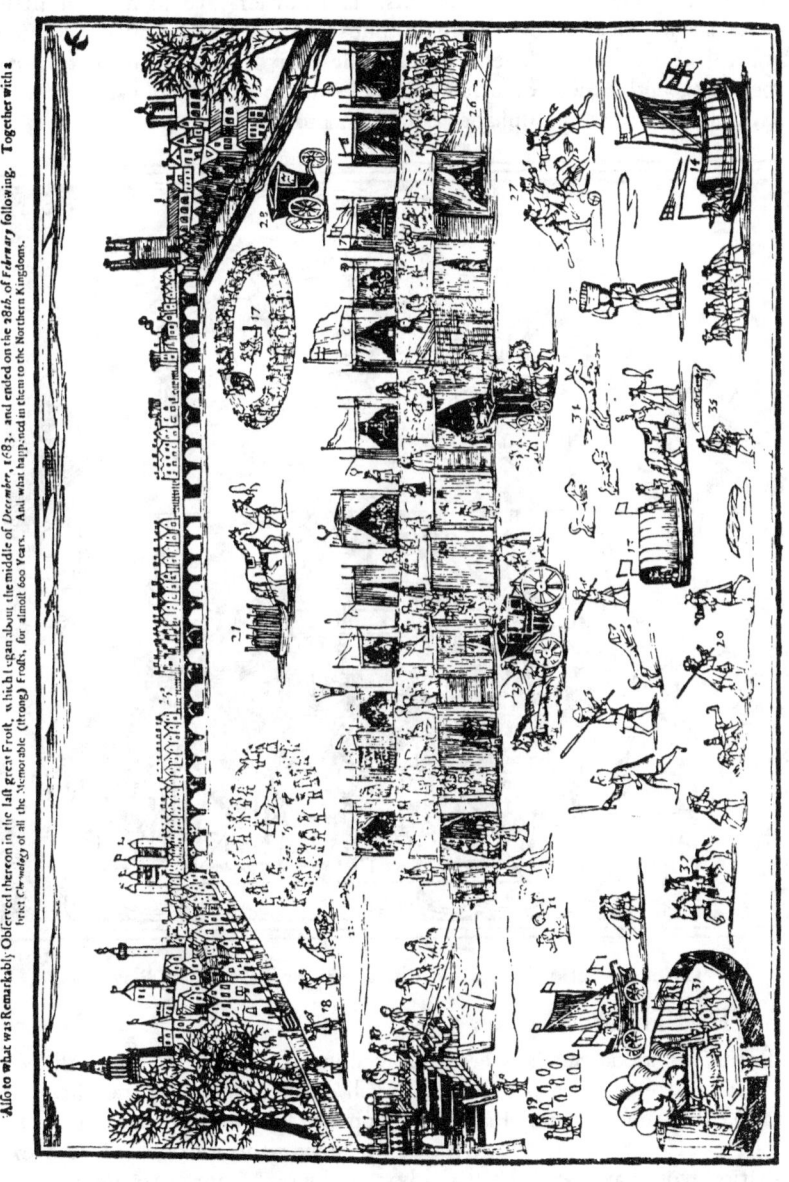

Wonders on the Deep; OR, The most Exact Description of the Frozen RIVER of THAMES:

Also to what was Remarkably Observed thereon in the last great Frost, which began about the middle of December, 1683, and ended on the 28th of February following. Together with a brief Chronology of all the Memorable (strong) Frosts, for almost 600 Years. And what happened in them to the Northern Kingdoms.

Broadside Souvenir of the Thames Frost Fair in 1683

Some of the most attractive of the educational prints are the decorated writing sheets (**45**), with a space left blank in the middle for the children to inscribe texts and suitable sentiments in their best copperplate, often as a "Christmas piece" for their parents. The borders are formed of little printed scenes usually from the Bible, but sometimes historical also, which are brilliantly coloured. Then there are the many little cut-out or turn-up paper toys, and a host of others, often with most ingeniously movable bits, dolls for dressing, alphabet counters, puzzles and many more.

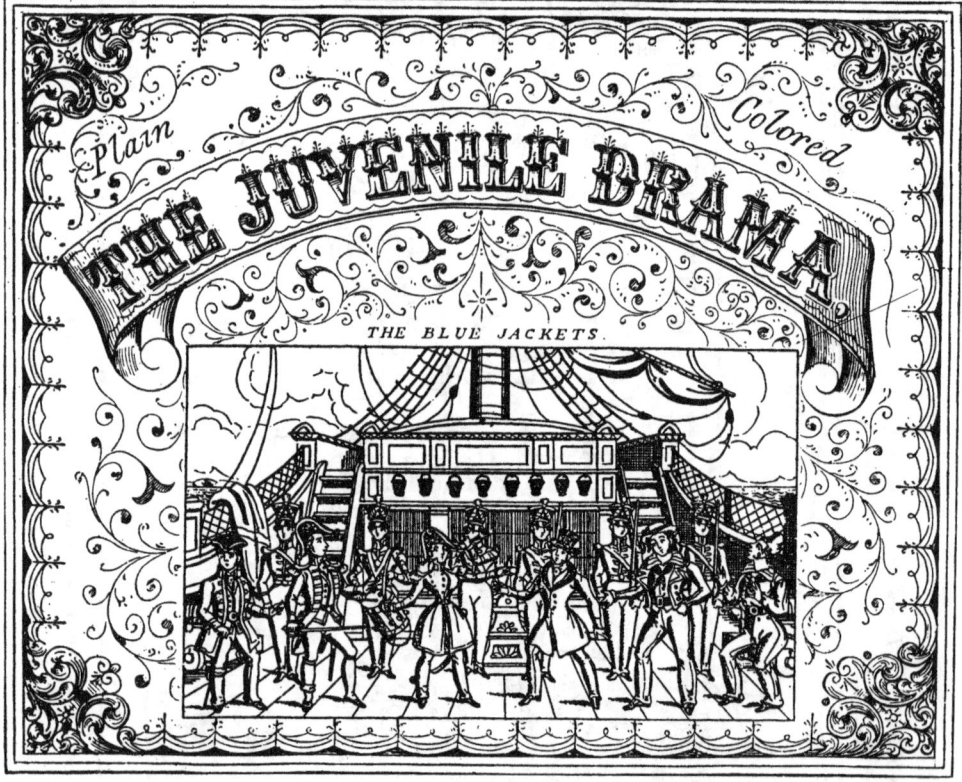

Cover for Set of Scenes and Characters for Toy-theatre Play

The Toy Theatre

Prints, booklets, games, were produced in the popular art idiom all over Western Europe. But a peculiarly English development was the "Juvenile Drama," the famous "Penny Plain and Twopence Coloured" theatrical sheets. Their precise origin has been much discussed; the most reasonable explanation would appear to be that advanced by Mr. George Speaight,[1] who

[1] In *Juvenile Drama—The History of the English Toy Theatre* (London, 1946), which is a mine of information on its subject.

thinks they were a development of the portraits of theatrical celebrities sold in the eighteenth and early nineteenth centuries as a form of souvenir. Howsoever this may be, by the 1820's they were in full swing and continued so till about the 1860's, when a slow decline set in. It was, however, still possible to buy a Juvenile Drama complete with little book of words, stage directions and instructions; a set of sheets of scenery—backcloth and wings—and another of characters, all printed from the old plates and hand-coloured in the traditional way, at the old price, right up until the middle of the war.[1] The sheets consisted of pictures in outline, printed from copper plates or later by lithography, and the cheapest from wood blocks. They were sold either plain for colouring yourself or, for an extra penny, hand-coloured by professionals with a verve and brilliance few amateurs could hope to achieve. The sheets were meant to be mounted on cardboard and cut out for use on little wooden frame stages, complete with gaily coloured proscenium, real drop curtain, and tin footlight holders in front. The scenery was set in wooden grooves, in imitation of the real theatre as it was in Regency days. The characters, in their appropriate attitudes, were slid on and off the stage from the wings, in little wooden or, better, metal holders, whilst the performer read their parts. The trick changes, so popular in contemporary pantomime, were done by dropping little flaps cut in the scenery to reveal a new picture. Fireworks could be introduced for the frequent storms, battles and conflagrations demanded by the plots; "red fire to burn" is a frequent stage direction and might be achieved by burning specially supplied chemicals in a little tin pan, though these particular effects were liable to set the whole stage alight. When set up, these little theatres gave a succession of set pieces, more like a peep-show than a puppet theatre.

The plays and pantomimes of the Juvenile Drama were taken direct from the contemporary stage, though simplified to suit the medium: plots, the book of words (much abridged), scenery and costumes. In the early days many of the characters were faithful portraits of famous players, including the superb stance, the strut and swagger with exaggerated gestures, of the romantic acting then fashionable. The stage fronts might be taken from well-known theatres; Mr. A. E. Wilson [2] has identified one of Reddington's as "The Old Brit." at Hoxton. Street scenes too might show real places; one of Pollock's includes his own shop as it existed till damaged by flying-bombs. The Juvenile Drama provides a mine of information on the early nineteenth century theatre and social life, preserving vanished splendours and even topical jokes.

It is, however, the decorative side that most concerns us here. In their style of drawing and dramatic use of colour the toy theatre sheets do not break new ground; they follow the same line as the coloured prints for

[1] They are again obtainable at Messrs. Benjamin Pollock, Ltd., 16 Little Russell Street, London, W.C.1.

[2] In *Penny Plain and Twopence Coloured*, a beautifully illustrated record of the plays, plots, their publishers and clientele.

cottage walls or frontispieces to Dream Books. But their intimate association with the theatre gives them a special flavour; they epitomise all the romanticism of fairground art, its unreality and wonderland qualities. Robert Louis Stevenson, taking the name of a well-known Juvenile Drama publisher, Skelt, coined the word "skeltery" for these scenes that never were on land or sea, the excessively bosky foliage, gnarling of the oaks, rockiness of the crags—fairytale castles, palaces, pavilions, with their grotesque jumbles of architectural styles, often suggesting in their treatment that very homely models may have posed for the more exotic creations—the beloved Victorian indoor fern in its bepinnacled ferncase, perhaps, for some of the more luxurious tropical vegetation and flights of architectural fancy. It is indeed amusing to try to trace the origins of some of the more fantastic motives. We catch reflections of some eighteenth-century folly in the grottoes of a submarine palace or of a Bernini fountain in the chubby trumpeting Tritons, for all their John-Bullish air of robust stolidity.

Immediate inspiration came, of course, from the contemporary stage, which in Regency and early Victorian days lent itself exceptionally well to the purposes of Juvenile Drama. Indeed, one cause of the latter's decline is undoubtedly the switchover to more naturalism in the theatre: the return to the comedy of manners which relies more on skilful characterisation and dialogue than on action and spectacle. Till then, what with the Romantic movement, the vogue for the picturesque and the Gothic revival, scenic design, like all the arts, was luxuriating in a riot of mediaeval, oriental and even nautical splendour, uninhibited by the insistence of a later date on historical accuracy. Plots too were wildly improbable, whilst the fashion for melodrama, burlesque and pantomime was fostered by the curious licensing laws, whereby only three London playhouses were entitled to put on straight plays. To meet the public demand for what we should call "actuality," recent events, like the battles of Waterloo and Trafalgar or the burning of Moscow, were put on the stage, providing opportunities for *tours de force* in scenic display, including aquatic and equestrian spectacles. Equally they found their way into the humbler sphere of the toy theatre and fairground peepshow.

All this splendour, however, had to be simplified and translated to suit the toy-theatre medium; it is this distillation that gives the results so much character and charm. The means available were of the simplest—outline drawings with the minimum of line shading. In professionally coloured sheets, the basic colours are usually limited to four; gamboge, carmine, prussian blue and the black of the print. Skilful gradations and mixings produced luscious browns, purples, greens, pinks, whilst the imaginative skill shown in juxtaposing one colour with another, enhances the effects. It is no small tribute to the quality of the water-colour pigments that sheets over a hundred years old retain all their brilliance. The colours were applied in flat washes, at first directly by hand, later by stencil. This latter process, though it cannot give the same fine tone gradations as direct painting, has its own attractions in the firmer outline and freer sweep.

Remarkable, too, is the amount of ingenuity and imagination shown within the limits of conventional representation. Mr. A. E. Wilson has managed to list some forty-nine names of publishers of Juvenile Drama, and Mr. Speaight over a hundred; yet a surprising number of them manage to

GREEN'S SCENE IN { *Harlequin Robin Hood, S.ᶜ 10 N.ᵒ 10*

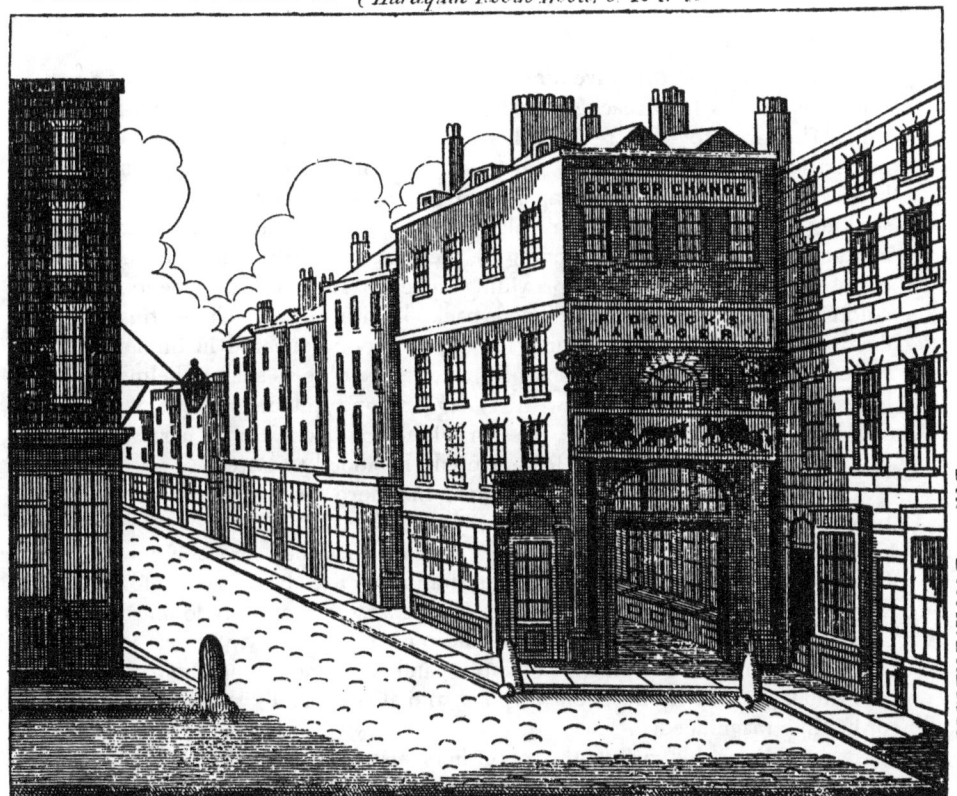

London, Pub. Dec. 26, 1843, by J.K. GREEN, 16, Park Place, East Street, Walworth. Price Halfpenny.

Sold by J.REDINGTON, 208, Hoxton Old Town.

Toy-theatre Sheet

give their representations of the same play an individual character, for all the practice of buying up old stock, or making an old plate do service in a new situation, was as prevalent in this branch of cheap publishing as elsewhere. Equally remarkable are the number and variety of plays produced. Mr. A. E. Wilson found as many as a hundred and seven plays published by William West, one of the most successful and prolific of these publishers.

1 Mr. Speaight, in *Juvenile Drama*, has compiled an exhaustive list of these publishers, with names and dates of their productions.

The toy-theatre sheets are, of course, meant to be cut out, but in their pristine state they have their own attractions, particularly the pantomimes with their trick items. Pantomime tradition demands that Harlequin with his bat or Clown with the poker shall transform everyday objects into something unexpected—an egg into a huge hen bigger than a man, and so on. The tricks as printed for the Juvenile Drama, with their juxtaposition of odd objects, drawn to different scales and at different angles to fit the sheet, give a fine effect of fantastic inconsequence.

Tinsel Pictures

Closely allied to the Juvenile Drama, and equally attractive, are the tinsel pictures, which reached the height of their popularity at the same time. The same toy-theatre publishers also provided these large prints of celebrities, mostly theatrical, but including also royalty and popular heroes. The fashion for making "patch portraits," decorating prints by sticking on bits of silk, satin or coloured paper, existed in the eighteenth century, but not till the beginning of the nineteenth did the publishers themselves take a hand by providing special "stick-on" ornaments of coloured metal foil, embossed and backed with paper. These "tinsel" decorations, sold in packets for a few pence, soon appeared in immense variety—stars, dots, rosettes, spangles, and larger objects such as helmets, breastplates, plumes, even swords, daggers and pistols. There were standardised tinsels and special ones provided for decorating a particular picture. Silk, satin and bits of feather could be added to taste.

The typical tinsel picture represents the hero in theatrical stance, brandishing his weapons. Some of the most attractive are equestrian portraits. Behind, on a much smaller scale, is a landscape, sometimes with figures enacting some high spot of the drama, whilst above, an explosive sky reinforces the sensational effect. The characters are predominantly masculine, though we find a superb heroine from time to time. Most dramatic of all are the villains, stamping and scowling, slung about with an armoury of heavily tinselled weapons, and at their best rising to heights of horrific magnificence.

Besides these big prints the publishers also issued smaller pictures, "fours," "sixes" or even "eights" to a sheet, for cutting out and decorating, perhaps by mounting them on a differently coloured background. Even background scenes were provided to choice.

Like the Juvenile Drama, the tinsel picture reflected the vogue for romantic acting of the barnstorming type as exemplified by Mr. Vincent Crummles in *Nicholas Nickleby*. With the rise of naturalism and the advent of cheap colour productions tinsel pictures too went out of fashion.

Valentines and Christmas Cards.

Another form of decorated picture, which also seems to have no precise counterpart abroad, is the Valentine, which flourished alongside the tinsel picture. Paper Valentines, made by embellishing a set of verses with a picture, seem to have arrived at the end of the eighteenth century; by the early nineteenth they had become very popular amongst all classes of society; Pickwick fans will remember Sam Weller composing one, and no

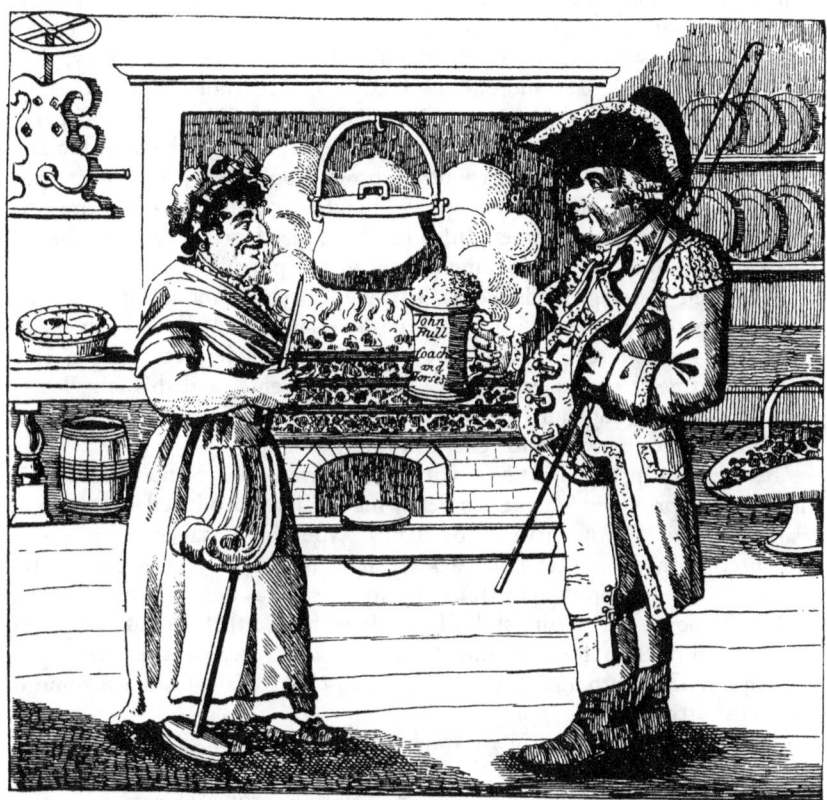

Says Coachee to Cookey, so charming you look,
You've drove through my heart or I am mistook;
My Horses are harness'd let's go to the Church,
Nor leave your true lover to sigh in the lurch,
Says Cookey to Coachee, I'll down with the beef,
And hasten to give your fond heart its relief.

Early nineteenth-century Comic Valentine

doubt the advent of the penny post in 1840 encouraged Valentines still more. The first ones were entirely amateur, and often show much skill and ingenuity; verses are composed and arranged to form patterns, such as a heart, and decorated with painted pictures, paper cut-outs or bits of silk and satin.

As in the case of the theatrical portraits, the printers soon realised the value of providing ready-made Valentine accessories. Those who could not compose their own verses were provided with valentine writers' books, like the letter writers.' By the beginning of the nineteenth century, delicate machine-made lace and embossed papers were available as frames and borders for the central picture, which might perhaps be an amateur painting on satin, framed with an embossed paper, and then edged with a lace one, mounted of a coloured ground to show through (50). A favourite picture was a posy of the striped, splashed and speckled "Florists' Flowers," like those illustrated with delightful hand-coloured prints in the *Floricultural Cabinet* and other gardening papers of the period.

Coloured paper grounds were also much used for mounting the many forms of paper "cut-outs"—hearts, true-love knots and the like, or sometimes the whole inscription cut out of paper in a single piece. The essence of a Valentine is the suggestion of secret sentiments, and this is reflected by the increasing ingenuity invested in devices for pulling up, folding back or sliding off one picture to reveal another.

Besides equipping amateurs with accessories, the printers and publishers also provided Valentines ready made. They produced an immense variety of the "transformation" or "fancy" type; for instance, a picture of a church with doors that fold back to show bride and bridegroom at the altar. Or the pull-up type of transformation, such as a little hand-coloured print of a posy, the picture skilfully cut in strips, so that it could be pulled up by a thread to form a miniature cage and reveal a heart or cupid, perhaps, underneath (48, 49). These "mousetrap" Valentines are some of the most attractive.

But by no means all printed Valentines had such tricks. Many of them are merely pictorial, such as the delightful trade Valentines, representing the different occupations in full panoply with appropriate verses, such as the Chymist, the Barmaid, Pastry Cook, Hatter, Draper, Housemaid and many more, all delicately engraved and coloured.

More purely typographical are the many jokes and puns—matrimonial ladders, cupid thermometers, the many adaptations of documentary forms, I.O.Us., wills, licences; so realistic was the £5 note drawn on the "Bank of Love" that it had to be withdrawn lest it aid forgers.

In glaring contrast to the sentimental Valentines are the cynical comic ones, which also seem to have been very popular, judging from the number that have survived. Some of the earlier forms, engravings or woodcuts, with flat washes of colour, are good humouredly satirical of foppishness and extravagance in the various characters they portray; they have much of the charm of other early prints. Later ones became savagely insulting, such as, for instance, the picture of a man or woman with a fold-back flap to show the same subject minus hair, teeth and so on—advancing age was indeed a stock joke.

Ridicule may perhaps have contributed to the decay of the Valentine. For instance, items such as a coloured woodcut printed on a narrow strip of paper, and representing a baby in long clothes, with the caption "Ah, Papa!" scarcely foster the Valentine spirit. But it seems more likely that they went out of favour in response to the rising popularity of Christmas cards.

Christmas cards were a surprisingly late introduction into England; they

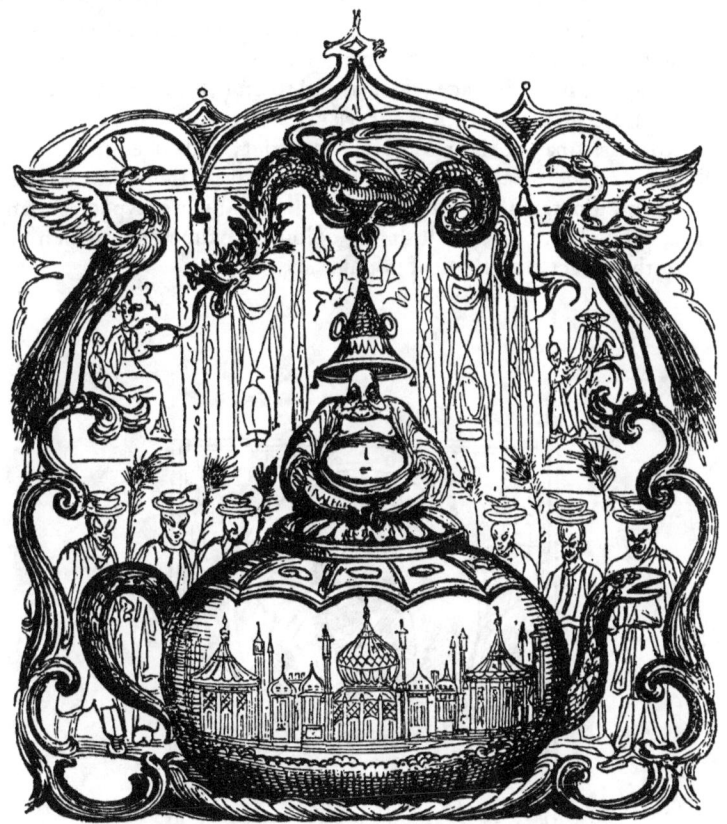

Printer's Catalogue of Metal Ornaments

are only about a hundred years old, though on the Continent they were the fashion from the end of the eighteenth century, much as Valentines were here, though of course Christmas cards were not restricted to lovers. It may be that their late introduction here is partly due to the fact that in Protestant England the little religious pictures of the Christ Child did not play the same part in popular imagery as they did in the Catholic countries of the Continent. In England, Christmas cards were started as the whim of a few well-known literary figures who commissioned artists to design them special Christmas greeting cards—a development of the visiting card. This idea was soon taken up by the publishers of Valentines and others who saw in it a much more profitable, because wider, market than the Valentine could provide. By the 1860's, Christmas cards were well launched on their career and have never looked back since. As far as popular art is concerned they are, perhaps, a borderline case. Coming later, they miss much of the simplicity and directness which go to make up the aesthetic appeal of the Valentine, although we can see how closely they are related by the many subjects and treatments common to both—flower posies, domestic scenes, puns, adaptations of documentary forms, with cut-out or pull-up devices, embossed papers, machine-lace edgings, and so on (**51**). Looking through an old album of Christmas cards, it is surprising to see how few bear any direct relation to Christmas in their motives. In variety and ingenuity as well as in skilful use of the machine, they were probably at their best in the last quarter of the nineteenth century. Mechanical and stereotyped as many of them are, they often possess a lush and colourful exuberance which brings them into the direct traditions of popular art.

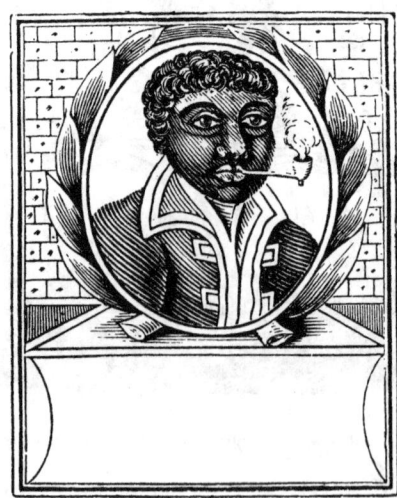

Tobacco Label

INDEX

(Numerals in *italic type* refer to the page numbers of the line illustrations;
numerals in **heavy type** refer to the figure numbers of the half-tone illustrations.)

Abbotts Ann (Hants), Maiden's garland at, *89*
Actors modelled in pottery, 75
Alphabets, **52, 55**
Andirons, *see* Firedogs
Angel and Royal Inn, Grantham, 14
Antwerp, 1, 3
Appliqué coverlets, 60; **24**
Armes, Miss Alice, "English Smocks," 62
Ashton, John (Antiquarian), 99
Ashton, Sir Leigh: *Samplers*, 64
Astbury, John (pottery), 73
Ath, 1
Axes, carved wooden, 5

Ballads, printed, 93
Balstone, Mr. T. (pottery collection), 74
Barley, Mr. M. W., on headstone lettering, 19
Barley Mow Inn sign by J. Crome, 49
Barnes, William (quoted), 30
Bavaria, wall-paintings in, 44
"Bear Inn," Devizes, 14; Woodstock, 28
Bellarmine stoneware bottles, 77
Bemrose, Mr. (Hanley Museum), 82
Beresina, Battle of, as a decorative motif, 56; **21**
Bettmann Archives, 69
Bewick, Thomas, 99
"Biddenden Maids," the, 25; **26**
Bideford Pottery, 68, 70
Billheads, 92
Bird in coloured spun glass, *85*
— whistle, brass, 42; *43*
Biscuit stamps, 24, 25, 26, *53, 55*
Blacksmith's work; *see* Smith's work
Bletchingley, White Hart inn sign-at, *28*
"Boot" hot-water bottle, 78
Bootmaker's shop sign, *13*; *14*
Bottles, carvings in, **22**
Bow, dragon weathervane at, 29
Brass ornaments, 40, 41
— birdwhistle, 42; *43*
— tobacco stopper, **15**
Brentford Election printed on handkerchief, 57

Bristol, Blaise Castle Folk Museum, 5
— Delft Tile, **28**
— Pottery 69, 71; **42**
Broadsides, 93; *94*
—, Catnach, *95*
—, eighteenth century satirical, *96*
Brontë sisters, samplers made by, 65
Brougham, Lord, portrayed as a stoneware flask 78; *77*
Brussels, 1
Bude, 7
"Bull and Mouth" inn sign, 11, 12
Buttons, glass, 86

Canal barges, painting on, 54
Caravans, painted, 53
Carpentry tools, carving on, 20
Carving, Chap. I; **7, 8**
Castle as motif in decoration, 54
— modelled in pottery, 76; **29**
Catnach, Jemmy, 95
— broadsides, *95*
— children's books, 101
Caudle Family portrayed as stoneware flask, 78
Chapbooks, Children's, 98; *100*
Charlotte, Queen, 79
Charmouth, St. Andrew's Church, fish weathervane on, 29
Chesham, George Inn, wall painting, 46
Chester giants, 2, 3
Children's books, 98, 101; *98*
— toys, 90; **54, 55**
Chimney-piece ornaments 41
Christmas cards, 115; **51**
Christopher, St., 4
Church Gresley, Mason's teacup factory at, 82
Cigarholders, Nailsea glass, 84; *91*
Circus placard painting, 53
Clay pipes, *91*
Cobalt, popularity of for pottery, 74
Coconut, carved, 21
Coconut flask, *21*
Concert bill, *105*
Copper engraving from Book of Common Prayer, *98*
Corinaeus, 1
Corn dollies, 88; **46, 47**
Coventry Giants, 2
— ribbons, 58; **25, 26**
— trade tokens, 37
— woven textiles, 36

Cricket as pottery ornament, *61*
"Cries of London" prints, 106
"Cries of Paris" prints, 106
Criminals as pottery figures, 75
Crock Street pottery, 69
Crome, John, 49

Dalmoningar wall paintings, 45
Darenth, tombstone, **6**
Darton, Harvey, "Children's Books in England," 99
Delany, Mrs. (silhouettist), 50
Delftware, 71
— tiles, 71
Demeter, Goddess, 88
Denby stoneware, 78; **28**
Devizes, "Bear Inn" at, 15
Devon pottery, 68; **35–37**
— quilting, 60
— straw plaiting, 88
Dickens, Charles, on inn signs, 12
Dighton prints, 106
Dinant, 1
Dolls (toys) 90
"Dolphin" inn sign at Langport, *13*
Donyat (Somerset) pottery, 68, 69; **27**
Door fittings, 41
— knocker, brass, *41*
— stop, cast iron, **10**
Dragons in processions, 4, 5; **1**
Dream books, 106
"Dun Cow Inn," Shrewsbury, 16
Dunmow trade tokens, 37
Dunstable, "Sugar Loaf Inn," 16
Durham quilting, 60
"Dutch" dolls, 90
Dwight, John (potter), 72

Earthenware, 72; **18, 27, 31–34, 41–44**
— castles and windmills; **29**
— eggcup, 82
— lustred, 80
Egan, Pierce, *Life in London*, 97
Eggcup, glazed earthenware, *82*
Eggs, Easter, 89
Election handkerchiefs, 57
— mugs, **44**
Emblem books, 93
Embroidery pictures, 63; **20, 23**
—, sailor's, 66; **20**
—, table-vice, *40*

117

Essex, decorative plasterwork in, 47
— straw plaiting, 88
Evelyn, John (quoted), 37

Fairground painting, 52
Faker's forgeries, 35, **16**
Farm carts, decoration on, 55
"Farmer's Arms" transfer (pottery), 80
Farndon, slate headstone from, *17*
Fate, Books of, 106
Faversham tombstone, **4**
Festival of Britain, 14
Figureheads, 6; *7*
Figures, pottery, 74
Filpot jugs, 73
Firebacks and hearth implements, 38; *39*
Firedogs, 40
Fire insurance signs, 36, 37; *35*
"Fish" stone flask (Lambeth ware), 78; *66*
Fisherman's jersey, 61
Fishley family (potters), 68
Flasks, Nailsea glass, 83
Flat-iron stand in cast iron, *41*
"Floricultural Cabinet," 114
"Flying Stationer," the, 94
Forks, carved, *22*
"Four Swans Inn," Waltham Cross, 14
"Fox and Hounds" inn sign at Barley, Herts, 14
Fremington clay (pottery), 68
French prisoners as carvers, *22*
— — as straw-plaiters, 87
Frost fairs, 96
— — Broadside souvenir of, *107*
Fuddling cups (pottery), 68
Fulham stoneware, 78

Garner, F. H. "English Delftware," 69
Garsdale, Knitting at, 61
George of Denmark, Prince, *30*
"George Inn," Chesham, Wall-painting at, 46; **11**
Giants, Chester, 2, 3
—, Coventry, 2
—, Salisbury, 3, 4
Gigantic History, 1, 2
Gilray prints, 106
Gingerbread stamps, *24, 25, 53, 55*
Glass, Blown glass figures, 85; **56**
—, brilliant, 87
—, buttons, 86
—, engraved, 86
—, love tokens, 86
—, lustred, 8*5*
—, marbles, 86
—, nailsea, 83; *84*
—, painting, 52; *17*
—, polehead, 31

Glass, rolling pins, 86
—, spun and twisted, 84; **85**
Gog and Maygog, 1; *2*
"Golden Cross Inn," Oxford, 44
Golden Legend, 4
Goldsmith, Oliver, 49
Gothic influence on domestic art, 40, 42
Grammont, 1
Grantham, "Angel and Royal" Hotel, 14
Great Exhibition as a print pattern, 58
Green, J. K. (toy theatre printer), 111
Greenacre murder broadsides, 95
Greenwich, Royal Maritime Museum, 7
Guilds, 1, 5

Hake, Mrs. Elizabeth, *English Quilting, Old and New*, 60
Handbills, 101
Handbrace, carved wood, *7*
Handkerchiefs, printed, 57
—, election, 57
Harp Alley inn signs, 16
Hart, Miss Innes, on tombstones, 16
Hasselt giant, 1, 4
Heal, Sir Ambrose, *English Writing Masters*, 104
— — —, *Signboards of Old London Shops*, 13
— — —, *Tradesmen's cards of the XVIII century*, 102
Hearth implements, 38
Hentland Easter cakes, 25
"Highlander" shop sign, 13; *15*
Hindley, Charles (Broadside collector), 95
Hob Nob, the Salisbury dragon, 4
Hoddening Horse, 5
Hodgson, Orlando, 95
Hogarth, 49
Hone, William, *Ancient Mysteries described*, 1
Horniman Museum, 13
Horse brasses, 31-34; *32*
Horse, roundabout, 8-11; *9*
Horsham, Gingerbread stamp from, *24, 25, 53, 55*
Household ornaments, 40; *41*
Howitt, William, *Rural Life in England* (quoted), 60, 62, 89
Huish, Mr. Marcus, *Samplers and Tapestry Embroideries*, 63, 65
Huntingdon, "Fox Inn" sign from, 27

Inn signs, 11-16, 27; *12, 13*
Iron, cast, 38-40; *39*, **10**
— wrought, 27 *et seq.*

Jackson, Mrs. N., on silhouette-cutting, 50
Jekyll, Miss Gertrude, on smocking, 62
Jerrold, Douglas (quoted), 97
Jones, Frank (canal-boat painter), 54
Jones, Inigo, 29

Kean, Edmund, pottery figure of, 75
Kern maidens, 88
"Knights of St. John Tavern," St. John's Wood, decorative plaster on, 47
Knitting, 60
Knitting stick, carved, 20; *61*

Lambeth stoneware, 78
— —, sailor's flask, *66*
Langport "Dolphin Inn" sign, 14; *13*
Larwood and Hotton, *History of Signboards*, 11
Latticino glass decoration, 83
Leeds pottery, 80; **43**
Lille puppet show, *5*
Little Moor Fields, London, parge decoration, *48*
Liverpool pottery, 80
Longman, Mrs. Charles, sampler collection, 64
Longthorpe, wall painting at, *44*
Lord Mayor's Show, 1, 2
Loughton, L. G. C., *Old Ship's Figureheads and Sterns*, 7
Love tokens, carved, 20-22
— — glass, 86
Lowestoft trade tokens, 37
— glass, 85
Lustred earthenware, 80

Maiden's garlands, *89*
Maidstone, Dolphin weathervane at, 29
Malines, 1
Manchester Reform Meeting as print motif, 57
"Man loaded with Mischief," by Hogarth, 49
Marbles, glass, 86
Maris Marten broadsides, 95
"Mariner's Arms" transfer (pottery), 80
Marionettes, 5*1* 6; **2, 3**
Market Harborough, "Three Swans Inn," 27
Marlborough's battles as decorative motif, 57
Marriage, The Four Stages of (prints), 106
Mason, teapot-maker, 82
"Mason's Arms" transfer (pottery), 80
Mayhew, *Life and Labour of the London Poor*, 91
Meerschaum pipes, 91
Mere, "Ship Inn" at, 27

Mermaid, Rockingham earthenware, 77
Merry-go-round, *see* Roundabout
Messent, C. J. W., *Weathervanes of Norfolk and Norwich*, 30
Midway, Burton-on-Trent, Mason's pottery factory at, 82
Mons, 1
Morland, George, 49
Morwenstow, 7
Murals, *see* Wall paintings

Nailsea Glassmakers' Guild, Club Poles of, 31, 84
— glassware, 83
— — pipe, *84*
— — cigar-holder, *91*
Napoleon, pottery figures of, 74
Naval scenes, cheap prints of, 106
Needle's Excellency, The, 63
Newark frock (smock), 62
Newberry, John (publisher), 99
Newcastle pottery, 80, 81
New Tory Guide (quoted), 37
Norfolk, weathervanes in, 30
Norman Cross, French prisoners at, 87
Northumberland styles in quilting, 59
Norwich Dragon ("Old Snap"), 5; *1*
Nottingham "bear" jugs, 72; **40**

Oakwreath earthenware bottles, 78
Ornaments, Nailsea glass, 84
Oxford, "Golden Cross Inn," wall-paintings in, 44

Paine, Tom, *The Rights of Man*, 38
Painting 48 et seq.
—, Fairground and circus, 52
—, on glass, 52
Panoramas, 106
Paper games, 106
Paperwork, 51, 52; **50, 51**
Parge work, 47, *48*
Parlour pastimes, 52
Parry, Joseph, "Village Fair" (painting), 53
Paste eggs, 88
Pastrycutters, brass, *42*
Peepshows, 106
Pegsworth murder broadside, 95
"Penny plain and twopence coloured" sheets, 108
Pewter poleheads, 31
Philips, E., sampler by, 65
Pilgrim's badges, *34*
Pin-prick pictures, 51
Pipes, clay, *91*
—, meerschaum, 115
—, nailsea glass, 83; *84*

Pitts, Johnny (broadside printer), 95
Plastering, decorative, 47; *48*
Poleheads, village club, 30; *29*
—, glass, 84
Political figures in pottery, 75; *77*
Pollock's toy theatres, 109
Porcelain, 72
Porringers (pottery), 68
Portsmouth, man-o'-war weathervane at, 29
Pottery, Chap. V
Prayer Book, engraving from, *98*
'Primitive" paintings, 49
Printed textiles, 56 *et seq.*; **21**
Printer's catalogue, *115*
— ornaments, 104; *49, 79, 81*
Printing, Chap. VII
Prints, 106; **38, 39**
— hand coloured, 106
Punch, 6, 78
Puppets, 5, 6
Puttenham, George, *The Art of Poesie* (quoted), 3

Quilting, 59

Railway as decoration on pottery, 80
Railway map as decorative motif, 57
Reader, Francis, "Use of the Stencil in Mural Decoration, 46
Reddington's toy theatres, 109; *111*
"Red Lion" at Barnet, 14
Red Lion Brewery (South Bank of the Thames), 14
Reform Bill stoneware bottles, 77
Rejected Addresses (quoted), 36
Religious subjects in pottery, 75
Rhead, Mr. W., on pottery figures, 74
Ribbons, printed, 56
Richards, H. S., *All about Horse Brasses*, 34
Robinson, P. F., 76
Rochdale trade tokens, 37
Rochester Town Hall, frigate weathervane on, 29
Rocking horses, 11
Rockingham ware, 82
— mermaid (earthenware) 77
— tobies, 78
Rolling-pins, glass, 86
Roundabouts, 8–11
— horses, 8; *9*
Rowlandson, 73, 106
Royalty as subjects for pottery, 78; *77*
"Running Patterers," 93
Rural Industries Bureau, 59

Saffron Walden tradition in Wood carving, 22
— — wall paintings, 45, 46

Sailors carved work, 22–24; *21*
— embroidery, 66; **20**
— flask, Lambeth stoneware, 66
— mementos in lustre ware, 80
Saint (of Newcastle) (publisher), 100
St. George as tobacco stopper, 92
St. John's Wood, "Knights of St. John Tavern," 47
St. Nicholas' Priory, Exeter, tillet blocks at, 58; *57*
Salisbury, carved figures at, 13; *15*
— Dragon, 4, 5
— Giant 3, 4
— St. Thomas's Church, 4
—, tobacconist's sign, *15*
—, "White Hart Inn," 14
—, wood-figure of "Wisdom," 13; *15*
Samplers, 62–66
—, darning, 66; **19**
Sauce Boat, earthenware, **32**
Saunders, Capt. Richard, 2
Savage, Frederick, 8
Scilly Isles, figureheads in, 7
Scrimshaw work, 20, 21
"Seven Dials" literature, 95
Shepherds' crooks, *19*
Sheringham, tombstone at, 18; **5**
"Ship Inn," Mere, Somerset, 27
Ships' figureheads, 6
Ships in bottles, carved, 22
Shop signs, 12–16; *14, 15*, Plate I
Shorleyker's, *Scholehouse for the Needle*, 63
Shovel, Sir Cloudesley, frigate weathervane at Rochester, 29
Shrewsbury, "Dunn Cow Inn," 16
Signs, inn and shop, 11–16; *12, 13, 14, 15*
—, wrought iron, 27
—, painted, 49; **9**
—, plasterwork, 47
Silhouettes, 50; *51*, **12**
Skelt (toy theatre printer), 110
Skelton, John (quoted), 63
Slipware (pottery), 67
Smith's work, 27 *et seq.*
— weathervane, 30; *28*
Smocking, 62; **22**
Snuff-boxes, carved, 92; *23*
Sparrow's House, Ipswich, decorative plasterwork on, 47
Speaight, Mr. George, 5
— —, "Juvenile Drama," 108, 111
Spoons, carved, 21; *22*
Sport portrayed in pottery, 75
Sporting prints, 96

Spreyton, Devon, weather-vane at, 30; *28*
Spun glass, 84; *85*
Staffordshire pottery figures, 53, 54, 72; **18, 30, 31, 33, 34,**
— castles and windmills, **29**
— mugs, 80
— pipes, 92
Staybusks, carved, 20
Steele, Sir Richard, 99
Stevens, Thomas (Coventry ribbon maker), 58
Stevenson, R. L., 110
Stoneware, 72; **40, 41**
— bottles, *77*
Stratford-on-Avon, White Swan Hotel wall painting at, 46
Straw marquetry, 87; **53**
— plaiting, 87; **46, 47**

Street literature, 93 *et seq.*
"Sugar Loaf Inn," Dunstable, 16
Sunderland pottery, 90, 91
Sussex iron work, 38, 39, 42
— fire backs, 38, *39*
— grave slabs, 38
— pottery, 69; **41**
"Swan Inn" sign, 14; *12*
"Swan Inn," Stratford, wall painting at, 46
Sweden, wall painting in, 44, 45, 46
—, wood carving, 23

Tatler, The, 99
Taunton Museum, 69
Taylor, John, on samplers, 63
Teacups, village club, 31
Teapots, giant, 82;
"Tee Total" pottery group, 75; **33**
Tewkesbury, corn dollies at, 88
Text plaques (pottery), 81
Textiles, Chap. IV

Textiles, printed, 56
Thames, souvenir of frozen, *107*
Threadgill, Mr., 89
"Three Swans Inn," Market Harborough, 27
Tiles, delftware, 71; **28**
— North Devon pottery, 69
Tillet block for marking wool bales, 58; *57*
Tinsel pictures, 112
Tobacco jars, 91
— labels, *104*
— stoppers, 91, **15**
Toby jugs, 73
— Rockingham ware, 77
Toft, Thomas (slipware pottery), 67
Tombstones, 16–19; **4–6**
— in S.E. England, 16
— from Farndon, Notts, *17*
— from Whatton, Notts, *18*
— lettering on, 19
Toper stone bottle, 78
Toys, 90; **54**
Toy theatre, 108–112; *108, 111*
Trade cards, 101; *102*
Trade tokens, 37
Transfer printing (pottery), 78 *et seq.*
"Trick" pottery, 81
Tunbridge ware, 25
— snuff-boxes, 92
Tyrol, wall paintings in, 44
Tythe pig (pottery), 79

Valentines, 112; *113,* **48, 49**
"Vicar of Wakefield" (Goldsmith), 49
Victoria, Queen, as subject for coventry ribbons, 59
— — marriage recorded in broadsheets, 97
— — portrayed as stoneware bottle, 78; *77*

Wafering iron, 40
Walking sticks, carved, 20; **8**
Wall paintings, 44–46; **11**
— — at Willington, Kent, *45*

Water-colour painting, **13, 50**
Wattle-and-daub, 47
Watch papers, *102*
Weathercocks and vanes, 28; **14**
Wedgwood, Josiah, 79
Wesley, John, portrayed on pottery, 80, 81
Wellington, Duke of, pottery figures of, 74
Welsh quilting, 59
West, William (toy theatre publisher), 111
Whatton, Notts, slate headstone from, *18*
Whieldon, Thomas (pottery) 73
"Whifflers," the, 4, 5
White, Gilbert, 89
White Hart Inn, Bletchingley, *28*
— — —, Salisbury, 14
— — —, Scole, 14
Willet Collection, Brighton Museum, 53, 74, 76
Willington Shire Hall, wall painting at, *45*
Willow pattern pottery, 79
Wilson, A. E., "penny plain and twopence coloured," 109
Wincanton pottery, 69
"Wisdom" carving at Salisbury, 13; *15*
Woodcuts, 93 *et seq*; *94, 95, 96, 98*
Wood family (potters), 73
Woodstock, Bear Inn sign at, 28
Worcester, The Commandery, wall painting at, 46
Wren, Sir Christopher, 29
Writing master's sheet, 108; *103,* **45**
Wrotham slipware pottery, 67
Wrought iron, *see* Smith's work

Young Mary, sampler by, 65
Young Ladies' Annual, 51